Get the eBook FREE!

(PDF, ePub, Kindle, and liveBook all included)

We believe that once you buy a book from us, you should be able to read it in any format we have available. To get electronic versions of this book at no additional cost to you, purchase and then register this book at the Manning website.

Go to https://www.manning.com/freebook and follow the instructions to complete your pBook registration.

That's it!
Thanks from Manning!

Testing Web APIs

Testing Web APIs

MARK WINTERINGHAM
FOREWORD BY JANET GREGORY AND LISA CRISPIN

MANNING
SHELTER ISLAND

Manning Publications Co.
20 Baldwin Road
PO Box 761
Shelter Island, NY 11964

Development editor:	Sarah Miller
Technical development editor:	John Guthrie
Review editor:	Adriana Sabo
Production editor:	Keri Hales
Copy editor:	Pamela Hunt
Proofreader:	Melody Dolab
Technical proofreader:	Karsten Strøbaek
Typesetter and cover designer:	Marija Tudor

ISBN 9781617299537
Printed in the United States of America

For Steph: I promise I'll finish decorating the kitchen now.

brief contents

contents

foreword

This book, *Testing Web APIs*, is much more than you might expect from a book on how to test APIs. It presents API testing as part of a holistic, risk-based testing strategy. Mark guides you with a range of helpful visual models, asking questions to make you think, and takes you along as a participant, not a passenger.

Before he digs into details, Mark has a chapter on "why we test" and how to identify different types of risks. He takes this important topic one step further—matching risks with quality characteristics and how they relate to a test strategy.

Mark lists a set of prerequisites for getting the most out of the book. Practitioners who are comfortable with coding, HTTP, and various developer and testing tools will learn great tools and techniques to understand all aspects of how their APIs behave. However, it is also a book for people who may not have all those prerequisites. A first read-through will give you insight and inspire you to try the well-explained learning activities during your second time around.

The many examples in the book, as well as the exercises, are based on a realistic project using a real application. You can start exploring and learning about the product, its business domain, history, and existing bugs—just like in real life. You can even use the product's UI to get more familiar with it.

We love the way this book helps people apply a holistic approach to API testing. Have conversations about quality to agree on a level of quality you want and build a strategy to achieve it, collaborating with different stakeholders and disciplines. As he writes in chapter 4,

> *A good testing strategy is a holistic one that focuses on the many places in which risk can creep into our work.*

We also like the way Mark gives equal value to exploratory testing and automation when thinking about that all-important API testing strategy. He takes a very pragmatic approach to both, listing pros and cons, and using concrete examples while recognizing that every team has its own context. Another aspect of the book we love is how it continually reminds you to use that physical or virtual whiteboard and visualize whatever is being discussed.

The book guides you from strategy to implementation—planning for your context. The last five chapters are very specific for advanced API automation. They go broad and deep, covering contract testing, performance testing for web APIs, security testing, and testing in production. You can choose which of these topics you want to explore first.

One of our favorite models, used extensively throughout the book, is based on a model created by James Lyndsay. It's a Venn diagram of imagination—what we want in a product—and implementation—what we have in a product. It helps us think of questions like "Who will be consuming this API response" and "What if I hit that Add button a thousand times?" It's one of the many ways this book helps us to think "outside the box."

The use of APIs continues to grow as more applications incorporate microservices and the cloud. Using the techniques and models in this book will produce high-quality, reliable APIs. These same models and techniques can be adapted to help with many other kinds of testing as well. Read this book, and you will strengthen your foundation of testing skills.

—Janet Gregory, consultant, author, speaker, DragonFire Inc.; co-founder with Lisa Crispin of the Agile Testing Fellowship

—Lisa Crispin, test consultant, author; co-founder with Janet Gregory of the Agile Testing Fellowship

preface

I always felt that when I first started API testing, I was late to the game. Software as a Service was being widely adopted, and microservices were starting to gain traction. I had seen developers in my team working successfully with API testing in an automation context, but it wasn't until I was fortunate enough to work with one that my API testing journey began. Thank you, Upesh!

However, as I developed my skills and began to share my knowledge with video courses and in-person training, it became apparent that many are yet to start the journey—or have started but are looking to learn more. This was my motivation for this book: to create an expansive view of the many ways in which we can test web APIs and learn how they work.

When I first began to teach others about API testing, my focus was to help testers understand and leverage the power of HTTP to help them test faster and deeper. But as I developed my material and began this book, I began to appreciate that there was so much more to cover. That's why in this book we'll explore a range of testing activities that we can take advantage of when working with web APIs that span the software development life cycle—ranging from asking questions before a single line of code is created to building sophisticated automation that gives us valuable feedback.

I hope that by exploring these activities with you throughout this book, you'll have the tools at your disposal to be better API testers, regardless of your background and role.

acknowledgments

I would first like to thank those who actively helped me put this book together: my editors—Christina Taylor, who was so patient with me as I took a break to become a dad again, and Sarah Miller, who helped me get this book over the line, as well as to all the production staff at Manning. I'd also like to thank Abby Bangser and Bill Matthews who took the time to let me pick their brains about testing in production and security testing, respectively. Also a thanks to my *Automation in Testing* partner in crime, Richard Bradshaw, whose many discussions around testability and strategy helped inform the chapter on establishing testing strategies. Long may we continue to change attitudes towards test automation. Finally, thanks to all the people who have reviewed and given me feedback via MEAP and the review process: Alberto Almagro, Allen Gooch, Amit Sharad Basnak, Andres Sacco, Andy Kirsch, Andy Wiesendanger, Anne-Laure Gaillard, Anupam Patil, Barnaby Norman, Christopher Kardell, Daniel Cortés, Daniel Hunt, Ernesto Bossi, Ethien Daniel Salinas Domínguez, Hawley Waldman, Henrik Jepsen, Hugo Figueiredo, James Liu, Jaswanth Manigundan, Jeffrey M. Smith, Jonathan Lane, Jonathan Terry, Jorge Ezequiel Bo, Ken Schwartz, Kevin Orr, Mariyah Haris, Mark Collin, Marleny Nunez Alba, Mikael Dautrey, Dr. Michael Piscatello, Brian Cole, Narayanan Jayaratchagan, NaveenKumar Namachivayam, George Onofrei, Peter Sellars, Prashanth Palakollu, Rajinder Yadav, Raúl Nicolás, Rohinton Kazak, Roman Zhuzha, Ronald Borman, Samer Falik, Santosh Shanbhag, Shashank Polasa Venkata, Suman Bala, Thomas Forys, Tiziano Bezzi, Vicker Leung, Vladimir Pasman, Werner Nindl, William Ryan, Yvon Vieville, and Zoheb Ainapore. It's been difficult but valuable reading.

I'm also indebted to Lisa Crispin and Janet Gregory for their kind words and their time spent writing this book's foreword. Thank you also to James Lyndsay, Rob Meaney, and Ash Winter, whose work has helped frame my understanding of key aspects of testing and for letting me share and expand upon that work within this book.

There are also people I'd like to thank who unknowingly helped me with this book: people like Upesh Amin, who kindly took the time many years ago to teach me HTTP one afternoon, and Alan Richardson, who started me on the journey of writing this book during a Marketing 101 course, of all places!

This work is a culmination of my experiences working within the testing community, so thank you to everyone at Ministry of Testing and the many friends I've made over the years at various testing community events. Also, to everyone who has sarcastically asked, "Oh, are you writing a book?" I appreciate the free publicity and motivation.

But most of all, I want to thank Steph, who has always supported me through all of the crazy projects I've pursued, and who patiently and politely congratulated me each night as I excitedly told that her I had written "three more pages!" . . . for a year.

about this book

The intention of this book is twofold. The first goal is to get you, the reader, comfortable with a wide range of different testing activities that can be carried out against web APIs. As you go through many of the chapters, you'll learn both how to execute these different testing activities and to appreciate what types of risks they mitigate and information they reveal. The second goal is to help you toward creating and communicating a test strategy that successfully combines the different testing activities you've learned about in a way that works for your context.

Who should read this book

In writing this book, I've attempted to lay out each part and chapter in the book to help you build up a testing strategy brick by brick. However, in the spirit of different strategies for different contexts, I've suggested a few ways in which you might want to use this book to help you succeed with your testing.

Regardless of your motivation, I highly encourage you to read the whole of part 1. Chapter 2 will get you set up with the role-play project that all the book's examples are related to, which you will need if you want to try out a lot of the activities within this book. Chapter 3 is essential reading because it explores quality and risk in detail and how they inform how and what you test. I'm a firm believer that to be successful in testing, you need a clear understanding of what problem you're trying to solve. If you don't know what the problem is, how can you be sure you've picked the right approach, and how can you measure success?

The rest of the book is there for you to read at your leisure. My hope is that for some, the book will act as a guide through every step of building a testing strategy, and for others, it will act as a handy reference guide to remind you of specific techniques, resources, and skills as and when you need them.

A newcomer to building an API testing strategy

The book is structured so as to take you through the journey from starting with no strategy at all to building, implementing, and executing a successful testing strategy. Therefore, if you're new to building test strategies and/or API testing, then simply follow along with each chapter to build up your knowledge and skills.

Enhancing an existing API testing strategy

Not everyone involved in a project is starting from scratch, and you might be a member of a team looking to bolster an existing testing strategy. In that case, I recommend you read the material about building a strategy and reflect on how it relates to your own strategy to better understand what gaps you might have. That analysis will then help you decide which activities you feel are required to help support your team.

Interested in specific activities

For some, you may be looking to learn more about how to get started with specific activities and aren't necessarily thinking about the bigger picture (e.g., you might have been tasked with implementing specific activities for a wider strategy). If this is your motivation, I recommend that you focus on the case studies and example sections of each testing activity. For some, it's easier to get a sense of where an activity sits within a strategy by trying it out and then working backward.

How this book is organized: A road map

The book has been divided into three sections across 12 chapters.

Part 1: Establishing our testing strategy

In chapter 1, we'll focus first on asking ourselves why we need testing and why understanding the value of testing can help kick-start our testing strategy. Chapter 2 familiarizes us with a role-playing project we'll use as a guide throughout this book to learn a range of testing techniques to help us quickly establish an understanding of what we're testing and who we're testing for. Chapter 3 concludes this part of the book by exploring how to establish the goals we aim to achieve with our testing strategy, which helps us prioritize what type of testing we might want to do.

Part 2: Introducing testing activities to our strategy

In part 2, chapters 4 to 7, we'll begin to explore a range of testing activities available to us when testing web APIs. There are a range of activities to try out for yourself, examples to learn from, and case studies to reflect upon. I've ordered the chapters in this part of the book to follow the common software development life cycle starting with ideation to implementation to maintenance.

This part of the book concludes with a chapter on how our working context informs our strategy and how we can go about implementing our strategy in a way that supports a team's existing work. We'll then use that knowledge to piece together our testing activities to form the meat of our testing strategy.

Part 3: Expanding our test strategy

In the final part of the book, chapters 8 to 12, we'll continue to learn more about different testing activities available to us, as well as expand upon some of the activities we've already learned about. It's important to note that the activities we'll cover in this section aren't necessarily more advanced or requiring more skill. However, they may perhaps require a greater investment in time and a more mature testing culture to establish them alongside what we will have already learned.

Prerequisites

There will be an assumption that you are coming into this book with a range of preexisting skills and knowledge.

HTTP

To test web APIs, we will need to use HTTP extensively, and we will explore an aspect of HTTP in detail to leverage different test ideas. This book, however, doesn't offer an introduction to HTTP. Therefore, it is assumed you have some knowledge of HTTP rules such as the following:

- Uniform resource identifiers/locators
- HTTP methods
- HTTP headers
- Status codes
- Request and response payloads

Java

For the coding portions of this book, I've opted to use Java, based on its ubiquity in the API development world. Although this means we'll have to deal with additional boilerplate code that comes with Java, the examples we'll explore will reach the widest audience possible. Additionally, the examples contain a lot of design patterns for the automation code, and the approaches are universal across languages. So I encourage you to either read the exercises or give them a try. That said, to carry out these exercises, you should have a working knowledge of the following:

- Libraries
- Packages
- Classes
- Tests methods
- Assertions

Other tooling

This book will also explore a range of tools that can be used to support various testing activities. Although previous knowledge of these tools is not required, it's worth mentioning the following key tools to help you prepare/get the necessary tools installed:

- *DevTools*—An extension found in most browsers to help you debug a web page (https://developer.chrome.com/docs/devtools)
- *Postman*—A tooling platform that helps you build and test web APIs (https://www.postman.com)
- *Wireshark*—An HTTP sniffing tool that allows you to intercept HTTP traffic between APIs (https://www.wireshark.org)
- *Swagger*—An API documentation and design tool that provides living documentation that you can interact with to learn more about web APIs (https://swagger.io)
- *WireMock*—A tool for mocking web APIs to increase the controllability of your API testing (https://wiremock.org)
- *Pact*—A contract testing tool that checks the integration between web APIs (https://pact.io)
- *Apache JMeter*—A performance and functional testing tool for web APIs (https://jmeter.apache.org)

Feel free to research any of these tools before we begin our journey.

About the code

This book contains many examples of source code both in numbered listings and in line with normal text. In both cases, source code is formatted in a `fixed-width font like this` to separate it from ordinary text.

Additionally, comments in the source code have often been removed from the listings when the code is described in the text. Code annotations accompany many of the listings, highlighting important concepts.

You can get executable snippets of code from the liveBook (online) version of this book at https://livebook.manning.com/book/testing-web-apis. The complete code for the examples in the book is available for download from the Manning website at https://www.manning.com/books/testing-web-apis.

Additionally, you should be aware of two supporting repositories that will be referenced multiple times throughout the book.

Restful-booker-platform

Restful-booker-platform is our sandbox API platform that we'll be practicing different testing activities against. The codebase for this application can be found at https://github.com/mwinteringham/restful-booker-platform, and installation details can be found in the book's appendix.

API Strategy Book Resources

Many of the chapters have resources such as testing notes, example code, and performance test scripts that can be reviewed in their own respective projects within the following repo: https://github.com/mwinteringham/api-strategy-book-resources. All code sections can be run locally.

liveBook discussion forum

Purchase of *Testing Web APIs* includes free access to liveBook, Manning's online reading platform. Using liveBook's exclusive discussion features, you can attach comments to the book globally or to specific sections or paragraphs. It's a snap to make notes for yourself, ask and answer technical questions, and receive help from the author and other users. To access the forum, go to https://livebook.manning.com/book/testing -web-apis/discussion. You can also learn more about Manning's forums and the rules of conduct at https://livebook.manning.com/discussion.

Manning's commitment to our readers is to provide a venue where a meaningful dialogue between individual readers and between readers and the author can take place. It is not a commitment to any specific amount of participation on the part of the author, whose contribution to the forum remains voluntary (and unpaid). We suggest you try asking the author some challenging questions lest his interest stray! The forum and the archives of previous discussions will be accessible from the publisher's website as long as the book is in print.

about the author

MARK WINTERINGHAM is a tester, toolsmith, and COO of Ministry of Testing, with more than 10 years of experience providing testing expertise on award-winning projects across a wide range of technology sectors including BBC, Barclays, the UK government, and Thomson Reuters. He is an advocate for modern risk-based testing practices and trains teams in automation in testing, behavior-driven development, and exploratory testing techniques. He is also the cofounder of Ministry of Testing, a community raising awareness of careers in testing and improving testing education.

about the cover illustration

The figure on the cover of *Testing Web APIs* is "Boucbar de Siberie," or "Siberian Shepherd," taken from a collection by Jacques Grasset de Saint-Sauveur, published in 1788. Each illustration is finely drawn and colored by hand.

In those days, it was easy to identify where people lived and what their trade or station in life was just by their dress. Manning celebrates the inventiveness and initiative of the computer business with book covers based on the rich diversity of regional culture centuries ago, brought back to life by pictures from collections such as this one.

Part 1

The value of web API testing

What is the point of testing? This might seem like a sarcastic question to ask at the start of a book about testing. But knowing the reason why we test and the value it brings can help guide us in how we approach it. If we assume that testing is just pushing buttons and breaking things, then that is the level of testing we'll get. But we should appreciate that testing is a collection of skills, knowledge, and activities that, when brought together, can help elevate our team's efforts in building high-quality work. That's why, before we dive into specific testing activities, we need to learn the value of good testing and how to focus it in the right places at the right time.

In part 1, we'll explore why we test and how to begin the process of testing that delivers real value to both our teams and our customers. In chapter 1, we'll discuss the challenges around delivering high-quality web APIs and a way of understanding how testing can help solve those challenges. Chapter 2 will explore some ways to begin our testing journey and establish some of the activities we'll be carrying out within this book. Finally, chapter 3 will discuss in detail two key concepts that guide our testing: quality and risk.

Why and how we
test web APIs

This chapter covers

- The challenges of building complex API platforms
- The value and purpose of testing
- What an API testing strategy looks like and how it can help

How do we ensure that what we're building is of good quality and is valuable to our end users? The challenge we face when delivering a high-quality product is the sheer number of complex actions and activities that occur in our work. If we want to make informed choices that lead to improved quality, we need to overcome this complexity and develop an understanding of both how our systems work and what our users want from our products. This is why we need to adopt a valuable testing strategy to help us better understand what we're actually building. So before we begin our API testing journey, let's first reflect on why software is so complicated and how testing can help.

1.1 What's going on in your web APIs?

In 2013, the UK government set out a digital strategy to move each department to a "Digital by Default Service Standard," which included Her Majesty's Revenue and

Customs (also known as HMRC). HMRC's goal was to bring all the UK tax services online to improve services and cut costs.

By 2017, the HMRC tax platform boasted more than 100 digital services, created by 60 delivery teams across five different delivery centers. Each of these digital services is supported by a platform of interconnected web APIs that were, and still are, constantly growing. The number of APIs created to support these services is dizzying. Even when I joined the project in 2015 and there were approximately half the services, teams, and delivery centers that there are now, the platform contained well over 100 web APIs. That number has undoubtedly increased since then, which begs the question: How does a project of this size and complexity deliver high-quality services to end users?

I mention the HMRC project because it helps highlight the following two "levels" of complexity that we face regularly when building web APIs:

- The complexity that exists within a web API
- The complexity of many web APIs working together in a platform

By understanding both of these categories, we can begin to appreciate why we need testing and how it can help.

1.1.1   *Complexity within web APIs*

It might seem a bit simple to start with this question: What is a web API? But if we take the time to dive into the makeup of a web API, we can discover not only what a web API is but also where its complexity lies. Take, for example, this visualization of a bookings web API that we'll test later in this book, shown in figure 1.1.

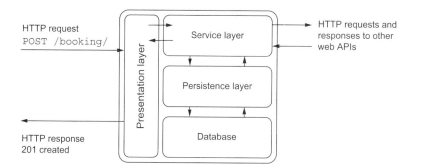

Figure 1.1   This visual model depicts a web API, its components, and how it works.

Using this diagram, we can see that a web API works by receiving bookings in the form of HTTP requests from clients, which trigger different layers within the API to execute. Once the execution is complete and the booking has been stored, the web API responds via HTTP. But if we take a more granular step through the API, we start to get a sense of just how much is going on within a single web API.

First, the presentation layer receives a booking HTTP request and translates it into content that can be read by the other layers. Next, the service layer takes the booking information and applies business logic to it. (E.g., is it a valid booking, and does it conflict with other bookings?) Finally, if the processed booking needs to be stored, it is prepared for storage within the persistence layer and then stored within a database. If all of that is successful, each layer has to respond to the other to create the response the web API is going to send to whomever sent the request.

Each of these layers can be built in different ways, depending on our requirements and tastes. For example, we have the option to design web APIs using a range of approaches such as the REST architecture pattern, GraphQL, or SOAP, all of which have their own patterns and rules that require our understanding.

Working with REST

Throughout this book, we'll predominantly work with web APIs that are built using REST architecture. Many different architectural styles exist, but REST is currently the most widely used. However, it is worth noting that although approaches such as GraphQL and SOAP use different approaches, the testing activities we will explore are equally applicable when you are working with any of these architecture types. Throughout the book, we'll discuss briefly how what we're learning can be applied to any architecture style.

The services layer also contains our business logic, which, depending on our context, will have many specific custom rules to follow. A similar case applies to the persistence layers. Each of these layers relies on dependencies that have their own active development life cycles. We need to be aware of a vast amount of information to help us deliver high-quality work.

Understanding what is going on in our web APIs and how they help others is an exercise that requires time and expertise. Yes, we might be able to develop some level of understanding by testing parts individually (which I encourage teams to do; check out J. B. Rainsberger's talk "Integrated Tests Are a Scam" to learn more: https://youtu.be/VDfX44fZoMc), but that knowledge gives us only a piece of the puzzle, not all of it.

1.1.2   *Complexity across many web APIs*

Think about the HMRC platform with its more than 100 web APIs, mentioned earlier. How do we maintain an understanding of how each one works and how they relate to one another? Approaches such as microservice architecture help reduce the complexity within singular web APIs by making them smaller and more focused. But, on the other hand, they can lead to even more web APIs being added to a platform. How do we ensure that our knowledge of a platform of web APIs is up to date? And how do we keep up with how each API talks to others and confirm that their connections to each other are working within expected parameters?

To build a high-quality product, we have to make informed choices, which means our knowledge of how our web APIs work and how they relate to each other and our end users is vital. If we don't make informed choices, we risk issues appearing in our products when we misinterpret how our systems work due to our lack of knowledge. It's from this perspective that we can begin to appreciate how testing can help us establish and maintain that understanding.

1.2   How does testing help us?

If we're going to be successful as a team with our testing, we require a shared understanding of the purpose and value of testing. Sadly, there are a lot of misconceptions about what testing is and what it offers, so to help us all get on the same page, let me introduce you to a model of testing that I use to better understand what testing is and how it helps, as shown in figure 1.2.

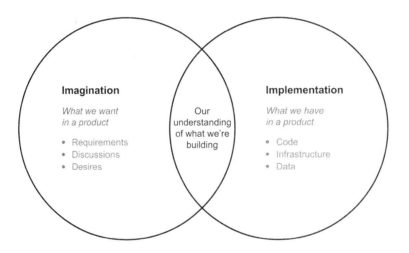

Figure 1.2   A model of testing helps to describe the value and purpose of testing.

The model, based on one created by James Lyndsay in his paper "Why Exploration has a Place in any Strategy" (http://mng.bz/o2vd), comprises two circles. The left circle represents imagination, or what it is that we *want* in a product, and the right circle represents implementation, or what it is that we *have* in a product. The purpose of testing is to learn as much as possible about what's going on in each of these circles by carrying out testing activities. The more we test in these two circles, the more we learn and the more we achieve the following:

- Discovering potential issues that might impact the quality
- Overlapping these two circles of information, ensuring that we understand what we are building and can be confident that it is the product or service we want to build

To examine this further, let's look at an example in which a team is delivering a hypothetical search feature that we want to ensure is of a high degree of quality.

1.2.1 Imagination

The imagination circle represents what we want from our product, which includes expectations that are both explicit and implicit. In this circle, our testing is focused on learning as much as possible about those explicit and implicit expectations. By doing this, we learn not just what has been explicitly stated in writing or verbally shared, but we also dig down into the details and remove ambiguity over terms and ideas. For example, let's say a representative of the business or a user, such as a product owner, has shared this requirement with their team: "Search results are to be ordered by relevance."

The explicit information shared here tells us that the product owner wants search results, and they want them ordered by relevance. However, we can uncover a lot of implied information by testing the ideas and concepts behind what is being asked. This might come in the form of a series of questions we could ask, such as the following:

- What is meant by *relevant results*?
- Relevant to whom?
- What information is shared?
- How do we order by relevancy?
- What data should we use?

By asking these questions, we get a fuller picture of what is wanted, remove any misunderstandings in our team's thinking, and identify potential risks that could impact those expectations. If we know more about what we are being asked to build, we're more likely to build the right thing the first time.

1.2.2 Implementation

By testing the imagination, we get a stronger sense of what we are being asked to build. But just because we might know what to build doesn't mean we will end up with a product that matches those expectations. This is why we also test the implementation to learn the following:

- Whether the product matches our expectations
- How the product might not match our expectations

Both goals are of equal importance. We want to ensure that we have built the right thing, but side effects—such as unintended behavior, vulnerabilities, missed expectations, and downright weirdness that might appear in our products—will always exist. With our search results example, we could not only test that the feature delivers results in the relevant order, but we could also ask the product

- What if I enter different search terms?
- What if the relevant results don't match the behavior of other search tools?

- What if part of the service is down when I search?
- What if I request results 1,000 times in less than 5 seconds?
- What happens if there are no results?

By exploring beyond our expectations, we become more aware of what is going on in our product, warts and all. This ensures that we don't end up making incorrect assumptions about how our product behaves and releasing a poor-quality product. It also means that if we find unexpected behavior, we have the choice to attempt to remove or readjust our expectations.

1.2.3   *The value of testing*

The model of testing the imagination and implementation demonstrates that the testing goes beyond a simple confirmation of expectations and challenges our assumptions. The more we learn through testing about what we want to build and what we have built, the more these two circles align with one another. And the more they align, the more accurate our perception of quality becomes.

> **Surprise—you're already testing!**
>
> Because the goal of testing is to understand and learn about what we want our products to do and how they should work, it's worth mentioning that you're probably already doing some form of testing. It can be argued that in any activity that you do, whether it's debugging code, loading an API and casually sending some requests, or sending some questions about how your API should work to a client, you're learning; therefore, you're testing.
>
> This is why testing is sometimes assumed to be an easy task to carry out. But there is a difference between ad hoc, informal testing and focused, intentional testing. We've learned how our product's complexity can overwhelm us, and it's only with a strategic approach to testing that we can really start to see a difference.

A team that is well informed about their work has a better idea of the quality of their product. They are also better equipped to decide what steps to take to improve quality, enabling us to decide to focus our attention on specific risks, make changes in our product to closer align with user's expectations, or determine what issues we want to invest time in to fix and which to leave. This is the value of good testing: it helps teams get into a position where they can make these informed decisions and feel confident in the steps they are taking to develop a high-quality product.

1.2.4   *Being strategic with API testing*

I find this model to be an excellent way to describe the purpose and value of testing; however, it can feel somewhat abstract. How does this model apply to API testing? What would an API testing strategy look like using this approach? One of the goals of this book is to teach you exactly that. To help us better understand this model, let's look at an example API testing strategy that could have been used for a different project than the HMRC project that I was part of.

The project was a service that allowed users to search and read regulatory documents as well as create reports on the back of said documents. The architecture of the system is summarized briefly in the model in figure 1.3.

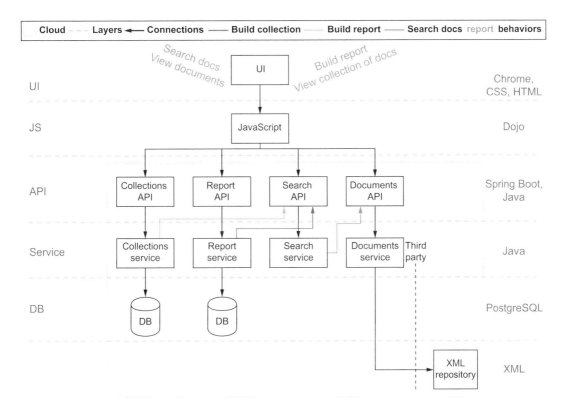

Figure 1.3 An informal visualization of the system architecture of a web API platform

Just for clarity, this is a stripped-down version of the application I worked on. But it gives us a sense of the types of applications we might work with if we're tasked with creating a strategy for API testing. We'll discuss this model further in chapter 2, but here it shows us that this application was made up of a series of web APIs that provided services to the UI and to each other. For example, the Search API could be queried by the UI, but it could also be queried by another API, such as the Report API. So, we have our example application, but how do we apply the testing model we learned about to this context? Once again, this can best be explained visually with the model shown in figure 1.4.

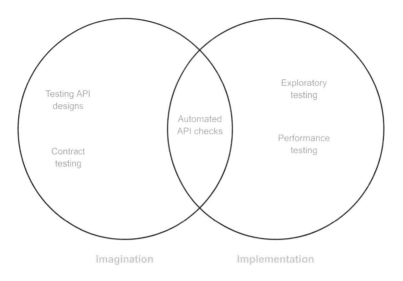

Figure 1.4   An instance of the testing model describes specific testing activities as part of an API test strategy

As we can see, both the imagination and implementation portions have been filled with a range of testing activities that can help us learn about how our web APIs work. On the imagination side, we have activities such as the following:

- *Testing API designs*— Allow us to question ideas and create a shared understanding around what problems we're attempting to solve
- *Contract testing*—Supports teams in ensuring that their web APIs speak to each other and are updated correctly when changes occur

On the implementation side, we have activities such as these:

- *Exploratory testing*—Enables us to learn how our web APIs are behaving and discover potential issues
- *Performance testing*—Helps us to better understand how our web APIs behave when under load

And finally, we have *automated API checks* that cover the areas where our knowledge of what we want to build (imagination) and what we have built (implementation) overlap. These checks can confirm whether our knowledge of how our APIs work is still correct and bring to our attention any potential regression in quality.

We will learn more about these activities throughout this book, along with other testing activities. But this model demonstrates how different testing activities focus on different areas of our work and reveal different information. It also shows us that a successful testing strategy for APIs is holistic in its approach, a combination of many different activities all working together to help keep ourselves and our teams informed. To create this strategy, we need to do the following:

1 *Understand our context and its risks*—Who are our users? What do they want? How does our product work? How do we work? What does quality mean to them?

2 *Appreciate the types of testing activities available to us*—Do we know how to use automation effectively? Are we aware that we can test ideas and API designs before coding begins? How can we get value from testing in production?

3 *Use our context knowledge to pick the right testing activities*—What risks matter the most to us, and what testing activities should we use to mitigate them?

This book will explore these three points to give you the necessary skills and knowledge to identify and deliver a testing strategy that works for you, your team, and your organization. As we progress through the book, we'll use the testing model to first help us understand which testing activities work best where and then establish a testing strategy that works for us. Before we dive too deeply into the many API testing opportunities that are available, let's first get comfortable with a few approaches that can help us rapidly learn about our web API platforms.

Summary

- Web APIs contain a range of layers. Each carries out complex tasks of its own that are made all the more complex when combined.
- Complexity scales even further when multiple web APIs work together to create services for an end user on a platform.
- Overcoming this complexity and understanding it are key to delivering a high-quality product.
- To establish understanding, we require a focused testing strategy.
- Testing can be thought of as focusing on two areas: imagination and implementation.
- We test imagination to learn more about what we want to build, and we test implementation to learn more about what we have built.
- The more we know about both the imagination and the implementation areas, the more the two overlap and the better informed we are about the quality of our work.
- The testing model can be used to show how different testing activities work in the imagination and implementation areas.
- A successful testing strategy will be made up of many testing activities that all work together to support a team.

Beginning our testing journey

This chapter covers

- Introducing our product
- Setting up our product
- Learning about what we're testing from our teams, the product, and its source code
- Capturing our understanding visually to share with others

Imagine it's our first day on an established project. We've joined a team, and we've been tasked with implementing a testing strategy to help the team and improve quality. Where do we begin, or what are our next steps for furthering an existing test strategy? We want to help our teams build high-quality products, but what is the best course of action to take? Are there new tools, techniques, or activities we should adopt?

This is the situation in which we find ourselves in this book right now. In the upcoming chapters, we'll learn different ways to test web APIs and how to build an API testing strategy, and to help us learn, we'll practice with an example product. Just like that imaginary first day, we're tasked with building an API testing strategy for an application and a context we're unfamiliar with. Therefore, in this chapter, we'll learn not only about our product that we'll be testing throughout the book but also how to begin our journey toward establishing a successful API testing strategy.

> **Getting set up**
>
> Before you begin this chapter, I strongly encourage you to download and install the sandbox API platform, restful-booker-platform, which we'll use throughout this chapter and beyond. You can find details on how to install the application in the appendix of this book.

2.1   Introducing our product

When beginning testing on a new product, it can be tempting to just dive in right away. However, we can get a lot of value from taking a step back and learning about the history of the product we're responsible for. By taking the time to learn about the journey our team and our product have been on, we'll reveal information on how the product works, what our teams hope to achieve, and what problems we're trying to solve for our users, all of which will help us become more familiar with testing the product and form our initial ideas on what our testing strategy should look like.

> **Already working on a product?**
>
> Although this chapter is framed as a situation in which we'll start fresh on a project without a testing strategy, many of us are more likely to be working on existing projects. However, the tools and techniques you'll learn in this chapter are of use to us regardless of our context. This chapter is here to help kick-start and accelerate your ability to understand how your API platform works and communicate that understanding to others.

To help us appreciate what we might learn, let's get acquainted with restful-booker-platform and learn what it does, why it was built, and what we are going to do to help improve its quality.

2.1.1   Introducing our sandbox API

To help us get into the mindset of building an API testing strategy, let's imagine that restful-booker-platform is a real-life product that we're responsible for. In our role-play, restful-booker-platform has been created for bed-and-breakfast (B&B) owners to manage their websites and bookings, with the following features:

- Creating branding to market the B&B
- Adding rooms with details for guests to book

- Enabling guests to create bookings
- Viewing reports for bookings to assess availability
- Allowing guests to send messages to contact the B&B host

The platform was initially built as a hobby project for a single B&B owner but has since grown and is now used by multiple B&B owners to take bookings. The project is slowly expanding both in scope and customer base but has suffered issues of late during its growth. Some B&B owners have expressed frustration with bugs, downtime, and incorrectly implemented features. Our goal is to provide a testing strategy that helps the team improve the quality of restful-booker-platform and ensures that both B&B owners and guests are happy with the product.

2.2 *Familiarizing ourselves with restful-booker-platform*

By reading about restful-booker-platform's short history, we've learned the following:

- The application is built for B&Bs, meaning we have two different user types, guests and B&B managers, to consider when designing our APIs.
- It contains multiple different features, which imply that multiple services are likely being processed by multiple APIs.
- The core of the product is built using Java, which suggests what languages and tools we might want to use to automate some of our testing.

But most important, we've learned that we're required to identify and implement an API testing strategy that can help our team improve the quality of our product.

We could dive right in and begin to use some preexisting techniques and tooling or just start sending requests to various web APIs on our platform to see what happens. This might deliver some value, but it's not really going to push forward our goal of creating an effective API testing strategy. A good strategy requires an understanding of what we're being asked to write a strategy for. Without knowledge of how our system works, how it is implemented, and by whom and for whom is it being built, how are we going to identify the right activities for our strategy?

Before we start making snap decisions, we need to build up our understanding of the product and project. This means researching various sources of information and using tools to help us learn more about the product for which we're going to build a strategy. As we begin our research, it's important to note that there isn't any priority on what to research first. Depending on our own preferences or learning style, we might want to start by reading documentation or source code first, ask for a demonstration from a team member, or play around with the product. Whatever we pick first, it's important to remember two things: first, the goal is to expand our understanding of the context for which we're being asked to build a strategy. This means focusing on learning and not on pushing systems to their limits to find issues (although sometimes finding issues will naturally occur). Second, we should take the time to research all facets of our products and project. The more we learn, the clearer our strategic choices will become when it comes to implementing our strategy. However, we do need to pick one place to start, so let's begin our research by looking at the product itself.

2.2.1 Researching the product

Because our focus for this book is on implementing an API testing strategy, we won't put too much of our testing attention on the user interface. However, that doesn't mean we can't use it to help our research. By using our product as a user would, we can begin to learn more about both the needs of our users as well as how our product is currently addressing them.

> **Activity**
>
> Take some time to book a room and contact the B&B as a guest. Also, try logging in as a B&B manager and creating rooms, updating the branding, reading reports, and accessing messages. The login credentials for a default administrator can be found in the README file. You can access restful-booker-platform via either http://local host:8080 or https://automationintesting.online, depending on whether or not you're running the application locally. Take notes about what you learn.

> **There's a UI in my API book!**
>
> By now you'll have discovered that our sandbox comes with a user interface because restful-booker-platform is used for teaching a range of activities beyond API testing. We'll take advantage of the UI initially in this chapter to demonstrate that if your API platform does have a UI, you can use it to help learn how your application works. But as we progress, the UI is out of scope for this book. If you require a test strategy that includes both API and UI testing, take some time to research testing activities that are relevant in the UI space.

DEV TOOLS

Navigating through restful-booker-platform via the UI helps provide some initial context about the product, but our goal is the web APIs that sit behind the UI. We can dig deeper into the product by using built-in tools for browsers like Google Chrome and Firefox. These tools, which we'll refer to as dev tools for consistency, come with features such as HTTP traffic monitoring, which allows us to capture the requests that come from the browser and the responses that come back. This traffic is then available for us to analyze and use to build up our understanding of what web APIs are being called and what details are being shared.

For example, let's look at the landing page for restful-booker-platform. First, open up dev tools (the quickest way is to right-click on the page and select Inspect Element), and then open the Network tab. Click the XHR filter, and then visit either https://automationintesting.online or http://localhost:8080.

XHRs, which stand for XMLHttpRequests, are HTTP requests sent from the browser to the API in the background. These can be used for situations in which we want to asynchronously modify data for either the UI or the backend without having to update the entire page. For example, an XHR request to `/branding/` could be used to update the home page images and details without having to do a whole-page refresh.

The network panel will show results similar to the ones in figure 2.1.

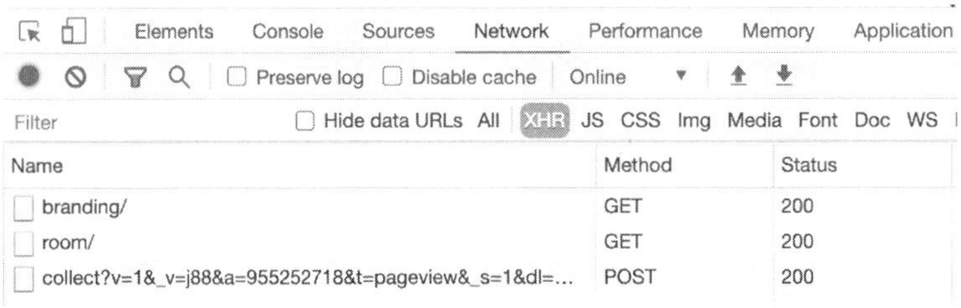

Figure 2.1 A list of HTTP requests in the Network tab of dev tools after calling the home page

From the results, we can see that there are at least two different calls made: one to `/branding/` and another to `/room/`. We can also open each call to see that specific information is being sent from these two web APIs to the UI to drive which images and text are shown on the landing page and which rooms can be booked. This demonstrates that an initial investigation with dev tools open can provide a lot of useful, actionable information that we can build upon in further activities.

Activity

Navigate to each of the pages we've identified in the previous activity while monitoring the traffic between the browser and restful-booker-platform's web APIs. Take notes on what traffic you discover, noting details such as the URIs in the HTTP requests, which tell you what web APIs restful-booker-platform might have. Look to see whether other APIs are being called and what their URIs are. Also keep an eye on what types of HTTP methods are being used.

TIP Clearing your network history between each call makes it easier to see what new network calls are being made. You can do this by clicking the Clear button, which you can find in the top-left corner, next to the recording icon.

HTTP CLIENTS

Now that we've identified HTTP traffic between the UI and web APIs, we can use that knowledge to expand our understanding of how each web API behaves. To do this, we're going to use the HTTP testing client, Postman.

We can download a free version of the tool from https://www.postman.com/downloads/, containing all the features we require for our research. If this is your first time working with Postman, ensure that you've installed the tooling, created an account, and created a new workspace. Once installed and set up, we can start copying the

HTTP requests we've discovered in dev tools over to Postman for us to work with. You can do this by following these example steps for one of the `room` endpoints:

1 Begin by opening dev tools and populating the Network tab view with HTTP requests by refreshing or loading the Admin panel.

2 Next, right-click on the HTTP request `/room/` and select Copy > Copy as Curl. (Select the Bash option if you are presented with the option to copy either Cmd or Bash.)

3 With your HTTP request now copied as a curl request, head over to Postman and click Import in the top left-hand corner.

4 Once the import popup appears, select Raw text, copy in your curl request, and click Continue > Import. You'll now see the HTTP request in Postman for you to use.

With the HTTP request now inside Postman, we can modify and execute the request to learn more about how the web API behaves. For example, with the `GET /room/` endpoint, we could do the following:

- Modify the URI to `/room/1` to discover an additional endpoint that shows specific room details.
- Change the HTTP method to `OPTIONS` to discover other HTTP methods that can be called on `/room/` in the response headers under `Allow`. (You can find the response headers by selecting the Headers tab in the bottom half of the window.)
- Investigate the request headers to discover custom cookies being sent (specifically, the mention of `token` in cookie value).

By simply making a few changes to the HTTP request, we can identify new information that we can add to our current understanding. Remember, we're not looking to test exhaustively at this time, but with a few changes, we can learn a lot.

Activity

Copy the HTTP requests you've identified from your investigations using dev tools into Postman. Once you've created the requests in Postman, try modifying the URIs, request bodies, and headers to learn more about the endpoints in each API and their behavior. Remember, the goal at this time is to learn, not to find bugs.

As a bonus, research how to create Collections in Postman and add your requests in there for future use. The Postman website has comprehensive documentation on how Collections work.

PROXY TOOLS

So far, our research has focused on the traffic between the browser and the backend web APIs. However, not all of the API platform's traffic is found between the browser and the backend, and in restful-booker-platform's case, there is much more to explore. We need to expand our research to start learning how many web APIs exist in this platform and how they talk to each other, which we can do with the proxy tool, Wireshark.

Wireshark is an advanced network-analyzing tool that can sniff traffic based on a wide range of network protocols. We're going to use Wireshark to monitor the local HTTP traffic between the APIs that exist in restful-booker-platform. Unfortunately, because this technique requires access to local traffic, we're going to need restful-booker-platform running locally. We also need to install and download Wireshark from https://www.wireshark.org/.

Once Wireshark is installed, we can start up the application and, from the Capture list, select the item in the list that has *Loopback* in the title, similar to the one shown in figure 2.2.

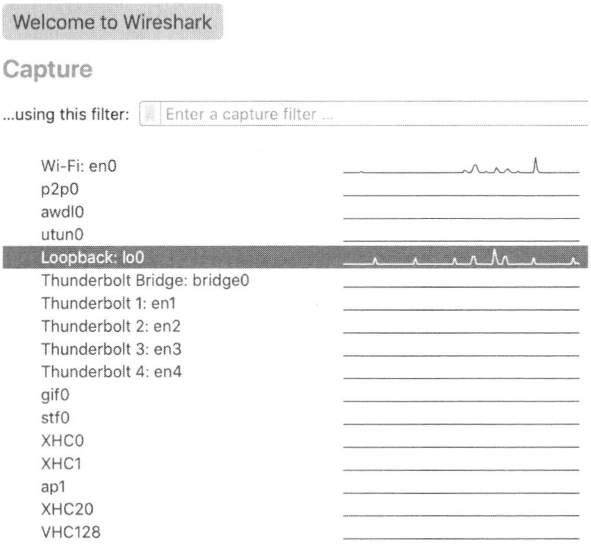

Figure 2.2   A list of networks to select in Wireshark with our desired network, Loopback, selected

If you don't see Loopback in the list, check to see whether you require additional permissions or plugins as part of your OS.

Troubleshooting Wireshark

If you are having issues with Wireshark, you might need to consider the following:

- If you're using Wireshark on a Mac, ensure you also install ChmodBPF because this is required to allow you to listen to traffic on localhost. You can find install details here: https://formulae.brew.sh/cask/wireshark-chmodbpf.
- Not all network cards support the ability to monitor internal traffic. If you are unable to get Loopback set up, consider searching online to see whether Wireshark works with your network card.

Wireshark will now monitor any network activity that is occurring internally in our machine. Once the Loopback interface is selected, we'll begin to see a list of every network request and response that has been triggered since Wireshark began monitoring. You might observe that the list fills up quickly with a range of network activities from different protocols (HTTP, TCP, UDP, etc.). To make our researching activity a bit easier, enter the term `http` into the filter view and press Enter. The list will update and show only HTTP requests and responses.

With Wireshark now set up, we can begin to monitor network activities between the various web APIs. For example, we've learned from the previous activities that there is a `POST /room/` endpoint that we can use to create a room. If we were to use the HTTP client Postman to create a room by sending the `POST /room/` request to the `room` API as shown in figure 2.3, we'd see in Wireshark both a request made to `/room/` and another to `localhost:3004/auth/validate`, as shown in figure 2.4.

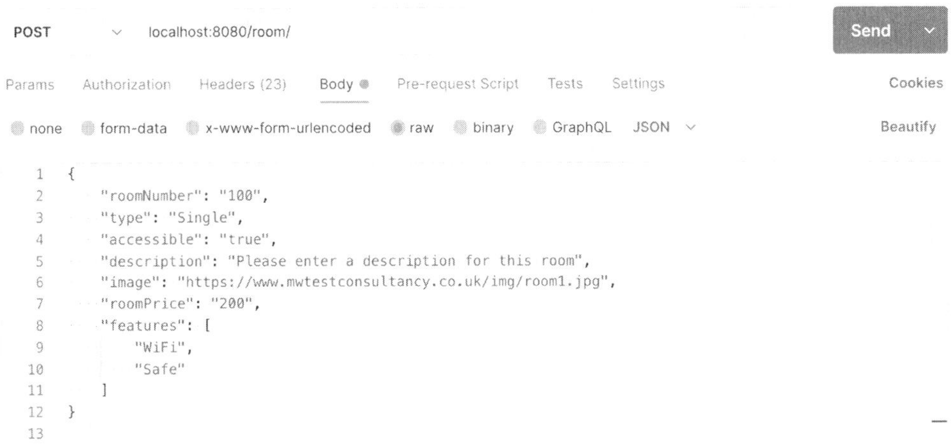

| POST | ∨ | localhost:8080/room/ | | | | | Send ∨ |

Params Authorization Headers (23) Body ● Pre-request Script Tests Settings Cookies

● none ● form-data ● x-www-form-urlencoded ● raw ● binary ● GraphQL JSON ∨ Beautify

```
 1  {
 2      "roomNumber": "100",
 3      "type": "Single",
 4      "accessible": "true",
 5      "description": "Please enter a description for this room",
 6      "image": "https://www.mwtestconsultancy.co.uk/img/room1.jpg",
 7      "roomPrice": "200",
 8      "features": [
 9          "WiFi",
10          "Safe"
11      ]
12  }
13
```

Figure 2.3 A POST HTTP request for the room API using Postman, which allows us to create a room

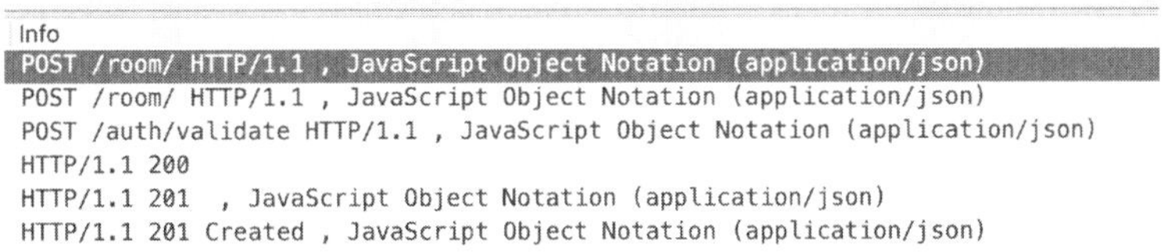

```
Info
POST /room/ HTTP/1.1 , JavaScript Object Notation (application/json)
POST /room/ HTTP/1.1 , JavaScript Object Notation (application/json)
POST /auth/validate HTTP/1.1 , JavaScript Object Notation (application/json)
HTTP/1.1 200
HTTP/1.1 201  , JavaScript Object Notation (application/json)
HTTP/1.1 201 Created , JavaScript Object Notation (application/json)
```

Figure 2.4 An example of an HTTP request that was captured by Wireshark, with the POST request to /room/ highlighted

Based on this information, we can conclude two things:

- There is a web API called `auth` that is listening on port 3004.
- The `room` API sends requests to `auth`.

This demonstrates that a tool like Wireshark can help us dig deeper to learn more details about our API platforms and how web APIs might depend on one another. It does, however, work only in a context in which you have the ability to listen in on network devices on a machine. If the API platform is deployed elsewhere and we lack access, this opportunity is not available.

> **Activity**
>
> Set up Wireshark to sniff for localhost traffic and show requests that are being sent between each web API. Once set up, trigger the various requests you've captured in Postman, and observe what additional traffic is being triggered between web APIs. As an example, try calling `GET /report/` and observe the other requests that the `report` API makes to the other APIs. Make note of what you discover, and update your Postman collection if desired.

Through a few simple activities with restful-booker-platform and through the use of a few tools, we've discovered that restful-booker-platform is made up of a collection of web APIs that offer different features, such as creating rooms, collating reports, and handling security for the product. By having a researching mindset as we go through the product, we've built up an initial understanding of how our product works and may even have begun to start thinking about certain strategic options. However, before that, let's look at some other sources of information that are worth spending time researching to expand our understanding even further.

2.2.2 *Researching beyond the product*

With restful-booker-platform, we've had the added advantage of having a user interface complete with a set of features to interact with. However, not all projects will have user interfaces or be in a completed state to analyze. We may need to consider other sources of information to help build up our understanding. Fortunately, as we build software, additional materials are captured, such as documentation, user stories, and source code, which can serve as excellent guides for us. Let's look at some examples of each for restful-booker-platform to demonstrate the type of additional information we might learn.

DOCUMENTATION

Although attitudes toward documentation have changed as agile became the dominant methodology for delivering software, it's unlikely that a project will have no documentation at all. For a lot of projects, the days of lengthy requirement documents are likely gone, but informal documentation such as Wikis, API documentation, and user stories can help expand our understanding.

For example, with restful-booker-platform, we can learn a lot from the project's README files found at http://mng.bz/nNna. They reveal details we already know about what versions of Java and NodeJS the product runs on and how to run the product locally. But the README file also leads us to other documentation, telling us that each API within the project has its own documentation. Opening up one of the API modules in the source code (more on that in a minute) reveals additional documentation, like the README found here: http://mng.bz/v6g7.

Reading this documentation shows more specific details on how the API is built and how it can be configured and run, as well as details on additional technical API documentation.

As we'll learn in the next chapter, modern API development tools offer a range of features to create rich, interactive API documentation, such as the documentation found here: http://mng.bz/44dw. Open this documentation, and not only will you discover a neatly presented list of all the endpoints we can call for the room web API, but we'll also be given the ability to interact with them through the documentation.

For example, opening room-controller reveals a list of requests we can use. Selecting GET /room/ presents us with a detailed technical view of how an HTTP request should be built for the endpoint and what is sent back in the form of a response. By clicking the Try it out button, we are presented with an Execute button that will send an example request to the web API for you and show you the response. This combination of detailed instructions on how each web API endpoint works and the ability to create and send requests is invaluable for exploring our web APIs in more depth. We have the ability to do the same level of research as we did earlier with the product research, with additional context and guidance in the documentation to learn from.

Finally, we can learn more about the history of our products by reviewing artifacts like user stories, feature files, and requirement documents in our project management tools. The artifacts that exist will depend on how we work as a team and how our captured information has been stored. For some, it's a simple case of looking through the completed work list in Jira; for others, it might require sifting through old emails to learn details. But it's worth taking the time to read through these artifacts to learn additional context such as the following:

- Potential features we missed during our product analysis
- The individuals in our team who were responsible for developing a feature
- The users and their problems we're hoping to solve
- The journey the product has taken as it's grown and changed

For restful-booker-platform, for example, we can look at the projects board on GitHub (http://mng.bz/QvGG) and discover the following:

- Bugs that have affected restful-booker-platform in the past
- Technical debt that reveals details about the implementation
- User stories about how each feature is expected to work

What is notable about looking through the information is the variety of things we can learn. For example, we can get more context about restful-booker-platform's features from user stories, but we can also learn technical details, such as what libraries and tools are used and what database we're using, from the technical debt cards.

SOURCE CODE

Looking at the source code may strike some as the most obvious and easiest place to learn how a product or platform works. For others, it might fill them with apprehension and worry. It totally depends on our experience with code. If we're comfortable writing code, looking at source code will feel natural. If we're not comfortable writing code, the unfamiliarity of it all can feel overwhelming and discourage us from taking the time to look at source code. If you are more on the uncomfortable side, though, you can consider a few approaches to make it more accessible.

First, it's important to remember that our goal for this chapter is to learn about restful-booker-platform. Our focus should be on understanding the existing code by reading it rather than writing code to come up with new ideas. Reading and writing code are two subtly different acts. Writing code involves a mix of understanding a language and using that understanding to solve problems. When we're reading code, we're making sense of a solution. Rather than solving problems, we're looking for things like

- Names for modules, like the names of the APIs in the root of the codebase that pop up regularly elsewhere in the codebase (such as `room`, `booking`, `branding`, etc.).
- Packages and class names that indicate behavior within each API. For example, the `room` web API has a class called `AuthRequests`. A name like that strongly signals that it is communicating with the other web API, `auth`.
- Looking at dependency files such as pom.xml and package.json, depending on which language our application uses, will tell us what types of libraries and technologies are being used.
- Code comments that describe how specific methods or functions work within the codebase.

These are just a few examples of details you can pick up from reviewing the codebase that don't require a deep knowledge of the language the web APIs are built in. Does it help to have that deep knowledge? Yes, it does. But we all have to start somewhere, and we can develop our skills, knowledge, and confidence by taking the time to explore code bases.

TALKING TO TEAM MEMBERS

Unless a completely new team has been assigned to take on an existing project and the previous team has been spirited away, never to return, there will be others with prior knowledge on the team to speak to. If we remember our testing model from chapter 1, we are looking to learn as much as possible about the following:

- *The imagination*—What we want to build
- *The implementation*—What we have built

We can learn more about these two areas by speaking with our teams and getting their insights and experience of working on the project.

IMAGINATION

Most of what we've discussed so far relates to understanding the product and its behavior, but it's also important to understand who we're building our product for and why. We can do this by speaking with individuals whose roles sit more in the imagination side of delivery, such as product owners, designers, and business analysts. The information they share will not just expand our knowledge of our products but also help frame our strategy. For example, with restful-booker-platform, we might learn that site reliability and uptime are of great importance to our B&B owners. Knowing this, we might prioritize testing activities in our strategy that mitigate reliability-based risks over other testing activities. We'll explore this approach of using what we know about our users and their problems to inform our strategy in more depth in the next chapter.

IMPLEMENTATION

We discussed earlier how reading through the existing codebase could be a valuable source of information. But it's important to remember that that is the output of work done by team members who will have a wealth of experience and knowledge of developing the codebase. You can tap into that knowledge by taking the time to discuss the work that has been created by specific individuals, perhaps through an informal chat about the product, sitting down for a pairing session in which the product is demoed, or getting a tour through the codebase.

2.3   *Capturing our understanding*

As our understanding of our web API platform begins to grow, one thing becomes clear: there is a lot to learn, and what we have learned is complicated. We can take notes and attempt to memorize different aspects of our API platforms, but at some point, we need to arrange our thoughts in a coherent manner that helps us make sense of what we've learned as well as communicate it to others. But how do we do this in a way that doesn't result in masses of additional documentation or complete confusion when we come back to our research after a week on holiday? We create a visual model of the product that captures our knowledge in a clear, succinct manner that is easily updated and shared with others.

2.3.1   *The power of models*

Imagine you're visiting a friend in a city you've never been to before, and your plan is to drive there. What do you do? Most likely, you'll open some sort of map, whether on paper or in an app, to work out the directions to your friend's city while also working out how long the drive will take and any potential stops. All the way through this process, you're using a model to solve your navigation problem.

In this example, the model is the map, and it demonstrates how we use models to make sense of the information around us. The map we use would most likely be one that highlights main roads and junctions available for us to take while removing other details such as terrain, speed limits, or traffic stops. Our map isn't an accurate representation of the geography and topography of the route we want to take, but it shares the important information we need to identify our directions. And that's by design.

You may or may not have come across the aphorism "All models are wrong, but some are useful," but it's an excellent phrase that cleverly captures the value of a good model. A good model shares the information that matters to us while removing other information that isn't necessary to us. If we're aware that models are fallible by nature, we can use this to our advantage. We can create models that are designed to amplify specific information that is useful to us while ignoring other items. For example, in our context, we could build a system architecture diagram that shows us specific details about our API platform to help trigger ideas around strategy, like the one shown in figure 2.5.

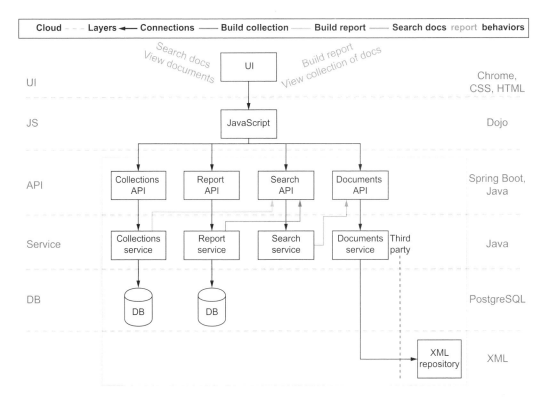

Figure 2.5   An example model of an API platform that demonstrates the different APIs that make up the platform and their relationships

2.3.2   *Building our own models*

Building diagrams of system architecture isn't a new concept. Many teams take advantage of different diagram types such as sequence, state, or system diagrams. But for our purposes, we need to be mindful that these diagramming approaches are models that are attempting to communicate specific information and solve specific problems. The way we model our systems will impact our decision-making. The goal of our modeling exercise is not to fit what we've learned into a preexisting way of thinking but to get our ideas onto paper in a way that helps us do the following:

- Make sense of what we've learned so far
- Trigger testing ideas and identify testing opportunities
- Solicit feedback from others that will help expand our understanding

This approach means we have the freedom to arrange our thoughts on paper in a way that communicates important information for us.

So, to help us better understand this, let's start a new model of restful-booker-platform that captures what we have learned so far. We can take advantage of many tools to model our products such as Visio, Miro, and diagrams.net. For these examples, we'll use diagrams.net to create our initial model, but it's up to you to decide what tool you want to use. Maybe experiment with a few, or just stick to good old paper and pen to begin with.

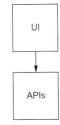

Figure 2.6   An initial model that helps us separate the system into two basic areas: UI and backend

Let's begin our model by first capturing the information we discovered about restful-booker-platform, consisting of a user interface and a backend, which we can visualize in figure 2.6.

This model is quite basic, but it immediately tells us that there are two main sections to restful-booker-platform and that they have a relationship. We then learn that our backend contains a few different web APIs, such as room and auth. We can expand our model to the one shown in figure 2.7, which begins to describe the backend in more detail.

Now we can see that restful-booker-platform has multiple web APIs that we need to consider. Finally, there is a relationship missing between the room API and the auth API in which the room API asks the auth API whether a room can be created. We can represent this by expanding the model once again to the model shown in figure 2.8.

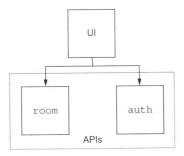

Figure 2.7   An expanded model that shows how the backend is made up of multiple APIs, not just one

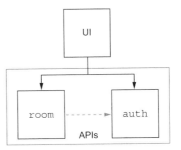

Figure 2.8   A further-expanded model that shows the relationship between two backend APIs

In this small fragment of a model of restful-booker-platform, we've built a visual representation that identifies the following:

- Multiple web APIs will require testing.
- `room` depends on `auth`, meaning `auth` might take priority in the order of testing.
- Our web APIs need to be able to send requests and receive responses from one another.
- The UI and API need to be able to send information to one another as well.

As we expand our model with new information, we begin to naturally see risks we will want to address and opportunities for testing.

ITERATING MODELS AND GETTING FEEDBACK

One last thing to note is that this model was built in an iterative manner. Models are an excellent way to show your understanding to others and have them provide feedback and share knowledge with you. When interpreting information, we all tend to have different models in our heads of how things work, which can be hard to communicate. As you attempt to explain information that is organized in a specific way in your head, the other person is trying to fit that information into their own mental model, which is a lot of work and may lead to misunderstanding. By presenting a visual model, either in person or via documentation, you share not just your knowledge but your interpretation of that knowledge. This makes it easier for the person giving feedback to understand where you're coming from and form their feedback in a way that makes sense to you. Additionally, it also brings about a shared understanding as your model and their mental model begin to align. This is why building and sharing models iteratively with others can be a hugely rewarding activity. We learn more together and gain a stronger, shared understanding.

Activity

Now that we have a better understanding of how models work and have seen some examples of how we can build our own, let's return to our original mission: to build an understanding of how restful-booker-platform works. Throughout the rest of this book, we'll research a range of different testing activities using restful-booker-platform that we can use to mitigate risks before organizing them into an API testing strategy. To do this, we need to understand how restful-booker-platform works, and as we've discussed, the best way to approach this is by creating a model.

So, to conclude this chapter, take some time to go through the different sources of information we've explored in the chapter. Learn as much as you can about restful-booker-platform, and then attempt to arrange what you've learned into a visual model. At a minimum, focus on creating a model that captures the various web APIs that exist within the platform, their relationships with one another, and the different endpoints they might contain. Remember, your model is there to help you make sense of what we're about to test, so arrange your model in a way that works best for you.

2.4 Congratulations—you're testing!

With our initial research complete, we're well on our way to putting together a web API testing strategy. Before we conclude this chapter, take a minute to reflect on the work we've done so far. If you remember from chapter 1, the goal of testing is to learn about what we are building and what we want to build. We also touched upon the fact that any activity we do that helps us learn about what we're building can be considered testing—the key is doing it with deliberate intention and focus.

The activities we've carried out so far—experimenting with the product with various tools and building visual models—demonstrate that it doesn't require much to begin testing. With a few simple tools and a mindset that focuses on not just confirming our assumptions but actively seeking new information, we can learn a lot. However, good testing is something that is easy to pick up but difficult to master. Our research has helped us establish an understanding of restful-booker-platform that aligns with our testing goal. However, our testing approach has been very informal and lacks deliberate thought and organization.

The time we have available to test will always have a constraint on it, so although what we've explored in this chapter serves as a starting point with our testing, we're going to need more deliberate and focused testing activities to discover the high-value information our teams need. This is why we need a clear, effective testing strategy. It's tempting to dive into testing activities that are familiar to us or sound novel. But by taking the time to work out our strategy, the goals that we want to achieve, and our plans for achieving them, we can begin to identify the right testing activities for a given context to help support our teams in building a quality product.

Summary

- We will use an example product called restful-booker-platform to learn about testing. It is available online or as a locally run application.
- Before we can start to design and implement our testing strategy, we need to learn about the context we are working in. We learn about the context by researching our products, their supporting documents and details, and our teams.
- Tools such as dev tools and HTTP(S) clients can be used to help us learn more about API platforms and how they work.
- We can also learn about our context from artifacts like documentation and source code and by speaking with team members.
- What we learn needs to be organized in a coherent fashion, which we can do with models.
- Visualized models can help us to identify potential risks and testing opportunities.
- The research we've been doing is a form of testing because it helps us understand our products and ideas better, but we need more deliberate testing to succeed.

Quality and risk

This chapter covers
- How to use quality to set goals for our strategy
- What quality is and how to define it
- What risks are and how they impact quality
- How to identify risks with various techniques
- How different risks are mitigated by different testing activities

Now that we're more familiar with our product, restful-booker-platform, the time has come to start considering our strategy. Specifically, we need to answer the following two questions:

- What are the goals we are hoping our strategy will achieve?
- How are we going to achieve our goals?

It's important to clarify these two points before we begin digging into specific testing activities to ensure the work we're doing is delivering value. Failing to do so will result in testing that, at best, will be inconsistent and, at worse, a waste of time. As the Japanese proverb puts it, "Vision without action is a daydream. Action without vision is a nightmare." We want to ensure that we have a clear goal so that we can not only begin to form a strategy but also assess the success of it. We've learned in previous chapters that it's easy to pick up some testing activities and explore a product. But the key to a successful test strategy is to test with purpose and direction. So, to answer our questions, we will require the following:

- A clear goal for our strategy, which we will achieve by identifying what quality means to our users
- A list of opportunities to test for in the form of risks

We can outline this as a model to complete, as shown in figure 3.1.

Strategy goal	???????
Steps to take	???????

Figure 3.1   An initial model for understanding strategies that highlights the need to identify a strategy goal and steps to take to achieve the strategy goal

In this chapter, we'll explore both questions so that we can complete this model and begin to prioritize the right testing activities.

3.1   Defining quality

Let us begin by talking about quality and what it means in a software development context. To do this, let's look at a quick analogy. Take a minute to search for a phrase such as "10 greatest albums," open the first few links, and compare the results. Most likely, we will see some similarities and some differences (and some truly excellent albums). But one thing that becomes very clear is that there isn't a unanimous agreement across each of the lists we find. Different people have different opinions about what is good and what isn't. In fact, sometimes people can't even agree with their own opinions over time. Compare the final 10 albums in *Rolling Stone*'s list of the top 500 greatest albums of all time from 2003 to their list from 2020, and you'll see a noticeable difference. For example, *Sgt Pepper's Lonely Heart Club Band* has inexplicably dropped from number one to number 24. The same publication, perhaps different authors, but the differences demonstrate how time also plays a factor in how we view something as having high/low or good/bad quality.

Quality is a highly subjective and fluid concept, which has been succinctly captured in this definition:

"Quality is value to some person who matters at some point in time."

The original quote, "Quality is value to some person," comes from Jerry Weinberg, and it reminds us that people are complex individuals with unique experiences, resulting in differing ideas on what quality is. We need to be appreciative of this when defining quality. User A may feel your product is of high quality to them, whereas User B may disagree. That said, User B might not be someone we are worried about, which is why James Bach and Michael Bolton added "who matters" to the quote. The products we build are providing specific solutions to specific people, so our definition of quality should be influenced by their needs and their views of quality. We want to prioritize the people who are helping us keep the lights on. Finally, we should also be aware that an individual's view of quality is also informed by their context, which changes over time, which is why David Greenlees added "at some point in time." A great example of "at some point in time" is the concept of "situational disabilities" in which a user's abilities are temporarily reduced by a specific situation. For example, imagine how a user's perception of the quality of an application like Siri changes when they're using it in the quiet of their house, compared to when using it on a busy street.

By being aware that quality is a fluid/subjective concept to individuals, we can use it to our advantage to help us identify our test strategy goals. By establishing a better understanding of what quality means to our users, we can use that knowledge to guide what we test and what we don't.

3.1.1   *Quality characteristics*

Every person's view of quality is subtly different, influenced by past experiences, biases, and their daily lives. So, how do we capture that information, analyze it to understand what a user's idea of quality is, and distill it into a set of clear goals to work toward? We have to strike a balance of capturing enough detail about quality to help keep us on the right track while not being so detailed that it's hard to see the forest for the trees. We can achieve this through the use of quality characteristics.

A quality characteristic is a way of describing a single aspect of quality in a high-level manner. For example, we could have the following:

- *Look and feel*—A product is deemed high quality if it looks good or feels good to use. It may have well-designed layouts and branding or sleek designs to make it easy to use. For example, Apple products might prioritize "look and feel" as an important quality characteristic.
- *Security*—A product is deemed high quality if it keeps individuals protected and secure. It may be that data is kept securely, or individuals have a certain level of privacy or protection from unwanted attention. For example, a password manager will want to give users confidence in its security.
- *Accuracy*—A product is deemed high quality if it processes information accurately. It may have to process complex details and return precise information. For example, a medical practitioner will view a medical diagnosis tool's accuracy of diagnosis as an important quality characteristic.

A large range of quality characteristics exists to pick from, and we can combine them to build up a robust picture of what quality means to our users. For example, the characteristics list captured by Rikard Edgren, Henrik Emilsson, and Martin Jansson in the

Test Eye Software Quality Characteristics list contains more than 100 different characteristics to consider that can be downloaded as a PDF file (http://mng.bz/XZ8v).

By analyzing feedback from users, we can use it to identify which quality characteristics are more important to them and then use those characteristics to inform our test strategy goals, helping us to align our work more closely with delivering a product that is viewed as having high quality. For example, users of a personal tax-filing service on an API platform might prioritize quality characteristics such as

- *Intuitiveness*—The user wants the filing process to be as simple as possible.
- *Accuracy*—The user wants it to calculate taxes correctly.
- *Availability*—The user doesn't want it to go down on filing day.

This would result in a strategy that prioritizes testing to learn more about these quality characteristics over others.

> **Activity**
>
> Think of a product that you use regularly, and go through the quality characteristics list from the Test Eye list. Pick out a handful of different characteristics and write them down. Once you're done, put them in the order of priority that matters to you. Are they ones you would have considered before using the list?

3.1.2 Getting to know our users

Capturing the right quality characteristics for our test strategy means getting to know our users better. The more we know about them, the more accurate we'll be in choosing our quality characteristics, which in turn will make our testing more targeted and more valuable. So before we start capturing quality characteristics, we should take the time to learn about our users through a range of different activities.

It's worth noting that user research and experimentation is a vast topic in its own right. If individuals in your team or organization are responsible for this type of work, it will be highly advantageous to you and your team to collaborate with them to identify quality characteristics. However, in the absence of people with those skills, here are a few ways in which you can learn more about your users to capture quality characteristics.

INTERVIEWING STAKEHOLDERS AND USERS

The quickest and easiest way to build up a picture of quality is to ask our users directly. Whether this is through a formal interviewing process or a casual talk over coffee, the conversations will help us better understand what quality means to them. One piece of advice I can give from personal experience is that it's best to facilitate a discussion in which quality characteristics naturally emerge. This simply means having a normal conversation rather than asking a user to pick quality characteristics from a list. If you present a list, they are likely to say that all of them matter equally, which doesn't really help.

Some of us might not have the ability to sit down with a user due to our working context. However, feedback from users will come to your team from some channel. (Otherwise, how else would you know what to build?) So if we can't speak to our users, we should try to speak to their proxy or representative. This might be a product owner, business analyst, or some other stakeholder in your organization. Speaking with them will help you to not only prioritize quality characteristics but also to advocate for the value of quality characteristics to them in the hopes that they will ultimately contribute toward exploring the idea of quality with end users.

OBSERVING LIVE BEHAVIOR

The tools that exist to monitor user behavior with our products have grown to such a level of sophistication that we can now infer user needs and attitudes toward our products without having to speak with them directly. We can use the information we gather from monitoring tools to inform us of certain aspects of quality. We can monitor the volume of traffic in our products to determine whether performance quality characteristics are a priority. Or we can measure user behavior after features are deployed. For example, if a feature is released that causes a high user drop-off, we can analyze that feature to see why it might have contributed to a drop-off. Perhaps it was hard to use, didn't look great, or was functionally broken. From that analysis, we might identify characteristics such as usability, attractiveness, or completeness.

As mentioned before, these are just a couple of approaches that we can employ to learn more about our users and their ideas of quality. Whatever approach we choose, the goal is to get into a pattern in which we're actively seeking out what our users want. As our work progresses, our products grow and change, and so will our users. This means we need to regularly check in with users to learn about their views on quality. Allow time in your strategy to "correct your course" and speak with users, reflecting on the discussions and updating quality characteristic priorities and goals for your test strategy.

> **Activity**
>
> Pick one of the techniques discussed here, and carry it out to see if you can learn something about your user base. See if you can capture at least one or two quality characteristics.

3.1.3   *Setting quality goals for our strategy*

Once we've spent time gathering information from our users, we need to analyze it to discover what quality characteristics are of importance to them and then use those as goals for our strategy. For example, although the users of restful-booker-platform are hypothetical, we could take the time to imagine a few quality characteristics for each. For a guest, it might be the following:

- *Completeness*—The user wants complete features to post bookings and get rooms.

- *Intuitiveness*—The user wants it to be easy to interact with our APIs.
- *Stability*—The user doesn't want crashes to occur or bookings to be lost (causing the user to turn up at a B&B with no booking).
- *Privacy*—The user wants their booking details to be secure.

And for an administrator, it might be these characteristics:

- *Completeness*—The admin wants all standard features to administrate bookings and rooms.
- *Intuitiveness*—The admin wants administrative features to be easy to use.
- *Stability*—The admin doesn't want the site to crash when they make changes to it.
- *Availability*— The admin wants the site to always be up.

As we can see, some characteristics for each user type match, and some don't. We could then sit down as a team and decide on a priority order for these characteristics. For example, we could prioritize the characteristics that matter to both parties over the individual characteristics, followed by the guest's characteristics (because they are a larger user base) and finishing with the admin characteristics. This list ultimately gives us our strategy's goal: our test strategy aims to support our team in improving the

- Intuitiveness
- Completeness
- Stability
- Privacy
- Availability

quality characteristics of restful-booker-platform, which we can reflect in an updated strategy model, as shown in figure 3.2.

Strategy goal	Quality characteristics Intuitiveness | Completeness | Stability | Privacy | Availability
Steps to take	???????

Figure 3.2 **An expanded model that shows how we can use quality characteristics as a basis for our strategy's goals**

Activity

Do you agree with these characteristics? Put yourself in the mindset of either a guest or administrator of restful-booker-platform. What quality characteristics would you add or remove? Write down your list, and set it to one side. We'll come back to it later in the book.

3.2   *Identify risks to quality*

The quality characteristics that we've identified set out the goals we aim to achieve and help us set a direction for our strategy. Now we need to consider what steps we want to take to reach our goals of improving quality. We do this by identifying situations in which our quality characteristics could be negatively impacted in the form of risks.

In the context of software development, risk, simply put, is the possibility of something negatively impacting our product's quality. For example, it could be the risk of us implementing an off-by-one error, causing us to accept incorrect data. Or it could be the risk of data being corrupted. When dealing with risks, we are essentially making a bet. We don't know at the time of identifying the risk whether it is actually going to manifest and become a problem or nothing will happen at all. This is where the information we learn from testing helps. By focusing our testing attention on an area of our work in which risk could have some impact, we can reveal information to determine whether the initial risk is actually an issue that requires mitigation.

The key with risks is that we won't know whether the risk is real until we carry out testing. As we build our products, we'll identify many risks in our work (and miss many more), but we won't have time to test for every single risk. So we have to be selective with the risks we test for and the risks we don't. This is how risk acts as a guide for our test strategy and the testing activities we do as part of it. We identify and select the risks that matter the most and test for them, making a bet that the other risks we've discovered will have a lower impact on our quality. We'll explore how to prioritize our risks and begin forming our strategy shortly, but first, let's look at how we can identify risks.

3.2.1   *Learning to identify risk*

We can use a range of techniques to guide ourselves and our teams in risk identification, but ultimately, identifying risks requires us to adopt a skeptical mindset. Being skeptical allows us to analyze what we know about a given context and ask ourselves questions that challenge our assumptions. For example, going back to our relevant search feature from chapter 1, we can ask questions such as the following:

- Can we be sure the search results are relevant?
- What if the search doesn't work as we expected it to?
- What search operators do we intend to support, and why?

By asking these types of questions and considering the responses we get, we can begin to identify risks.

Skepticism does not mean being negative or pessimistic about a given situation. Testing sometimes gets a reputation for being overly negative about the work people do, but the intention isn't to tear down the hard work of others. It's to question the unknowns around our work and ensure that they don't conceal unexpected or unwanted issues. By being skeptical, we're thinking about the truth of things instead of being motivated to prove that something is right or wrong.

When learning to identify risks, we need to focus on what we don't know about a given situation and then work from there to determine what risks lurk in those unknown areas that we might want to test for. This might feel like quite an abstract exercise, but fortunately, there are a few different techniques and tools we can use to help focus our attention on a given area of our work.

3.2.2 Headline game

The Headline game is an approach to risk identification that was popularized by Elisabeth Hendrickson in her book *Explore It!* (Pragmatic Bookshelf, 2013), in which she uses it as an approach for identifying areas in which we can target exploratory testing sessions (https://pragprog.com/titles/ehxta/explore-it/). We'll cover exploratory testing later, but the Headline game technique is worth exploring now because it's an effective tool for analyzing and identifying risks, regardless of the testing activity you want to carry out.

The technique works by taking time to imagine a range of made-up headlines and then working back from the headlines to identify risks that could potentially contribute to the existence of each headline. For example, we could come up with a headline for restful-booker-platform such as

Embarrassment for local business as B&B is overrun with double-booked guests

Working back from this headline, we could consider risks that could cause this scenario, such as the following:

- The double-booking validation feature is broken.
- Bookings are saved incorrectly.
- Stored bookings are cancelled without informing the guest.

The headlines we create act as triggers for us to start discovering risks that we might want to address. When combined with our quality characteristics, this becomes an excellent way to start identifying risks that matter to us. As we'll learn shortly using the technique RiskStorming, we can use a quality characteristic as a trigger to identify relevant headlines, which we can, in turn, use to identify the types of risks that matter the most. You can read a more comprehensive guide on how to run the Headline game in the article "The Nightmare Headline Game" (http://mng.bz/J2M0).

3.2.3 Oblique testing

The Headline game requires a certain degree of imagination to come up with material to jump off of, which may work better for some than others. Fortunately, those who struggle with that type of activity can use tools like Oblique testing as a trigger to begin risk analysis. Based on the Oblique strategy created by Brian Eno, in which Eno would use cards to help artists explore different creative avenues, the Oblique test cards were created by Mike Talks to use the Oblique concept to explore perspectives for testing. The deck contains 28 cards that each have fake one-star reviews that you pick at random to help trigger different ideas. For example, one card states

I thought this would make things easier to do! ONE STAR!!!

We can use this quote as a trigger to think of ways that our products might cause a user to write such as a review. For restful-booker-platform, it could relate to how well the APIs are documented, how they provide feedback, how many calls you have to make to achieve something, and so on.

What makes the cards effective at helping us identify risks is that the cards themselves straddle a fine line between specific enough to give us a jumping-off point when discovering risks but not so specific that when used repeatedly, we end up generating the same ideas over and over. To get a copy of the Oblique testing card deck, visit Leanpub (https://leanpub.com/obliquetesting).

3.2.4   *RiskStorming*

Although the Headline game and Oblique testing techniques are useful for triggering ideas, they are dependent on at least a basic level of experience and skill in risk analysis. For teams who are new to risk analysis, though, RiskStorming offers a structured way to guide a team to identify risk collaboratively.

The RiskStorming technique is based on a deck of cards called TestSphere, created by Beren Van Daele. You can find out more about TestSphere on the Ministry of Testing website (https://www.ministry oftesting.com/testsphere). Built in collaboration with Marcel Gehlen and Andrea Jensen, RiskStorming uses the TestSphere deck in a three-phase approach to guide teams to do the following:

1 Identify quality characteristics that might impact the product or specific feature.
2 Identify risks that can impact the quality characteristics.
3 Identify ideas around how to test the risks.

What makes RiskStorming so effective is the way it's structured and the cards that are in use. Similar to Test Oblique, the TestSphere cards can be used to help trigger ideas and discussion around quality and testing. But because the deck is quite large and comprehensive (there are 100 cards split into five categories that cover topics such as quality, testing techniques, and test patterns), RiskStorming gives enough structure to guide a team toward identifying risks while not being so restrictive as to prevent good ideas from flowing. Let's look at how we can use RiskStorming to generate risks by carrying out the first two phases of RiskStorming with restful-booker-platform.

PHASE 1: QUALITY

The first phase requires us to select six of the 20 quality aspect cards from the TestSphere deck. As we discussed earlier in the chapter, the quality characteristics (or quality aspects, as they are called in the TestSphere deck) will come from our understanding of our users. The cards we select will represent what quality means to our users. If we were to think about our users for restful-booker-platform, the guest and the admin, we could take our quality characteristics from section 3.1.3:

- Intuitiveness
- Completeness

- Stability
- Privacy
- Availability

Then we would pick six quality aspect cards from the deck that either match or are similar to our list (you can view the list of quality aspect cards by trying out the free online version of RiskStorming at https://app.riskstormingonline.com/):

- User-friendliness
- Functionality
- Availability
- Stability
- Business value capability
- Security and permission

PHASE 2: RISKS

With our six aspects selected, we can now go through each of the six quality aspects and generate risks that could potentially impact each aspect. What is great about this phase is that we can actually thread in other risk analysis techniques to identify risks. For example, we could use the Headline game to think of ways in which "User friendliness" could be negatively impacted if we want to come up with new ideas. During this phase, we're free to add as many risks as we like, but it's advised that the phase be time-boxed. This helps focus the work and stops the lists of identified risks from becoming too bloated. Remember, we can't test everything.

For our list of quality aspects, we'll limit the number of risks found to three per aspect. Our lists of risks are

- User-friendliness
  - Incorrect status codes or responses are sent on successful requests.
  - Vague or incorrect error messages are sent when a user makes a mistake.
  - Documentation for API requests is hard to decipher.
- Functionality
  - Existing features are broken when new changes are implemented.
  - Implemented features don't match what the user requested.
  - Validation on APIs doesn't work as expected.
- Availability
  - APIs fail under the stress of too many users.
  - Memory leaks cause APIs to fail.
  - Bookings can't be made on days that say they are available.
- Stability
  - APIs in the platform send incorrect HTTP requests and responses to one another.
  - The API fails to deploy correctly.
  - Intermittent failures come from APIs.

- Business value capability
  - The admin is unable to update the look and feel of the guest pages.
  - Details that the admin sets aren't saved or shared correctly.
  - The existing features don't match an admin's requirements.
- Security and permission
  - Functionality that is only for the admin is accessible to others.
  - Private data can be stolen.
  - The site can be manipulated to attack users.

These risks become our steps to take in realizing the goals of our strategy, meaning we can complete our strategy model with an abbreviated list of risks (I've picked one from each section), something similar to figure 3.3.

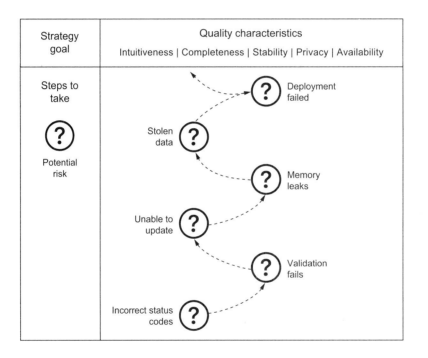

Figure 3.3   A completed strategy model that shows how the risks we identify and learn about are steps toward achieving our strategy's goals

Activity

To test out how RiskStorming works, head over to the Ministry of Testing RiskStorming page (http://mng.bz/woeq) and download either the Death Star or Iron Man suit activity PDF files. Attempt to carry out the first two phases of a RiskStorming session to see what risks you come up with. You can use the free online version of RiskStorming (https://app.riskstormingonline.com/) to help generate your risks.

These are just a few techniques to help get us started identifying risks, but the best way to improve with risk analysis is with practice. Much like we need to rereview our quality characteristics regularly, we should also be regularly assessing risks that could impact our work. Through this regular process, not only do we keep an up-to-date list of risks that we need to address with testing, but we improve our own skills in identifying risks.

3.3   A strategy's first steps

With our goals now in place and our risks identified, we're left with one last action: to prioritizing what risks we want to focus on and in what order. To do this, we can use three factors, the first being the quality characteristics themselves. For example, with restful-booker-platform, we listed intuitiveness as our first quality characteristic. Let's assume we added it there because it was the number-one characteristic. We might want to prioritize all risks associated with the quality characteristic first. This would be sensible, but we also have to consider the other two factors in risk: likelihood and severity.

We use likelihood to consider how likely it is that a risk will impact our quality. If we had data informing us that there was an 80% chance of rain, we would likely take a coat. If it was 20%, maybe not. Severity, on the other hand, is used to consider the size of impact that a risk might have on our quality. These two factors are used in conjunction to help us further prioritize our risks, as demonstrated in figure 3.4.

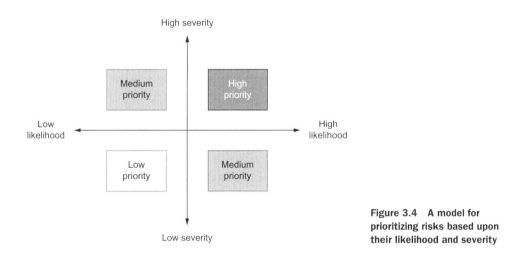

Figure 3.4   **A model for prioritizing risks based upon their likelihood and severity**

If a risk has a high likelihood and severity, then we will want to address it as a priority. Equally, if both likelihood and severity are low, then the risk can slip down the list. This can be useful when combined with quality characteristics. For example, say we have two risks:

- A booking made in the past sends an unclear error message (intuitiveness).
- Admin is unable to add rooms to be booked (completeness).

In our list, intuitiveness trumps completeness for priority in quality characteristics. But if the second risk has a high likelihood and severity, it makes sense to prioritize that risk first. This is a simplified example, because likelihood and severity aren't measured in just a binary high or low way. It's important to remember that prioritizing risks is ultimately a guessing game. We need to do our best to make sure that our decisions around prioritizing risks are as informed as possible, which is something that we can do by regularly reevaluating both our quality goals and associated risks.

> **Activity**
>
> Take the risks we identified from the previous section, and based on your knowledge of our quality characteristics and the product itself, attempt to order them in a priority list. Reflect on how you judge likelihood and severity. Do you go for a gut feeling or for a more formal approach, grading them high, medium, or low?

3.3.1   *Picking the right approach for testing a risk*

Our strategy is now beginning to come together. We have our goals and our risks to focus on; now we can begin to think about what testing we want to do and where. For example, if we were to pick the risk

Vague or incorrect error messages sent when a user makes a mistake

that could impact the intuitiveness quality characteristic. We might choose to implement API design-testing activities to ensure that the error messages we send are not incorrect or unclear during design discussions.

This is just one example. Our projects will have many risks that will need to be addressed in different ways. Some testing activities may be responsible for addressing a multitude of risks. But being able to identify a suitable approach to test for each risk requires some familiarity with the range of testing activities we can carry out. A successful strategy will take advantage of testing activities that range from the use of automation tools to testing abstract concepts and ideas, which we'll explore in part 2. We'll put our strategy on pause as we learn about the different testing opportunities we can use and the types of risks they can help address before we come back to our strategy to work out what testing we want to carry out and when.

Summary

- A successful strategy requires a goal to work toward; otherwise, it may become directionless.
- Our strategy's goal is supporting the improvement of quality.
- "Quality is value to some person who matters at some point in time," meaning we need to take the time to understand what quality means to our users.
- We can define what quality means to our users in many ways to help us measure it using quality characteristics.

- Once we've identified what quality means to our users and to us, we can use that as a launching point to identify risks.
- Identifying risks requires a skeptical mindset to identify unknowns to explore.
- We can use techniques such as the Headline game, Oblique testing, and Risk-Storming to help us identify risks.
- We prioritize risks based on likelihood and severity.
- Once we have our identified list of risks, we can begin to determine a suitable approach to test for each risk.

Part 2

Beginning our test strategy

There is almost a chicken-and-egg situation when it comes to working with test strategies. We want to take the time to understand our working context before we dive into specific testing activities. But to know which activities to execute first, we need to have an appreciation of how to carry them out. So before we start to form our test strategy, let's look at some key activities we can take advantage of across the software development life cycle before learning how to organize them into a coherent strategy that we can execute.

We'll do this by looking at how we can test ideas and designs before our web APIs are implemented in chapter 4, followed by how exploratory testing can help us discover how our web APIs truly behave in chapter 5. We'll then conclude our activities in chapter 6 by learning how to use automation to help support our API testing strategy. Finally, we'll conclude this part by discussing how we can form a strategy that uses the testing activities we've learned about in a way that addresses the specific challenges and risks our products face.

Testing API designs

Imagine that someone is assessing our restful-booker-platform API sandbox to determine whether it's an application that they would like to use for a B&B. As they begin to explore it, they discover that the room API needs to be called to create a room that can be booked. As they look through the API documentation, they come across details similar to the ones shown in figure 4.1.

45

CREATE ROOM

`/room/`

HTTP method	Description
POST	Creates a room for booking

Request arguments

`roomNumber`	The number of the room.
`type`	The type of room. Can be single, twin, double, family, or suite.
`accessible`	Sets whether the room has disability access.
`description`	Sets a description for the room.
`image`	Sets a URL of an image for the room.
`roomPrice`	Sets the price of the room.
`features`	Preset features a room can have including Wi-Fi, TV, safe, radio, refreshments or views.

Figure 4.1   An example of API documentation that might be found on a vendor's website

Based on this information, we build and send the following HTTP request to see how the API responds:

```
POST /room/ HTTP/1.1
Host: automationintesting.online
Accept: application/json
Cookie: token=r76BXGVy8rlASuZB

{
    "roomNumber":100,
    "type":"Single",
    "accessible":false,
    "description":"Please enter a description for this room",
    "image":"https://www.mwtestconsultancy.co.uk/img/room1.jpg",
    "roomPrice":"100",
    "features":["WiFi"]
}
```

However, rather than getting the expected room creation back in an HTTP response, the user receives a `500 Server Error` message. The error leaves them feeling a bit frustrated. They go back to the documentation to see what we might have missed but learn nothing new. In the end, they decide that this API isn't working correctly and move on, resulting in lost business for us.

What went wrong here? On the surface, it would appear that the `room` API is broken. But let's imagine we could be a fly on the wall and observe the decision process for creating the `POST /room` endpoint. From our perspective, the API is working correctly, built according to the requirements we were given and deployed without issue. In terms of our expectations, everything is fine. But this is where the problem arises: in the team's expectations. As our team began developing the API, they made the following design choice:

> The room identifier must always be a String because some users use nonintegers to identify rooms.

Our team missed a series of questions that we could ask: What if someone sent an integer? How should we handle that? If the team had allowed time and space for someone to ask that question, it might have resulted in a decision to send a `400 Bad Request` HTTP response with additional information to let the client know that a String was required. A further discussion might have identified that, in fact, `roomNumber` is a misleading parameter name and that renaming it to `roomName` would make things clearer. These additional discussions and questions could have been the difference in whether the person assessing our platform decided to use it or not.

This example demonstrates that the decisions we make and the assumptions we derive from those decisions influence the quality of the products we build. More often than not, the issues that appear in our systems don't come from incorrect code but from risks such as

- Misinterpreting user requirements
- Making incorrect assumptions
- Violating architectural guidelines

Ignoring these risks can result in teams delivering products that don't behave in the way the user expects or wants, resulting in a negative impact on team dynamics or unexpected bugs or vulnerabilities appearing in our software. Part of building a quality product means ensuring that everyone has a clear and shared understanding of what needs to be built. That's why in this chapter, we'll learn how to use testing techniques to question designs and ideas upfront to eliminate misunderstandings, discover potential issues, and contribute to improving the quality of your product.

4.1 How do we test API designs?

Unlike testing an application, testing API designs means using our testing skills to question less-tangible items such as ideas, documentation, and visualizations. Before code is created, a team will ideally work together to discuss the problem or feature they need to solve, resulting in some sort of design or an agreement on what to do. It's during these discussions that we can listen, learn, and question what is being proposed to help teams establish a shared understanding and catch issues earlier.

4.1.1   *Tools for questioning*

The key challenge when testing API designs is learning how to ask the right questions at the right time. Although this takes time and practice to become adept, we fortunately have techniques to help kick-start our questioning straight away.

One common technique is "five Ws and an H"—a phrase that helps us to remember the following six keywords that can inspire different types of questions:

- Who
- What
- Where
- When
- Why
- How

We use this technique by picking one of the six items in the list, for example, *What*, and using it as a trigger to see what sort of questions you could come up with. For example:

- What happens when the user isn't authorized?
- What will we do if an API we're dependent on isn't available?
- What information will we send?

The order in which the keywords are listed doesn't indicate a priority or order in which you should use them. But each word in the list allows you to explore ideas in different ways. By using a technique like the five Ws and an H, we can quickly prime ourselves for questions we might ask, and as we listen to the information being shared, we can use our critical thinking skills to dig deeper or use our lateral thinking skills to explore different ideas.

To help us better understand the power of questions, let's start testing a proposed API design that focuses on the /room/ endpoint, which is part of the room API in our sandbox. In our role-play, a member of our team has presented the following user story:

> In order to allow bookings to be made for a room
> As a B&B owner
> I want the ability to create a room

The the team has proposed the following details around how we will design the request and response for the room API:

REQUEST

```
POST /room/ HTTP/1.1
Host: example.com
Accept: application/json
Cookie: token=abc123

{
    "roomName": "102",
```

```
    "type": "Double",
    "accessible": "true",
    "description": "This is a description for the room",
    "image": "/img/room1.jpg",
    "roomPrice": 200,
    "features": ["TV", "Safe"]
}
```

RESPONSE

```
HTTP/1.1 201 OK
Content-Type: application/json

{
    "roomid": 3,
    "roomName": 102,
    "type": "Double",
    "accessible": true,
    "image": "/img/room1.jpg",
    "description": "This is a description for the room",
    "features": ["TV", "Safe"],
    "roomPrice": 200
}
```

With this information available to us, let's apply the five Ws and an H technique to learn more about our design choices and identify potential issues.

WHO

Who questions are useful for learning more about the people or systems interacting with our APIs. The more we learn about who is using our APIs, the better we can understand what their needs are and how we can deliver value to them. Questions might include:

- *Who is going to use this?* We would ask this to get a better sense of who or what is going to use the /room/ endpoint we're discussing. We may discover that another API or a UI library will be consuming the response, or it might be used by an individual. What we learn might inform other questions we ask. For example, I may ask more technical or architecture-based questions if it's another API that is using /room/.
- *Who should have access?* We can also consider risks around security during this activity. In the API design, there is mention of a Cookie header with a token, and we might want to learn more about the security controls around this token. Although this is a surface-level question to ask around API security (we'll explore security testing in more depth in chapter 9), answers from this question might allow us to dig deeper into how we're securing our APIs and explore risks that might result in vulnerabilities.

WHAT

What questions can be used for hypothetical situations: *What if X happens?* These are useful for thinking laterally, proposing scenarios that we might not have addressed already. A useful way to use *what* questions is to take existing information that has been shared and use it with *what* to push our thinking a bit further. Examples of *what* questions might include

- *What if we send incorrect details? What happens?* These questions are reminiscent of the initial example we explored in this chapter. Not all hypothetical questions result in a positive result, and we need to be mindful of how we handle the negative ones, too. At a minimum, we might want to discuss how to minimize the damage that can be done to our systems. But given that we're working with APIs, we might also want to discuss how we provide feedback for errors in a clear, readable manner.
- *What format will the payload be in, and why?* Again, here we're focusing on learning more about potential technical decisions that have been made. On its own, "What format will the payload be in?" could result in a simple response—JSON. But by adding a *why* in at the end, we're asking for a deeper explanation. We may discover that there are assumptions being made about who might use the response.

WHERE

Where questions can be used to expand our view of what is being discussed. We can use them to discover potential dependencies and learn more about what impact our design choices will have on potential consumers of our responses. For example, you might ask questions like

- *Where will the room be saved?* A question like this can help reveal implementation details and where they might exist. This might trigger discussions around how the implementation choices we are going to make might fit into architectural conditions we need to meet. For example, if we were working in a microservice architecture, would this work mean we needed to create a new API?
- *Where will the room be used?* A slightly different question from the "Who will use it?" question earlier, this question is attempting to understand how the design choices we make fit into the wider scope of a platform or user features. Learning where something will be used could help reveal new users or APIs that will rely on our design.

WHEN

When provides a focus on time. It can help us to identify questions that are tied to events that might occur in the future and what will happen during those events. Examples of when questions might be

- *When we make changes to the API contract, will we version the URI?* When we're thinking about how we're going to solve a particular problem, it's important to consider the long-term future of a solution. How might it change over time, and how frequently will we make changes? What might cause it to change? How will we handle said changes? Asking about versioning will have implications not just for our API designs but also for how we document our changes and share them with our users.

- *When this goes live, do we want to cache the requests?* The interesting part of this question is the first part: "When this goes live . . . ." Here we can use our understanding of a release process and how our production environments behave in our questioning. This can help us identify additional considerations that need to be made to ensure our designs work in line with existing rules and patterns in our platforms. For example, this question is trying to reveal whether we want to cache the response. If the answer is yes, this could have an impact on our designs (e.g., ensuring no randomized variables are used in URIs that might break caching rules).

WHY

Why questions allow us to probe deeper into the desires and meaning of the decisions we are making. It can help us question the value of the work we're doing and explain our decision-making process to others. Example questions might include

- *Why are we building this?* Perhaps a little contrary, but still an important question to ask. If we're to invest our time and money into delivering features, it's best that we are aware of what the value is in the work we're doing. A question like this can help us to understand and empathize with the end user. Any answers we explore from this type of question are going to give us more details about the problems our user might be facing, which will help us make an informed decision as to how we can solve it.
- *Why have we chosen to list features as an array?* This type of questioning is focusing more on design choices. Why are the features in an array? If it's a fixed list of features to pick from, why not have parameters for a sub-object? The goal is not to criticize the decisions that have been made but to explore alternatives and understand the choices that have been made.

HOW

Finally, *how* questions help us to understand how something is going to work or the tasks we need to consider to deliver our work successfully. Example questions could include

- *How will it work?* When asking questions in a collaborative context, there will be times in which you'll have a feeling that the question lacks value. A question like "How will it work?" is a great example because on the surface, it feels like you're opening yourself up to criticism for not understanding what is being discussed. However, a question like this can reveal a lot of misinterpretation between team members. Personally, I've asked this question to get a response from one team member who offers a conflicting view to other team members. Sometimes the basic questions work the best.
- *How will we test this?* Not all questions have to be about understanding the design. We can also question how we are going to respond to the decisions we make. Asking a question like this helps our testing because it can highlight any potential blockers. For example, if we've designed something that relies upon a scheduled task that triggers at specific time intervals, we might ask how we are

going to test it and start a conversation around having more control over the time intervals to help speed up our testing.

Activity

Using the five Ws and an H technique, look over the POST /room/ endpoint again, and write down a list of questions you might ask a team to learn more. Try to capture at least three for each W and H.

Testing ideas is about asking questions

Although techniques like five Ws and an H are a great place to start, to develop our questioning skills further, it's worth understanding how critical and lateral thinking play an important role in our testing.

Let's go back to our model of testing, shown in figure 4.2. As we can see, just as we can ask ourselves a question like "What if I press that Add button a thousand times?" when testing an application, we can also use those skills to ask questions such as "Who will be consuming this API response?"

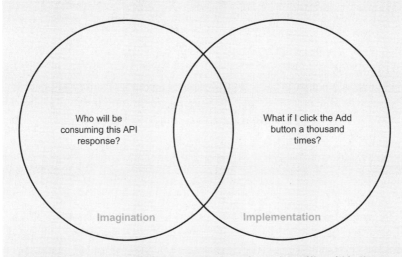

Figure 4.2   A demonstration of how asking questions might differ within the imagination and implementation areas of our testing

Although our focus might be slightly different—perhaps on software, perhaps on an idea—what drives our ability to ask useful questions is our critical and lateral thinking. With critical thinking skills, we can identify questions that dig into the truth and meaning behind ideas, revealing the motivations behind the decisions we make and highlighting assumptions that might lead to errors. With strong lateral thinking skills, we can develop questions that help us expand the impact of our ideas and the consequences of decisions we've made that might not be considered. Crudely speaking, critical thinking lets us dig deeper and lateral thinking lets us go broader.

Honing both critical and lateral thinking skills helps us to come up with more impact-ful questions. However, when learning to improve them, it can feel abstract. The best way to improve both skills is to think of them as a muscle. By finding opportunities to exercise both by testing ideas and code, this approach to thinking and analysis will become stronger, making your testing skills more effective.

These questions we've explored are just a small demonstrative sample. There are many questions we can ask to learn more about the choices we've made for an API design, how it might impact consumers of the API, and what might happen in specific situations. We will inevitably come to a point, though, when the well of questions run dry. This isn't an inherently bad thing, but it can be a clear sign that we've exhausted all the avenues we can identify and might mean that it's time to stop testing. However, we can use some additional techniques and tools to help us generate other ideas and questions.

4.1.2 Expanding your API design-testing techniques and tools

Five Ws and an H is a fundamental technique for testing API designs, but it can be built upon with the use of additional questioning techniques, data type analysis, and visualizations. Each of these techniques provides ways to generate new ideas or develop new perspectives that you can use in combination with five Ws and an H to test further and deeper.

FURTHER QUESTIONING TECHNIQUES

Along with five Ws and an H, you can use two other techniques to expand your questioning: *else* questions and funnel questions.

You can use *else* questions in conjunction with five Ws and an H by adding an *else* after one of the keywords. The idea is that the *else* primes us and our team to think laterally with questions like

- Who else is going to use this?
- What else might happen?
- How else could an error occur?

If *else* questions help us to think more laterally, then funnel questions can help us become more critical. Unlike the other techniques that use keywords to trigger questions, funnel questions are about reacting to the response of an initial question and then asking further questions to dig deeper. For example:

Q: How does a user add an image?
A: The user adds an image by providing a URL as a string to the image they want in the payload.
Q: Why does the user have to provide a URL for an image and not an image upload?
A: Because we don't have an upload feature as of yet.
Q: When will we be creating one?
A: Maybe we should prioritize that now.

In this example, the aim isn't to make the person answering look foolish but to dig into the reasoning behind the decision that was made. To be successful with this approach, we need to incorporate other skills into our questioning. We need to employ active listening skills in which we make the conscious effort to listen to responses and react to them. And we also need to be aware of the way we phrase our questions to make them inquisitive but not combative.

If you are struggling to remember all these questioning techniques or would like to mix things up by randomizing which approach you take, you can download Discovery Cards for free from Hindsight Software to use as questioning cue cards: https://www.hindsightsoftware.com/discovery-cards.

Activity

Using your original questions from the previous activity, see if you can expand them using the *else* keyword. Reflect on how they change the question. Write down each of the *else* questions you might ask.

DATA TYPE ANALYSIS

With data type analysis, we can observe proposed data types that exist in our API design and pick out specific questions related to a data type. As an example, let's briefly remind ourselves of the proposed payload that we can send to create a room:

```
{
    "roomName": "102",
    "type": "Double",
    "accessible": "true",
    "description": "This is a description for the room",
    "image": "/img/room1.jpg",
    "roomPrice": 200,
    "features": ["TV", "Safe"]
}
```

We can see in our payload that we send a `roomPrice` in the form of an integer. With this information in mind, we can ask questions that focus on the general rules related to the data type, such as

- What if we send a float instead of an integer?
- What if we send an overflowing number?

Or we could ask questions related to business rules behind the data type, such as

- What if the `roomPrice` is set to zero or below?
- What if the `roomPrice` is not sent?

By using our knowledge of how the integer data type works along with our knowledge of business rules, we can drill down into specific details to get answers.

Each data type has its own considerations that you can use for questioning, which requires an understanding of how they work and their limitations. Fortunately, cheat sheets have been created for this type of work; for example, we can use the Test Heuristic Cheat Sheet PDF created by Elisabeth Hendrickson, which can be found here: http://mng.bz/Ay5K. We'll discuss heuristics in more detail in chapter 5 when we discuss exploratory testing, but for now, you can use them as a means to help trigger questions quickly.

> **Activity**
>
> Using the Test Heuristic Cheat Sheet, write down a list of questions you might ask that relate to the POST /room/ payload.

VISUALIZATIONS

Cliché as it sounds, a picture is worth a thousand words, and when we're carrying out an activity in which we are trying to establish a shared understanding and reveal assumed information, visualizations can be extremely valuable. Consider the question we asked earlier.

HOW WILL IT WORK?

Imagine that instead of giving a verbal answer, a member of a team walked over to a whiteboard and drew out the diagram in figure 4.3.

Although not the most elaborate visualization, it shares information about dependencies between APIs and demonstrates a security mechanism in play. It can also serve as a launching point for more questions, such as

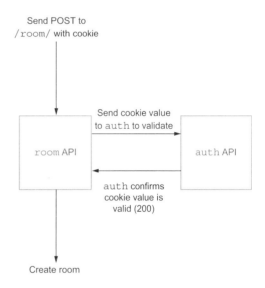

Figure 4.3   An example of a visualization we can create of an API design to facilitate conversation

- What if the Auth API connect fails?
- What if the Auth API returns an error code?
- How does the Auth API tell the room API whether the security check passed?

The visualization acts as a source for asking new questions as well as a tool for clarifying your own understanding. Offering up your own visualizations and asking the team "Is this how it works?" can yield excellent feedback as team members use your visualization to communicate to you the differences in their understanding of what is going to be built.

> **Activity**
>
> Using your knowledge of restful-booker-platform and the model you created in chapter 2, try creating a stripped-down visualization of the POST /booking/ process. Once you've completed the visualization, review it and complete your list of questions with additional questions you might ask that are triggered by looking at the visualization.

As mentioned earlier, testing API designs and testing abstract ideas and requirement artifacts is a skill that comes with practice. But these techniques and tools we've explored can help kick-start conversations and generate questions. There is one other approach we can explore, though, that can help trigger conversations and increase shared understanding, and that's documentation.

4.2 *Using API documentation tools to test designs*

Documentation is sometimes a loaded word. Some push back and say that documentation is wasteful, hard to maintain, and rarely used, citing images of specification documents that are hundreds of pages long. But when done right, documentation strikes a balance between being lightweight and easy to maintain while capturing what we intend to create. Our documentation can become a source of agreement between individuals and an effective way to communicate our work to others outside of the team.

As we test API designs, we're not just revealing information and discovering issues. We're helping teams to capture our shared understanding to do the following:

- Remove any assumptions and ambiguity by explicitly stating how we expect our API to work
- Identify new information that we can use to trigger further questioning
- Set out clear details of how we expect our APIs to work to the consumer of our APIs, whether it's another team developing APIs on the same platform or a third-party user on the other side of the planet

The key is creating good documentation that is useful for everyone and easy to maintain. Fortunately, as we'll learn, modern documentation tools are designed with those values in mind.

4.2.1 *Documenting APIs with Swagger/OpenAPI 3*

There are many tools we can use to document APIs with a range of different features, but for our documentation, we'll use the Swagger toolset. Swagger offers a range of tools that we can take advantage of that we'll discuss shortly, but for now, our focus will be on using the specification schema called OpenAPI 3 to document our API design.

The OpenAPI 3 schema started life as part of the Swagger toolset. But in an effort to help develop an industry standard in documenting APIs, the Swagger team donated the schema to the open source community OpenAPI Initiative (https://www.openapis .org/). Since then, the OpenAPI Initiative has evolved the original Swagger schema into the OpenAPI 3 schema specification, which can be used to specify APIs in a way that is open and easy to validate, helping to mitigate risks around the misinterpretation of designs and documentation.

To understand how OpenAPI 3 works, let's create an API design using the schema for our `POST room` API design. Let's remind ourselves of the proposed design:

REQUEST

```
POST /room/ HTTP/1.1
Host: example.com
Accept: application/json
Cookie: token=abc123

{
    "roomName": "102",
    "type": "Double",
    "accessible": "true",
    "description": "This is a description for the room",
    "image": "/img/room1.jpg",
    "roomPrice": "200",
    "features": ["TV", "Safe"]
}
```

RESPONSE

```
HTTP/1.1 201 OK
Content-Type: application/json

{
    "roomid": 3,
    "roomName": 102,
    "type": "Double",
    "accessible": true,
    "image": "/img/room1.jpg",
    "description": "This is a description for the room",
    "features": ["TV", "Safe"],
    "roomPrice": 200
}
```

First, we need to decide where we want to capture our design. Because the preferred format for OpenAPI is YAML, the easiest option is to fire up an editor and get to work. Depending on your editor or IDE of choice, you can install plugins or linters to ensure your documentation follows the correct OpenAPI patterns. Alternatively, if you're looking for additional features, there is SwaggerHub, which offers an online editor that is free to sign up and use (https://swagger.io/tools/swaggerhub/), although more advanced features require a paid subscription. Alternatively, if you're comfortable with using Docker, you can also pull down a Docker image of the editor to use. Details of the Docker image can be found on the swagger-editor GitHub page (http:// mng.bz/7yx9).

Alternative API design tools

If for any reason Swagger is not a toolset that works for you, other tools offer API design tooling, such as the Postman API design and Stoplight, which both support the OpenAPI format.

Regardless of the tooling you select, let's begin by creating a new YAML design document and add in the following:

```yaml
openapi: 3.0.0
info:
  description: An example API design
  version: 1.0.0
  title: SandBox Room service
  contact:
    name: Mark Winteringham
```

We begin on line 1 by declaring the schema type for the documentation. This is essential for validating the format of our design with the OpenAPI 3 schema and for using our design with other Swagger tools. Next, we provide contextual information under the `info` section to help describe the API and track versioning for the design. With those details in place, we can now document the request and response by adding the following details to the YAML file as follows:

```yaml
servers:
  - url: https://example.com/
paths:
  /room/:
    post:
      tags:
        - room
      parameters:
        - in: cookie
          name: token
          required: true
          schema:
            type: string
      requestBody:
        content:
          application/json:
            schema:
              $ref: '#/components/schemas/Room'
        description: roomPayload
        required: true
      responses:
        '201':
          description: Created
          content:
            application/json:
              schema:
                $ref: '#/components/schemas/Room'
        '403':
          description: Forbidden
```

As we'll learn in the next section, the design documentation we create can be consumed by one of Swagger's tools to create interactive API documentation. This allows us to send requests and receive responses. To enable that feature, we need to provide one or more entries under the `servers` section for the documentation to consume.

Then we begin to map out the `room` API endpoint starting with the specification of the URI in the form of `/room/` with the following four sections:

- *tags*–The tags allow us to give our URI specification a name to make it easy to find in documentation.
- *parameters*—In the design, we can specify items such as headers that will go into the request. In our request, we require a `Cookie` header with a `token=abc123` value.
- *requestBody*—Although we haven't yet specified what the body of the request will be, we do need to declare it later in the design. The `content:` section tells us that the request body will be in `application/json` format before creating a reference to the schema we intend to create.
- *responses*—The `responses` section allows us to list out expected status code responses by declaring each status code as a subsection of `response` and add additional details. For example, the `201` section has additional details to show that a payload that follows the `room` schema is added in the response.

With the last two sections, we've referenced a `room` schema with the use of `$ref:` `'#/components/schemas/Room'`, so let's complete our YAML file by creating a schema for the following JSON body

```
{
    "roomid" : 1
    "roomName" : "101",
    "type": "Single",
    "accessible" : false,
    "description" : "A room description",
    "image" : "link/to/image.jpg",
    "roomPrice" : "100",
    "features" : ["TV", "Refreshments", "Views"]
}
```

by adding in the following:

```
components:
  schemas:
    Room:
      title: Room
      type: object
      properties:
        accessible:
          type: boolean
        description:
          type: string
        features:
          type: array
```

```
        items:
          type: string
          pattern: Single|Double|Twin|Family|Suite
      image:
        type: string
      roomName:
        type: string
      roomPrice:
        type: integer
        format: int32
        minimum: 0
        maximum: 999
        exclusiveMinimum: true
        exclusiveMaximum: false
      roomid:
        type: integer
        format: int32
    required:
      - accessible
      - description
      - features
      - image
      - roomName
      - roomPrice
```

Notice how the first three lines of this section have the same hierarchy as the $ref:
'#/components/schemas/Room' reference. This is how we tie schemas to the
paths section.

Under the Room section, we declared the schema structure, starting with the root
object and its name, followed by the properties section where we declare each item
we want in the object. Each property has rules to determine what type it is (string,
array, integer, etc.) and any rules around each property's boundaries.

For example, with roomPrice, we've used minimum and maximum to set a low and
high boundary. The exclusiveMinimum and exclusiveMaximum tells us whether
we include the value set in our boundary. So, for example, minimum is set to 0 and
exclusiveMinimum is set to true, meaning anything less than 1 is out of bounds.
Finally, we can set which properties are required and which are optional with the
required field.

Putting all of that together, we end up with an API design document for the
/room/ endpoint that looks like this:

```
openapi: 3.0.0
info:
  description: An example API design
  version: 1.0.0
  title: SandBox Room service
  contact:
    name: Mark Winteringham
servers:
  - url: example.com
servers:
  - url: https://example.com/
```

```
paths:
  /room/:
    post:
      tags:
        - room
      parameters:
        - in: cookie
          name: token
          required: true
          schema:
            type: string
      requestBody:
        content:
          application/json:
            schema:
              $ref: '#/components/schemas/Room'
        description: roomPayload
        required: true
      responses:
        '201':
          description: Created
          content:
            application/json:
              schema:
                $ref: '#/components/schemas/Room'
        '403':
          description: Forbidden
components:
  schemas:
    Room:
      title: Room
      type: object
      properties:
        accessible:
          type: boolean
        description:
          type: string
        features:
          type: array
          items:
            type: string
            pattern: Single|Double|Twin|Family|Suite
        image:
          type: string
        roomName:
          type: string
        roomPrice:
          type: integer
          format: int32
          minimum: 0
          maximum: 999
          exclusiveMinimum: true
          exclusiveMaximum: false
        roomid:
          type: integer
          format: int32
```

```
required:
  - accessible
  - description
  - features
  - image
  - roomName
  - roomPrice
```

Using a tool like OpenAPI, we can quickly develop documentation that is easy to read and, in turn, can help us to test. We can look at the `properties` list with each of the type fields and apply the data type analysis we discussed before. In the `responses` section, we could ask questions about different errors and the feedback we send. The reason this becomes easier to do is that the design idea is no longer inside the head of one or more team members but concretely documented for the whole team to review.

Activity

Using OpenAPI is relatively easy, but it does require some familiarity with the rules of the schema. To help you come to grips with documenting with OpenAPI, using what we've learned, build an API design document for the `/booking` endpoint you tested earlier:

REQUEST

```
POST /booking/ HTTP/1.1
Host: example.com
Accept: application/json

{
    "bookingdates": {
        "checkin": "2021-02-01",
        "checkout": "2021-02-03"
    },
    "depositpaid": false,
    "firstname": "Mark",
    "lastname": "Winteringham",
    "roomid": 1,
    "email": "mark@example.com",
    "phone": "01234567890"
}
```

RESPONSE

```
HTTP/1.1 200 OK
Content-Type: application/json

{
    "bookingid": 2,
    "booking": {
        "bookingid": 2,
        "roomid": 1,
        "firstname": "Mark",
        "lastname": "Winteringham",
        "depositpaid": false,
```

```
        "bookingdates": {
            "checkin": "2021-02-01",
            "checkout": "2021-02-03"
        }
    }
}
```

4.2.2 Beyond documentation

One of the benefits of using OpenAPI for our documentation is the other opportunities it offers to us after our documentation is complete. By designing our API in OpenAPI, we can then use Swagger tools to speed up our development and improve our public documentation with a range of tools, such as those covered next.

SWAGGER CODEGEN

Swagger Codegen offers the ability to turn our API design documentation into code. Apart from the value in potentially saving time to build a new API from scratch, it also helps ensure that what was agreed during the design discussions is implemented, while leaving freedom to add the necessary business logic to complete the work. This does mean you are entrusting the generation of your production code to a third-party tool, which may come with additional risks that can be tested for using other testing activities we'll explore in this book.

You can find out more about Swagger Codegen here: https://github.com/swagger-api/swagger-codegen.

SWAGGER UI

If you went through the previous section using SwaggerHub, you would have already seen Swagger UI in the form of interactive documentation to the right of your design file. Swagger UI has the ability to take your API design documentation and present it in an easy-to-read UI that clearly presents your API's functionality. In addition to that, if configured correctly, you also have the ability to build requests using the documentation to send requests to your API and view the responses. This tool provides an excellent way to test your APIs because they're built quickly. But more importantly, it can share accurate documentation with your users of what your APIs can and can't do, resolving any risks around misunderstanding how our API works, so it can't be incorrectly dismissed as not working correctly.

You can find out more about Swagger UI here: https://github.com/swagger-api/swagger-ui/.

Documenting GraphQL APIs

Because GraphQL doesn't use OpenAPI for defining schemas, the Swagger toolset (at the time of writing) doesn't support GraphQL. However, open source libraries offer a similar experience for GraphQL, such as graphql-playground and graphiql, which are maintained by the GraphQL community (https://github.com/graphql/).

4.3   Encouraging teams to test API designs

Having the knowledge and skills to analyze and question API designs is essential. But without the opportunity to test, it's hard to help teams improve quality. Yes, we can test API designs in an asynchronous manner, taking the time to go through the designs, jot down questions, and then send them to your team. But this approach is time-consuming with potential issues being identified after implementation has begun, negating the value of the activity. Additionally, the lack of a collaborative discussion means opportunities to spot discrepancies will be missed. Sending emails or instant messages is never going to be as subtle as a good conversation.

To truly get the most from this testing activity, it's best carried out in a collaborative discussion as a group. Having different stakeholders and disciplines will provide different perspectives and sources of information that can be shared during a conversation. Asking a question about the product might trigger a discussion about architectural constraints. Getting clarification on a specific point may flag differing assumptions across the team.

4.3.1   Getting buy-in and initiating opportunities to test API designs

An important contributor to these types of discussions is the cultural mindset of a team. It's easy for me to say that you should use the existing conversations that are being had or kick off collaborative sessions with your team and start testing. But for some, the reality is that teams may exclude certain roles from discussions either by accident or deliberately. To combat this exclusion, some might say that you should just invite yourself. However, even if you get past the initial shock of just inviting yourself to a session, it doesn't necessarily ensure buy-in from a wider team.

As we will discuss in later chapters, encouraging a team to incorporate testing activities during the ideas phase requires a strategy. Experimentation can be a great way to incorporate testing API designs. Start small with your experiments. For example, start with pairing sessions with like-minded individuals and measure success. Share the value of your pairing with the team and perhaps expand pairing sessions to gain more traction. Once there is a critical mass of interest, discuss with the team as a whole whether to agree to formalize this type of testing activity. Or, if it works, keep doing the work you're doing as a team.

4.3.2   Taking advantage of existing sessions

Fortunately, the activity of testing API designs slots nicely into other approaches our teams might take to discuss designs. Whether the current discussions are being had in a formal or informal style, we can bring in testing to help clarify ideas and think deeply about what we're building.

FORMAL APPROACHES

Agile ceremonies have become a staple in team software-development life cycles. Regardless of choice, it's not uncommon for teams to have some sort of activity in which upcoming work is discussed before it's begun. Ceremonies such as sprint planning or story kick-offs can offer opportunities to begin testing API designs. Typically, these types of ceremonies will already have people from different roles collaboratively discussing ideas and informally testing. By bringing a testing focus into the mix, you can expand the conversations that are already being had.

If you want to take advantage of existing ceremonies, keep in mind that there are potential limitations. Some sessions can be quite large and go on for quite a while, having to fit a lot of discussions into a time-boxed session. This can lead to fatigue in attendees, which can have a negative impact on how team members communicate. Additionally, larger groups of people can mean some members are less willing to share.

INFORMAL APPROACHES

Although taking advantage of formal ceremonies can offer you an "out-of-the-box" solution, sometimes a more informal approach can be more successful.

Pairing, for example, can offer an excellent opportunity for testing. It could be argued that pairing activities already have testing baked in implicitly, with pairs discussing ideas and sharing solutions. However, if a pair is focused on implementation, it's easy to become biased by the task at hand. By agreeing as a pair to spend time discussing and testing ideas before implementation, we allow ourselves to think more widely and deeply about our work before we begin implementing.

Beyond pairs, team members may get together for informal discussions about design ideas. For example, if we worked on a project that had split roles for backend and frontend developers or APIs providing data and consuming data are handled by different teams, this might result in informal conversations about API designs. This could be an excellent opportunity to bring a formal testing perspective into the discussions. By observing how our teams work, we can sometimes spot these informal discussions to join.

4.3.3   *Establishing your own sessions*

Although taking advantage of existing ceremonies or discussions in teams can offer a quick path for testing API designs, sometimes it might not be the best fit for what we want to achieve. Sprint planning might already be too long, while pairing might be too informal or lack the level of information sharing we desire. So we may look to implement a new approach to allow us to test API designs.

For some teams, adopting the "Three Amigos" approach can create a space in which a team's members can get together with the sole focus of discussing design ideas and gaining a better understanding of what they need to deliver. Traditionally, a Three Amigos session can be a formal or semiformal meeting that is run when a new user story or piece of work is ready to be considered for design and development, in which a tester, developer, and product owner (or similar) come together to collaborate and discuss the delivery of said story or work. The goal is that everyone leaves with a clear, shared understanding of what needs to be done.

The Three Amigos approach for collaborative discussion is straightforward and easy to adopt and can be an excellent way to encourage testing API design activities. But as you progress and mature with this approach, you can adapt to your context. We can make Three Amigos sessions a formal part of our software development cycle, adding an Analysis column to our Kanban board. Or we can choose to keep it as an informal affair, encouraging team members to come over and speak to one another when required.

Additionally, we can consider adding more people to our conversations. It doesn't have to be Three Amigos—it could be four, five, or more. Having other roles involved offers different perspectives; for example, if we have split disciplines for development, we could invite one member of each discipline. Or perhaps we would invite a team member responsible for UX. The key thing to remember with Three Amigos is that it's flexible. As long as you're collaborating and discussing, there's value.

4.4 *Testing API designs as part of a testing strategy*

For some, testing API designs might feel like an unusual place to begin our journey into learning the many ways in which we test APIs. However, it highlights dynamic testing as craft and how it can fit into many different situations and deliver value. A good testing strategy is a holistic one that focuses on the many places in which risk can creep into our work.

If we recall the testing model we explored in chapter 1, the goal is to ensure that what we want to build matches what we're building. But that requires us to have a good understanding of what we want to build in the first place. If we are misinformed about what we want to deliver as a team, it can lead to frustrating rework or the delivery of work that doesn't match what the user wants. Therefore, to ensure that we build the right thing, we should focus our attention on two specific areas shown in our highlighted test strategy model in figure 4.4: testing what we know as a team (the area overlapped with Implementation) and what we don't know as a team that matters (the rest of the Imagination area).

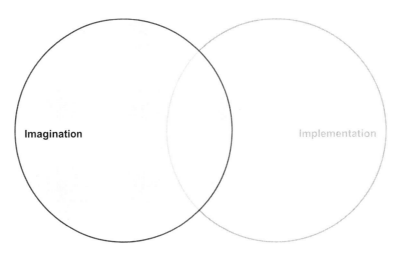

Figure 4.4   Using the test strategy model to demonstrate how testing API designs focuses the Imagination side of testing

Unlike other testing activities, this type of testing focuses on questioning requirements, designs, and ideas. When done correctly, the questions we ask can help a team develop a shared understanding of what they're being asked to build. We can use questions to probe the problems we're being asked to solve, reflect on whether our solutions will deliver value, and uncover any issues or ideas that haven't been discussed yet (like sending incorrect status codes). The more we collaborate, question, and discuss ideas and designs, the easier it will be for us to expand what we know as a team and reduce what we don't, resulting in a better-informed team with a clearer idea of how to improve the quality of the product they are building.

Summary

- We're at risk of delivering poor-quality work if we don't take time to discuss and test design requirements and ideas.
- By questioning API designs up front, we can capture issues earlier and dispel assumptions and misconceptions.
- At its essence, testing is about asking questions. We can use those questioning skills to test ideas and designs.
- Questioning requires strong critical and lateral thinking skills.
- We can use techniques such as five Ws and an H as a way to identify questions quickly.
- We can also use techniques such as *else* and funnel questions, data type analysis, and visualization to expand our questions.
- To help facilitate collaborative discussions and testing, we can use modern documentation tools like Swagger.
- Swagger uses the OpenAPI 3 schema to help us accurately and clearly describe our API's design.
- We can use designs with other Swagger tools to share clear documentation and quickly build code for us.
- Joining or starting new collaborative sessions provides an excellent opportunity to test designs.

Exploratory testing APIs

Before we dive into exploratory testing, let's start with a short activity. Find a piece of paper and a pen, and write down a script that guides a reader from point A to point B. This could be from the office front door to your desk or from the front door of your house to your kitchen. Try not to worry too much about the route. With your script written, if you can, give it to someone else, and ask them to start at point A and use your script to get them to point B. Once they've completed the journey, ask them a simple question: What things did they see as they followed your script? For example, was there anything interesting on the walls? Did someone have an unusual item on their desk? It doesn't matter what they say; note it down, then ask them to do the same activity again. But this time, don't give them a script to follow. Tell them they have 10 minutes to get from point A to point B, but during those 10 minutes, they can write down everything they see around them as they make their journey.

Once they're done, compare the differences between what was observed when using the script to what was observed without the script. It's very likely the volume and detail of feedback from the second iteration were much higher. That's because during the second iteration, your volunteer was carrying out an informal session of exploratory testing. During that session, they explored a constrained area with purpose to learn about what was around them. They've demonstrated to you how, at its core, exploratory testing works and its value. In this chapter, we're going to analyze an exploratory testing session and learn more about what exploratory testing is, how to explore with purpose and structure, and how to execute exploratory testing.

5.1 The value of exploratory testing

Exploratory testing has reached a point at which many are aware of it but are unsure how it works or what it entails, with some misinterpreting it as an ad hoc, made-up, or structureless approach toward testing that is hard to practice or to use to deliver value. There is some truth regarding the free nature and flexibility of testing that can be found in exploratory testing. But as we'll learn, exploratory testing is a highly disciplined approach toward testing that balances structure and freedom to help enable the "explorer" to learn as much useful information as possible.

5.1.1 The testing cycle in exploratory testing

In Elisabeth Hendrickson's book, *Explore It!*, which offers a deep dive into exploratory testing, she states that exploratory testing is

> *"…simultaneously learning about the system while designing and executing tests, using feedback from the last test to inform the next."*

What she is saying is that during exploratory testing, we repeat a loop many times over during a session, as summarized in figure 5.1.

Each step of the loop works as follows:

1. *Design*—At the beginning of a loop, we have some knowledge of the system we are testing. Based on that knowledge, we identify new questions we might want to ask or gaps in our knowledge we want to fill, so we come up with a new test idea and design it.

2. *Execute*—Once we have designed our test, we'll execute it, perhaps with the assistance of some tools.

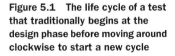

Figure 5.1   The life cycle of a test that traditionally begins at the design phase before moving around clockwise to start a new cycle

3   *Analyze*—After the execution is complete, we analyze the results.

4   *Learn*—Our analysis will update our understanding of our system, and we begin the loop again with an updated understanding.

All of this happens at a relatively fast pace, typically in our heads, with the help of some sort of note-taking. To put this into a more concrete example, let's imagine we're exploring a form field that has been designed to accept "valid" phone numbers as follows:

1   *Design*—We know that the form field should accept only valid phone numbers, so we come up with a test that tests two valid phone number formats from two different countries (UK and United States).

2   *Execute*—We create two valid phone numbers for each country and submit each one.

3   *Analyze*—We observe that the UK number is accepted whereas the US number is not.

4   *Learn*—We learn that not all phone numbers are considered "valid" phone numbers. At the moment, only UK phone numbers are valid, so perhaps we could try other countries to see what happens.

This short loop demonstrates how we can rapidly test and learn during exploratory testing because we will go through the loop many times over and over in one exploratory testing "session" (more on sessions soon). The loop itself allows us to follow a pattern that gives us structure in our testing, but it also gives us the freedom to choose what we want to focus on and what tests we can design. It's this loop that enables us to test further with exploratory testing, but it is a double-edged sword. As we've learned before, we can't test everything because our time is limited. We want to ensure our testing is delivering value which means we need guidance as to what to focus on and what to leave for another day.

5.2   *Planning to explore*

We've learned that exploratory testing is a structured approach to testing, but where does the structure come from? It comes in the form of *charters*, which are brief, specific, measurable goals that we hope to achieve through the execution of exploratory testing "sessions." For example, a charter could be the following:

- Explore the `branding` API
- With different B&B details
- To discover whether the `branding` API saves B&B details correctly

Or it could be in the following format that my colleague, Dan Ashby, has shared with others to use:

- Look at updating in the `branding` API
- To test for issues when saving branding details

The purpose of a charter is to set out clearly what we hope to achieve in our exploratory testing without being too overly prescriptive. For example, reflecting on the charter just mentioned, we could come up with tests for details such as B&B names, locations, and addresses and feel confident that those ideas are in line with the goal of the charter. We also know that if we're identifying test ideas that look at response codes of the `booking` API, we've gone "off-charter," and we might not be discovering information that is of use to our team.

5.2.1   Generating charters

When thinking about charters, we may conjure images of famous explorers chartering adventures in unknown lands or ancient ruins. That's because charters are statements that describe what an explorer aims to discover, and the same works for exploratory testing. Just like an explorer would create a charter to discover some unknown area of the world, we use charters to discover a different type of unknown: risks. We identify risks and then capture them into charters to use in exploratory testing sessions.

We've already explored risk analysis in detail in chapter 3. But as a recap, we can identify risks by adopting a skeptical mindset, with the aid of tools such as RiskStorming, to question our assumptions and hypothesize situations where the quality of our product might be negatively impacted. Through this process, we'll identify risks that might impact our product, and it is these risks that we can turn into charters that we'll use for our exploratory testing purposes.

For example, let's take the following risk we identified in chapter 3 and turn it into a risk that is more relevant to restful-booker-platform's APIs:

- Admin is unable to use the `branding` API.

This can be tweaked to

- `PUT /branding` endpoint fails to update details in the `branding` API.

We have a brief, specific description of the risk we want to test for, but in its current form, it isn't measurable and lacks focus. This is where a charter can help. For example, let's update our risk using a common charter template that was popularized in *Explore It!*:

```
Explore <Target>
Using <Tools>
To discover <Risk/Information>
```

Using this approach, we can translate our risk into the following charter:

```
Explore the PUT /branding/ API endpoint
Using different data sets
To discover issues in which data is incorrectly handled
```

By converting the risk into a charter, we have a clearer goal of what we hope to achieve when we use the charter for an exploratory testing session. We know what the focus is and what tools we might employ and can use the charter to help us get started with our testing as well as determine the success of our exploratory testing.

To generate charters, we identify risks and then capture them using a templated format that describes our intention during an exploratory testing session. Much like other aspects of testing, chartering takes practice, but to help us create charters, we can use a range of templates, such as Dan Ashby's template we saw earlier:

```
Look at <Target>
To test for <Test Idea>
```

We could write this as

```
Look at PUT /branding/
To test for issues in which data is incorrectly saved
```

Another template that I have found particularly useful when starting out with charters is one from Michael D. Kelly, which he shares in his webinar "Tips for Writing Better Charters for Exploratory Testing Sessions" (https://youtu.be/dOQuzQNvaCU):

```
My mission is to test <Risk> for <Coverage>
```

We could write this as

```
My mission is to test for issues with data not saving for the PUT /branding/
API endpoint
```

Which format you choose to use is up to you. The goal, ultimately, is to identify a series of charters that each capture different risks we want to explore so we can begin to plan what exploratory testing we are going to do and when.

Activity

Either pick one of the risks you identified back in the RiskStorming activity in chapter 3 or sit down and think of a risk you could explore in the API sandbox. Write out one or more charters, using the templates we've explored, that capture the focus for an exploratory testing session.

Finding the right time to pick out charters

One of the great things about charters is that there is a lot of flexibility when it comes to picking times to generate them. Charters can be created during formal meetings, such as sprint plannings or user story discussions, but they can also be captured as you run an exploratory testing session. The most successful approach is to have a mix of both. Taking advantage of times when a team is together is a valuable way to identify a range of different charters. But don't be afraid to add more when exploratory testing or sharing your discoveries with others.

5.2.2 *Charters and exploratory testing sessions*

Once we've generated our charters, our next step is to plan what exploratory testing sessions we want to run. An exploratory testing session is a single time-boxed instance of exploratory testing that is guided by a charter. For example, we may plan to run one exploratory testing session for a charter we've identified, as demonstrated in figure 5.2.

However, it can at times be more beneficial to run more than one exploratory testing session for a charter, as demonstrated in figure 5.3.

This is because every exploratory testing session will be different. Who is running the session, our knowledge of what we're testing, our skills as a tester, and many more factors will contribute to how we test and how we observe the system. By running multiple testing sessions that all focus on the same charter, we will likely end up with different discoveries to share.

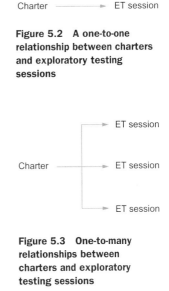

Figure 5.2 A one-to-one relationship between charters and exploratory testing sessions

Figure 5.3 One-to-many relationships between charters and exploratory testing sessions

5.2.3 *Organizing our exploratory testing*

The number of exploratory testing sessions we choose to do for a single charter as well as which set of charters are a priority will depend on the amount of time we have to test. Charters are not just a way of guiding our testing, but a way to organize what we want to do exploratory testing on and in what priority. For example, with restful-booker-platform, let's say we have identified the following three charters in priority order:

1 Explore the `Create Room` API to discover risks around rooms not being stored correctly.
2 Explore the `Delete Room` API to discover risks around rooms not being deleted correctly.
3 Explore the `Create Room` API to discover risks around incorrect responses being sent.

We ideally want to run at least three exploratory testing sessions for charter 2, but we only have enough time to run four sessions in total across our whole list. Our options might be the following:

- Run charter 1 once and charter 2 three times, and have a clear indication that charter 3 is still unknown to us, which can trigger a conversation about freeing up time for more testing or accepting the risk of the unknown.
- Run each charter in order of priority, starting with charter 1, then moving to charter 2 and finally charter 3, before coming back to charter 2 again for a second exploratory testing session.

Both options have their benefits and drawbacks. The point of this example, though, is to show how we can use charters to organize our work and to communicate what exploratory testing we want to do, when we want to do it, and, importantly, what exploratory testing we won't do. By creating charters, we're not just identifying a way of guiding our testing—we're also identifying a way to organize our exploratory testing and sharing what can be done or what has been or will be done, which can be used to communicate the progress of our exploratory testing.

> **Charters and regression testing**
>
> Charters can also be used to help organize exploratory testing sessions for regression testing purposes. If we organize our charters in a place in which we can track what charters have been run and when, as well as what their focus is, we can use this to determine what regression testing we might want to carry out. For example, we might choose to rerun charters that haven't been run for a certain amount of time, or we might pick out charters that cover areas of the system we're concerned might have been affected by recent changes.

5.3   *Exploratory testing: A case study*

Because exploratory testing allows a person to run a session how they want (within a certain level of constraint), it can make learning how to perform exploratory testing a bit tricky. As we discussed earlier, every exploratory testing session will be different. The differences might be subtle, or they may be dramatically different, but whatever they are, we can't just copy what someone else does in exploratory testing. There are, however, patterns and techniques that we can employ in our exploratory testing that, once identified, can be used regardless of what we're exploring. So, to help us learn different aspects of exploratory testing, we're going to analyze a session that has already been carried out to determine what occurred during the session, what techniques and tools were employed, why we used them, and what the thinking is behind each.

For our use case, we'll look at an exploratory testing session I ran based on the following charter:

- Explore booking a room
- Using different data sets
- To discover issues that might cause bookings to fail or be in an error state

We'll start by breaking down the test ideas that were generated as the exploratory testing progressed before diving into more details. During this exploration of the session, I will be refer to specific sections of my testing notes. If you would like more context, you can review my complete testing notes that have been captured as a mind map and stored on GitHub (http://mng.bz/1oDV).

5.3.1   *Beginning the session*

One of the trickiest aspects of exploratory testing is knowing where to start. We usually begin in one of two states. We either know very little about what we're about to test, making it hard to make decisions in your testing, or we know too much, and the possibilities are a little overwhelming, making it hard to pick a place to begin. I find it best when beginning an exploratory testing session to first spend some time learning about what we're going to test before digging into the test ideas.

For example, in my exploratory testing session, for the room booking request, I began by establishing my testing notes in the form of a mind map and added some session information, such as when I started, what version I'm testing, and what environment I'm using. I also added details around the HTTP request that is used for successfully making a booking, including details around the URL, HTTP headers, and the HTTP body, all of which can be seen in figure 5.4.

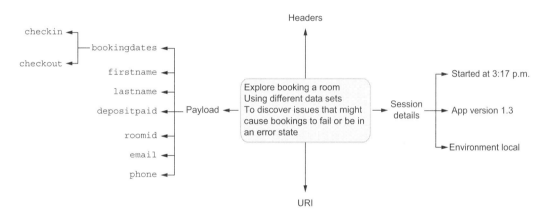

Figure 5.4   The initial notes taken at the start of an exploratory testing session

I discovered this information based on what I learned when going through the activities I outlined in chapter 2, specifically, using developer tools to capture the POST / booking HTTP, which I then copied into the HTTP testing tool, Postman. I could, however, have learned about the request by reading documentation or source code or having a conversation with the individual who created the web API endpoint in the first place.

With this information added, I could then begin testing. For me, my next step was to pick one of the nodes from the mind map and add in test ideas that came to mind. For example, in figure 5.5, we can see a series of test ideas for the bookingdates object in the HTTP body payload that have been added in the form of questions.

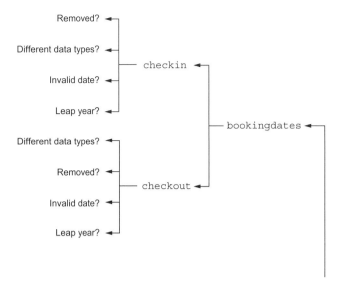

Figure 5.5   Testing notes describing different testing questions around the check-in and checkout dates

I'm able to do this because I've established an understanding of what the booking dates are used for when creating a booking. And by exploring and reflecting on that understanding, using critical and lateral thinking, I identified my test ideas. If we remember from chapter 2, critical thinking lets us dig deeper into ideas and concepts, and lateral thinking lets us go broader, which means I can use these skills to ask questions such as

- What if the check-in or checkout dates are on a leap year?
- What if the date format was different?
- What if I added in some other incorrect data?

Each of these questions are opportunities to find out new details about the application by devising a test, executing it, and observing what happens, such as

- Setting dates in check-in or checkout to 29-02-2020
- Updating date formats to 01/01/2000 or 2000-30-12
- Changing dates to null, integers, or strings

Exploratory testing with GraphQL

Although the structure of GraphQL is different from the REST approach that we're working with in this case study, how we approach our exploratory testing is similar. For example, let's take this simple query for a character:

```
query Character {
  character(id: 1) {
    name
    created
  }
}
```

We could apply a similar approach as before, considering what other fields we can query on and what IDs and filters we could add. For example, we're providing a character ID that takes an integer. I could ask questions such as these: What if I query for characters that don't exist? What if I remove the value? And what if I provide a different data type other than an integer?

Activity

Think of a series of different test ideas/questions for the `checkin` and `checkout` dates. Write down each of the ideas, and put them to one side for later use.

5.3.2   *Knowing when something isn't right*

A concern some individuals have when adopting exploratory testing is knowing when to raise an issue and when not to. Unlike scripted approaches that are designed specifically to test requirements or acceptance criteria, exploratory testing doesn't have explicit expectations. It's up to the person doing the exploratory testing to decide whether something is worth raising as an issue, and that can be a problem for some when starting out.

Although this might seem like an issue at first, through the use of oracles, we can overcome it quite easily and start to discover issues that violate our expectations as well as the expectations of others. An oracle is a source of information that may be explicit, like requirements, or may be tacit, such as the rules of language. Oracles are used when we reflect on new information presented to us to help us determine whether that information conforms to our oracles and is fine, or doesn't and is a potential issue that needs resolving. There are many different oracles that we can use to help us decide if something we're looking at feels right. To help us get a better understanding of how oracles work, let's look at some examples of oracles I used in my exploratory testing session to discover issues:

- *Product oracle*—With the product oracle, we're using our knowledge of our system to determine that it behaves in a consistent manner. For example, during my testing, I found that sometimes, when a 400 error was returned, it would return an error message that I could action (e.g., a field cannot be blank in my payload). At other times, however, I found that a generic 400 error message was returned with no error message. My product oracle might be that the application should always return a 400 with a clear error message. The inconsistency of behavior within the product violates my product oracle, which indicates a potential issue. Which error message should be sent? The generic one or the one with detailed error messages? This is something to investigate further.
- *Statutes and standards oracle*—Many projects are subject to rules, regulations, and laws that need to be adhered to. Examples might include medical software

following specific health codes, financial products following financial regulations, or, in the case of another issue that I discovered, architectural standards. While I was exploring the different `checkin` and `checkout` dates, an issue was revealed—when setting the `checkin` and `checkout` date on the same day, it would return a 409 error. A 400 type error makes sense if we review the definition for a 409 status code in rfc7231:

The 409 (Conflict) status code indicates that the request could not be completed due to a conflict with the current state of the target resource.

For our issue, this doesn't match up. There is no conflict because there is no booking to conflict against, so a 409 is the incorrect status code to use.

- *Familiarity oracle*—This oracle is based upon our experiences and knowledge of systems beyond just the product we're testing. Our ability to spot issues doesn't just come from our domain knowledge of a specific product we're testing but from the accumulation of experiences from every piece of software we use, whether it's something we work with professionally or use in our personal time. It's this knowledge that helped me identify an error in which a 500 server error is returned if I attempt to make a booking when the `message` API is unavailable. Specifically, it's not the 500 error that is the problem, but rather the fact that the booking is actually saved. My familiarity oracle when witnessing the 500 error was to interpret it as something that had failed to complete. In this situation, though, the booking process had actually partially completed, which didn't match my past experiences with other APIs that returned 500 errors.

These oracles demonstrate that as we observe our systems, we have different ways of interpreting information to determine issues beyond the more common approach of comparing what we see against a written requirement. Becoming comfortable with oracles takes time and practice before it becomes second nature. So to begin with, it's good to have a list of oracles in front of you as a quick reference to help trigger ideas as a heuristic, a technique that we'll explore next.

Triaging bugs together

We'll discuss sharing what we've learned during our testing in more detail later, but at a minimum, I always advise you to at least have a conversation with your team about the bugs you've raised. Oracles are fallible, meaning they work only in certain situations, and sometimes that means we raise issues that aren't actually issues. This is why it's useful to have a conversation with our team after our session to confirm which are actually issues. Speaking with a developer or product owner will help highlight what to fix, as well as demonstrate the value of our work to others.

Activity

There are more oracles you can use that have been summarized nicely by Michael Bolton in his article "FEW HICCUPPS" (http://mng.bz/5QrB/). As an activity, read through each of the oracles, and then think of an example issue or bug that describes how the oracle works.

5.3.3 *Coming up with ideas for testing*

At some point during an exploratory testing session we will run out of test ideas. Although this can be a cue that our session is complete—we'll explore this in more detail shortly—through the deliberate use of heuristics, we can continue to expand our testing ideas to discover even more.

As Richard Bradshaw and Sarah Deery put in their article, "Software Testing Heuristics: Mind The Gap!" (http://mng.bz/6XVo)

> "[H]euristics are cognitive shortcuts. We use them under conditions of uncertainty, often automatically without knowing using system 1 thinking, to rapidly solve problems and make decisions."

We use heuristics every day to solve problems, both consciously and unconsciously. As an example, I have a personal heuristic that I used to use consciously for getting into my shed, which is padlocked. I have two keys on a red keychain—one for the shed padlock and the other for a different door. The issue is that they look almost alike, meaning I was constantly using the wrong key, which was a source of frustration. However, I developed a heuristic that took advantage of the fact that one key is slightly warped and the other is not. The heuristic is the phrase "Red is right."

Whenever I would have the keys in my hand, the phrase "Red is right" would trigger me to remember that the shed key is not warped. By reciting the phrase, I would know which key to select. This phrase is interesting for a couple of reasons. First, it demonstrates the fallible nature of heuristics because "Red is right" works only if I have the red key chain. If I had the spare green key chain, it won't work. So, the heuristic helps me solve only a specific problem, much like other heuristics are designed to solve other specific problems. The second reason is that at some point, I stopped reciting the phrase; I reached a point when I knew that the untwisted key on the red key chain was the right key. The heuristic has become an unconscious one because I have practiced it many times. I don't doubt that I'm still using the heuristic, but I have internalized it somewhere deeper in my subconscious.

The same theory applies to using heuristics to create test ideas. A lot of my initial test ideas of trying out different dates, date formats, and data types come from internal heuristics that I've developed by testing other date fields in the past. The more I have tested, the more internal heuristics I've developed. However, as mentioned earlier, there comes a point when we will exhaust those ideas and heuristics. Rather than stopping, though, we can switch and start using explicitly stated heuristics to help identify new ideas.

For example, a great resource that I use a lot in exploratory testing sessions is the Test Heuristic Cheat Sheet (http://mng.bz/Ay5K) created by Elisabeth Hendrickson, James Lyndsay, and Dale Emery. The cheat sheet compiles a list of heuristics and data type attacks to help trigger test ideas. For my session, I used them to create new test ideas around

- Simulating blank first names and last names by filling the field with whitespace characters
- Trying out a range of accented characters and emojis, which resulted in discovering an issue
- Trying out dates that are incorrect, for example, February 30

Not only do the different items that exist in the cheat sheet trigger ideas to try out, but those explicit ideas themselves open up new avenues to explore, which in turn create new ideas.

Mnemonics are also frequently used as heuristics for triggering ideas. I've used the following to help generate more test ideas:

- *BINMEN*—Created by Gwen Diagram and Ash Winter, it stands for *boundary, invalid entries, nulls, method, empty, negatives,* each of which can be used to trigger different ideas. When I reviewed the BINMEN mnemonic, *method* stood out to me because it was something I'd not explored, and it triggered test ideas around learning what HTTP methods are available for the `/booking/` endpoint.
- *POISED*—This stands for *parameters, output, interoperability, security, exceptions, and data* and was created by Amber Race. The *exceptions* part of the mnemonic triggered ideas around questioning the error handling. Do the returned errors match what I would expect to see? (Remember our familiarity oracle.) Are the errors messages useful? Can they be actioned easily?

Many more mnemonics can be used to help trigger new ideas, and people have very handily collated them together into useful heuristic collections, such as the following:

- Lynn McKee's collection on the Quality Perspectives website (http://mng.bz/ZANO)
- Del Dewar's heuristic mind map (http://mng.bz/R4z0)
- The periodic table of testing by Ady Stokes (https://www.thebigtesttheory.com)

The important thing to remember is that tools like the Test Heuristic Cheat Sheet and mnemonics aren't list-checking exercises. They are ways to help us trigger ideas. There is no correct way to use heuristics; what matters is our relationship with them. If they trigger ideas, use them. If they don't, leave them and move on.

Activity

Go back to your test ideas that you created for the dates section of the booking request. Review the different resources we've learned about, such as the Test Heuristic Cheat Sheet, and use them to generate new test ideas.

5.3.4 Using tools

We've explored tools and techniques to expand the generation of test ideas during exploratory testing. Now let's look at how we can use software tools to help test further, deeper, and faster. During my exploratory testing session, I used a collection of tools during my session, which I captured in my test notes, as shown in figure 5.6.

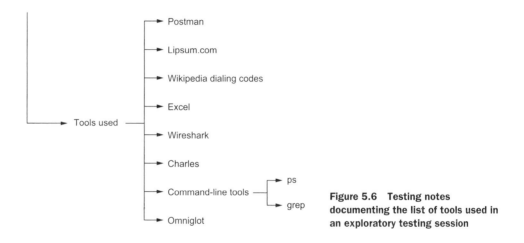

Figure 5.6 Testing notes documenting the list of tools used in an exploratory testing session

As we can see, there is a range of tools that served different purposes. Let's explore how they were used and how they helped expand my exploratory testing session.

EXCEL AND HTTP CLIENTS

The first example involves the `phone` field in the body of the HTTP request. During the session, a test idea came to me around trying different phone number formats to see whether the validation would support each of them. The problems I had with this idea follow:

- I needed a list of international numbers.
- There are a lot of international numbers to try out.

The first problem was solved through the use of Excel and Wikipedia. An initial search for international numbers returned a table on a Wikipedia page that showed different formats and lengths for numbers. I took those details, added them into an Excel spreadsheet, and, with the use of Excel formulas, generated a list of randomized international numbers that matched each format, similar to what's shown in table 5.1.

Table 5.1   Data-driven table example

id	country	code	length	example
1	Afghanistan	93	9	93212264949
2	Åland Islands	358	10	3583415884081
3	Albania	355	9	355224314764
4	Algeria	213	9	213941947247

With the list of numbers created, it was time to try each one as a test. Carrying this out "by hand" would be a slow process, so instead, I took advantage of the API testing tool Postman to do the work for me. The process I used follows:

1 I captured the POST /booking/ HTTP request in Postman and added it to a collection.

2 I then updated the JSON body to turn the values for id and phone into Postman variables (notice how the variables match the names of the rows in the CSV file):

```
{
    "bookingdates": {
        "checkin": "2022-12-01",
        "checkout": "2022-12-04"
    },
    "depositpaid": true,
    "firstname": "Mark",
    "lastname": "Winteringham",
    "roomid": {{id}},
    "phone" : "{{example}}",
    "email" : "test@test.com"
}
```

Finally, I used the runner tool in Postman to import the CSV file and run the collection with my modified request multiple times. Each iteration would pull a new row from the CSV file and inject it into my JSON body before sending the request. You can learn more about how to use this feature on the Postman website (http://mng.bz/2nld).

As each request was sent, a new phone number was injected, and the response was saved. Once the run was complete, I then reviewed the results to discover that not all international numbers were supported, which struck me as something to raise as a potential issue.

Activity

A similar test idea can be applied to the email parameter in the body for POST /booking. Using the Postman's runner and CSV files, create a new data-driven experiment to test out a range of different email formats, both valid and invalid. After running the experiment, analyze the results and see what you discover.

PROXIES AND MOCKS

For my second example, I used a combination of proxies and mocking tools to help discover and execute a relatively technical test idea. As we explored back in chapter 2, we can use the proxy tool Wireshark not only to monitor HTTP traffic between a user interface and backend APIs (similar to other proxy tools) but also to monitor traffic between APIs. In this instance, using Wireshark detected a relationship between the `booking` API and the `message` API, as shown in figure 5.7.

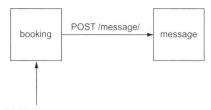

Figure 5.7   A model describing the relationship between the `booking` and `message` API

Leveraging system knowledge

Although in this example I've explained how I used Wireshark to detect the relationship between the `booking` API and `message` API, we could easily have done this as part of the initial product investigation in chapter 2. Having preexisting knowledge of the system could help us arrive at similar conclusions to what had been discovered as part of this example.

Knowing that this relationship exists, I thought of a new test idea around what would happen if the `message` API sent back an unexpected error or an incorrect status code. The problem I had, though, was sending those unexpected errors and incorrect status codes to the `booking` API. So, another tool was required—an API mocking tool called WireMock.

With WireMock, we can simulate the request and response behavior of a web API to give us more control over the information that is being sent between our APIs. For my test idea, I could use WireMock to mimic the `message` API's behavior, allowing me to send a series of different status codes back to the `booking` API. To do this, I downloaded the standalone version of WireMock that can be found in the documentation (http://wiremock.org/docs/running-standalone/). After I downloaded WireMock, I first needed to kill the current `message` API that was running by finding its PID number and then executing `kill {pid_number}` before starting up WireMock with the following command:

```
java -jar wiremock-jre8-standalone-2.28.0.jar --port 3006
```

NOTE   The version number may have changed. Be sure to use the latest version number.

This turned on WireMock and set up the tool to sit in the `message` API's place because of the argument `--port 3006`, which matched the port number for the message API. WireMock also created a `mappings` folder, into which I added the following JSON file:

```
{
  "request": {
    "method": "GET",
    "url": "/message"
  },
  "response": {
    "status": 400
  }
}
```

This configured WireMock to respond to requests sent to `GET /message` and return a response of 400. I loaded this mapping by restarting WireMock, and with the mapping loaded, I could send a request to `POST /booking/` and observe what would happen when a 400 status code was returned from WireMock. I could modify the JSON mapping with different status codes or connection errors, which resulted in uncovering issues like the `booking` API responding with a 500 error, but the booking is saved.

> **Activity**
>
> Similar behavior exists between the `room` API and the `auth` API in which a call to `POST /room` will send an additional call to `POST /auth/validate` in the `auth` API to determine whether room creation can be done. Try mocking the `auth` API with WireMock and having the mocked API send different status codes back to `room`.

These two examples show that through the use of automated tools, we can imagine and execute sophisticated test ideas that return interesting results. When doing exploratory testing, it's useful to keep an eye out for opportunities to use tools to support and expand our testing. As an additional recommendation, outside of exploratory testing, spending time familiarizing yourself with a range of tools is a great way to build up a collection of tools that can be used at a later date.

5.3.5   *Note-taking*

We've explored the process of identifying and applying different test ideas, but we also need to be mindful of the fact that the things we discover will at some point need to be shared with our team. We'll discuss options for sharing our learnings shortly, but when it comes to sharing details, we need some form of notes to help us in that process.

Note-taking in exploratory testing is essential, not just to communicate what we've learned but also to help us keep track of our testing and trigger new ideas. As long as we ensure that the notes we take help us to track and share our testing, how we record our notes is up to us. A few common approaches that have been employed by exploratory testers are described next.

MIND MAPS

To begin, let's discuss the format I opted to use for the session we've been analyzing. The mind mapping approach involves setting a root node, to which I added the charter for the session, and then branching off in different threads of exploration. The value of this approach is that as you discover new information, it can be recorded in subnodes that highlight a relationship between the testing that has been done and the information discovered. During my session, I would add information to the map, followed by questions and test ideas, which would eventually turn into more information. As I tested, the mind map grew organically, helping me keep track of the information I found and identify what to work on next during my session.

Additionally, if you look at the testing notes (http://mng.bz/mOor), you'll see that the mind map was made with mind mapping software that enabled me to do things like these:

- Organize different threads of thinking by different colors
- Highlight nodes that are answered questions (green) and nodes that are questions that need following up (yellow)
- Add in icons to highlight discoveries, such as bugs

These formatting tools become very useful when taking a snapshot of the results of the testing that was done. For example, in a quick look at the test notes, we can see a lot of red nodes, meaning that the session discovered a large number of potential issues to address.

One criticism of mind maps is that they are simply checklists in a different format. It is possible to end up recording a mind map that lacks detail and just reads like a list of testing that was done. We can ensure that our mind maps capture both our testing and our thinking through the use of formatting tools (different colors for different events), capturing additional information, and reducing the word count for each node. A trick I was once told was to keep your nodes down to three words max to force you to break out your thinking.

PEN AND PAPER

Sometimes getting away from software or a screen can be of benefit when taking notes, which is why a lot of individuals prefer using pen and paper. Personally, I find the act of drawing my attention away from the screen to pen-and-paper notes very useful in switching my thinking from observing the system to formulating ideas. Plus, there is something very satisfying about writing notes with a good pen.

Additionally, with pen and paper, we have a lot of flexibility as to how we take our notes. We might choose to use a formal note-taking approach such as the Cornell method, which structures a page into note-taking areas such as main notes, keywords/comments, and summaries. Others might prefer a more visual medium. The modeling activities we carried out in chapter 2 are a form of note-taking that help us organize our thoughts and capture ideas in a visual medium that is easy to share. Some take it further by adopting the sketch-noting technique, in which pictures and icons along with short phrases of text are used to capture the testing that was carried out, which is a great approach to sharing not just what was being tested but the thoughts and feelings behind it.

Each approach requires good habits in note-taking and discipline. We need to ensure that we capture the right balance of detail. Too much detail, and our focus on the testing is lost, which is disruptive. Too vague, and it will be harder to share what we learned later. Additionally, building up a visual language to detail what happened during a session with sketch-noting takes practice, and diagramming needs to be captured in a way that is easy to interpret at a later date.

SCREEN RECORDING

One final approach some individuals use is setting up a screen-recording tool that will record the entirety of the session as a video that can then be played back later. Some find this useful because it accurately captures not just what has been observed but all the information that resulted from testing. This will helpfully include not only details that we have noticed, but all the information we might not have noticed due to "functional fixedness"—a cognitive bias in which we are so focused on observing one event that we completely miss another.

By being able to review the recording, new details may be discovered, and testing work can be reviewed easily. However, this is a laborious process, especially if a session is multiple hours in length. Additionally, it records only what happens on the screen and doesn't capture any of the thought processes behind the session, making it hard to review the quality of the testing itself.

Experiment with note-taking

Finding the right note-taking approach for you can make a big difference in your exploratory testing. Ideally, we want to find an approach that doesn't distract us as we test but also ensures we capture the right amount of information to share at a later date. The best way to find out what works for you is through experimentation, so as you execute different exploratory testing sessions, try out different note-taking styles and reflect on what works and what doesn't. You'll eventually find the right approach for you.

5.3.6   *Knowing when to stop*

Eventually, at some point, an exploratory testing session has to end. But how do we identify the point at which to stop? Our goal in a session is to learn as much information related to the charter we set as is reasonably possible. But it's up to us to determine whether we feel we've captured all the relevant information we can find. To help us determine when we are done, we can employ/observe a few techniques or cues to help trigger the decision to stop.

No more test ideas

We discussed earlier how we could start a session by identifying test ideas that come to us naturally, through the use of subconscious heuristics, before using heuristics explicitly to generate other test ideas. But a point will come when those heuristics stop bearing fruit. A typical sign that this is happening is when we find our minds wandering a bit as we lose focus, or we find ourselves repeating test ideas (perhaps with minor changes). This is usually a sign that we've exhausted our ideas and we're not going to come up with any more, and that is perfectly fine. Remember, we'll never be able to test everything, so stopping is acceptable. As we'll discuss, there should be opportunities to reflect on our testing after that session, and that reflection may reveal new ideas. If so, we simply run another session.

Fatigue

Exploratory testing demands a lot from us mentally, and at some point, we'll start to slow down. Tiredness and low energy is usually a sign that it's time to stop. Even if we feel like there is still more to do, there is a risk that if we're feeling fatigued, we may miss things in our observations, much like in the "no more test ideas" scenario. It's OK to stop, reflect, and then run further sessions later. We can always use our test notes from previous sessions as an aid for future sessions.

Time-boxing

Time-boxing can be useful for a few reasons. First, it can help combat the feeling of fatigue by organizing sessions into manageable chunks, allowing us to take regular breaks in between to keep us fresh. They also enable us to manage and prioritize which sessions to run if time is short. Time-boxing sessions is an approach that has been popularized in session-based test management, a technique for managing exploratory testing sessions created by James and Jon Bach (http://mng.bz/PnY9). Sessions can be allocated small, medium, and large time boxes that refer to a fixed time amount with a variance of time added to it to allow the individual to complete a session. For example, a medium time-boxed session might be an hour in length, give or take 15 minutes. The idea is that if we have reached the one-hour mark but still want to continue testing for 15 minutes, we can. With this approach, we can give ourselves a deadline to complete but still have some allowance when stopping our work. And once again, if we're not done, we can always run further sessions.

Going "off charter"

Finally, we find ourselves going "off charter" during a session, meaning we're exploring areas of the system that no longer relate to the intended charter for a session. This may be because we're drawn toward another feature, or we may have discovered other issues that are worth exploring. The degree to which we go off charter is flexible, and it's common for a small amount of off-charter work to happen during a session. For example, in my session, I captured the off-charter work I did in my notes, as shown in figure 5.8.

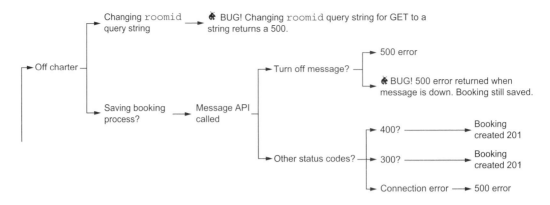

Figure 5.8   Testing notes describing activities that happened that are considered going off charter

We're not required to stop when going off charter. In fact, we can simply accept that the original intent of the session has been superseded by this new focus. But at times, it might be sensible to stop, take a step back, and reflect on this new area that we're exploring and capture it as a new charter to explore.

5.3.7   *Running your own exploratory testing session*

That concludes the exploratory testing use case. We've explored many facets of what happens during an exploratory testing session, and the best way to become comfortable with each of them is through practice. As an activity, take the charter you captured earlier in the chapter, and run an exploratory testing session using the charter as your guide. Experiment with the following:

- Different heuristics to trigger test ideas
- Different tools to support your exploring of APIs
- Different approaches to taking notes

5.4   *Sharing your discoveries*

Once our session is complete, it's important that we find time to share how the session went with others. The information we've discovered has value only if our team is aware of it and is using that new knowledge to help them plan the next steps.

A common approach to concluding an exploratory testing session and sharing information is to have a debrief with other members of our team. With the support of our testing notes, during a debrief, we have the opportunity to share details such as

- What was the focus of the session?
- What testing was done?
- What issues were found?
- What blockers that prevented testing arose during the session?
- Did we stay on charter?
- Are more sessions required?

These are just a few of the topics we can discuss during a debrief because the nature of the conversation allows us to tell our story about how the session went, much like how I have shared parts of my exploratory testing session with you.

Another benefit of a debrief is that we also have the opportunity to reflect on the quality of our testing. We can discuss potential gaps and missed opportunities and identify areas to improve, meaning we grow as exploratory testers as we share. How the debrief is structured is entirely up to the individuals involved. It can follow a structured checklist of questions, or it can be an informal chat that is time-boxed to ten minutes. The important factor is that by sharing what we've learned, we can help our teams reflect on the quality of what we've built and make changes if required.

ACTIVITY

Find a colleague and share with them what you've discovered during the exploratory testing session you've carried out. Share details about what you learned, the types of test ideas you came up with, and your reflections on the quality of your testing. Encourage your partner to ask questions to dig deeper into your testing. Once done, reflect on what you shared and how it helped you understand the value of the testing you did.

5.5   *Exploratory testing as part of a strategy*

James Lyndsay first created his model in his paper, "Exploration and Strategy," which we are using to better understand our testing strategy. He used it as a device to explain how scripted testing and exploratory testing come from different identified risks. He also explained how both are required to create a successful strategy.

To get a better understanding of this, remember the original activity at the start of the chapter in which we followed a script, explored a space, and then compared the differences in what we learned about both. The first task of following a set of directions simulates a test script and has the individual focusing on specific instructions that come with expectations and knowledge we already have. To put this into context using our testing model from chapter 1, test scripts only ever focus on the overlap of imagination and implementation, as shown in figure 5.9.

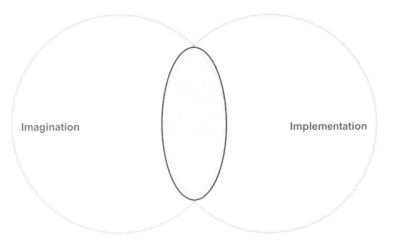

**Figure 5.9
A demonstration of the focus of test scripts within a testing strategy**

Test scripts require us to have some knowledge of what we expect from the system. A common source for test scripts are requirements, and this is why they can focus only on the overlap of imagination and implementation because the implementation is derived from the same requirements the test script is using. For example, if a requirement states that a form field should accept valid phone numbers, that's what will be developed, and that's what the test script will test for—checking valid phone numbers, nothing more, nothing less. And this is what occurs during the first round of our activity; the individual focuses on our directions while ignoring other details around them.

The issue with this approach, as we can see in figure 5.9, is that it leaves a lot left untested. With our phone number field, we might want to test for other valid phone number formats, invalid numbers, alphas and symbols, different ranges of numbers, character overflows, repeated submissions, and so on. Our products are of such a level of complexity that we need to explore beyond our expectations to learn what is actually occurring in our products, as shown in figure 5.10.

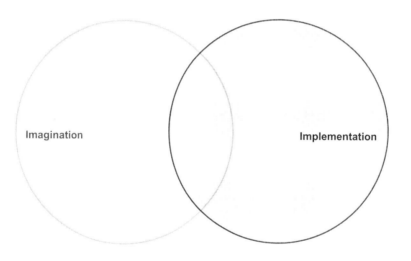

Figure 5.10   A model demonstrating how exploratory testing focuses on the whole of the implementation side of the testing strategy model

We've learned throughout this chapter how exploratory testing can help us expand our investigation into how the application works beyond our own expectations. Therefore, a good strategy can benefit from both scripted and exploratory testing. As we'll see in the next chapter, our test scripts can be excellent candidates for automation, because test scripts tend to be algorithmic in nature. But to really appreciate how our applications work, when creating a strategy, we want to be able to give our teams the opportunity to explore with purpose, while ensuring that there is enough structure to plan where our explorations will deliver the most value.

Summary

- Charters are short, specific, measurable phrases that help guide our exploratory testing.
- Charters are statements of intent to explore risky areas of a system.
- We can use different types of charter templates to form our charters.
- Charters are executed in exploratory testing sessions. A charter may be explored multiple times with many exploratory testing sessions.
- Charters can be used to help us organize what exploratory testing we want to do and to communicate our testing progress.
- We use heuristics to help us generate test ideas both subconsciously and consciously.
- Oracles are a way of determining whether the things we've observed are issues. There are many different types of oracles we can use.
- We can use software to help expand our exploratory testing.
- Note-taking is an important aspect of exploratory testing, and there are many approaches we can use.
- Observe your behavior when testing. If you are running out of energy or ideas, it may be time to stop.
- Sharing what we've learned during a session via debriefs is essential.

Automating web API tests

According to Global Market Insights, in 2019, the "automation testing market" was worth $19 billion, with projections that it could grow to $36 billion by 2026, which reflects the demand for automated testing. As teams are expected to deliver faster, more complex products, the desire to implement automated testing as a testing strategy has increased. Unfortunately, this automation gold rush comes with many misconceptions about what it can achieve and its value, potentially misleading teams into a false sense of security about the product they're delivering and its quality.

The issue, though, lies not in the tools themselves but the perception of how they can be used. When automation is used correctly, it can be a major asset to a team's testing strategy. But it requires us to know the limitations and advantages of using automation in a test strategy, as well as understanding how to implement automation in a clean and maintainable manner. So for this chapter, we'll begin by discussing how to get the most out of automation before exploring how to implement our own automation.

6.1 Getting value from automation

As we learned in the previous chapter on exploratory testing, we can apply automation in many different ways in testing. But when automation is normally discussed in the context of testing, it's usually referring to *automated regression testing*, an activity in which a collection of tests is run by a machine and the results of each test are reported as a pass or fail to detect potential issues that might regress the quality of our product. In this chapter, we're going to explore how to create automated regression testing that is of value to us. To do this, we need to consider two challenges:

1 Picking the right things to automate
2 Implementing our automation in a way that is reliable and easy to maintain

We'll come to challenge two shortly, but first let's tackle the task of picking the right things to automate, because it doesn't matter how great your automation code is if you're automating the wrong things.

6.1.1 The illusion of automation

The allure of test automation can be very strong. Using machines to do our testing for us conjures ideals of faster delivery, increased productivity, and reducing costly "manual" testing (I recently saw a tongue-in-cheek webinar titled "QA Retirement Party"—at least, I hope it was tongue-in-cheek!), but the reality can be very different. Automation requires a large amount of upfront investment. It can slow teams down as they attempt to fix unreliable automation, and worst of all, it can mislead teams about the quality of the product they are building.

This is not to say that automation doesn't have value. It does. But too often, the discussions around automation testing assume that there is a one-to-one relationship between the testing an individual does and the testing a tool can do. To give an example, let's imagine we've built an automated test that needs to check a website's home page (a departure from APIs, but it helps illustrate a point). The page has a call to action that shows the next available training event to sign up for, as shown in figure 6.1.

The automated test works by opening a browser, loading the home page, and locating an element in the browser that has a class of `next-training-label`. If the element exists and is displayed, then the automated test passes. If it doesn't, then it fails. Now let's imagine that we run that automated test again, but this time, the browser renders the page differently, as shown in figure 6.2.

Web element we're checking to see is displayed

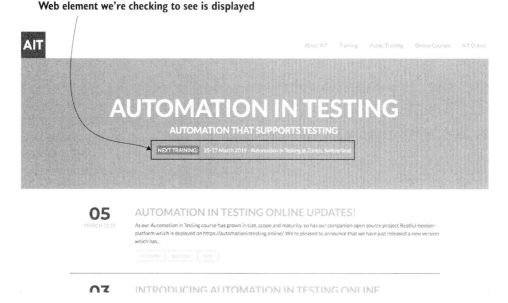

Figure 6.1   An example of a web page with working CSS that shows the event details we want to check

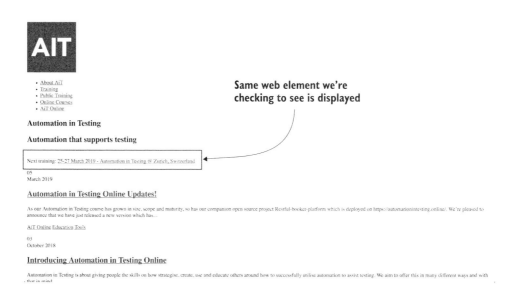

Same web element we're checking to see is displayed

Figure 6.2   An example of a web page with broken CSS that still shows the event details, albeit in a less-polished format

As an individual, when comparing figure 6.2 to figure 6.1, we can automatically see that something is amiss and that the quality of the home page has dropped. Who would want to buy training from someone with such a broken and ugly site? The automated test, however, still passes. (Side note: visual testing tools are available for this example, but the point is related to our assumptions around what automated tools can do.)

Does this mean that the human is better than the machine? Not really. Automation tools are very good at giving us rapid feedback in a consistent manner based on explicit instructions we set. But we get out what we put in, nothing more. Skilled testing done by an individual can be slower and harder to repeat in a deterministic manner. But we as individuals are amazing at spotting patterns, and our ability to simultaneously observe many things both consciously and unconsciously is what makes us so good at testing. Automation will tell us only what we asked it to tell us and nothing more.

Checking and testing

To help clarify the difference between the "testing" done by automation and by humans, some individuals (including myself) like to distinguish the two activities as "checking" and "testing." Because a machine is providing feedback based on explicit steps we've set, this is referred to as "checking," whereas a human who uses heuristics, biases, oracles, and much more is "testing." To help distinguish what we'll do in the rest of this chapter, I will use the terms *checking* and *checks* going forward. But ultimately, it doesn't matter what we call it as long as we appreciate the difference between what a human and a machine can bring to a testing strategy.

This becomes a problem when a team opts for a "monoculture" testing strategy that focuses purely on automating as much testing as possible. Although the automation may "test" quicker, the richness of feedback and observation is lost. Automation testing sacrifices the quality of information we need for speed and efficiency. Again, this doesn't mean that automation is bad, but by appreciating that tools, by design, will only provide feedback on what we explicitly ask them to tell us, we can use automation to our advantage. We can use automation in conjunction with other testing activities to balance the quality of information that we gather in our testing with the speed and efficiency of automation.

6.1.2 *Automation as change detection*

In Michael Bolton's 2012 webinar, "Things Could Get Worse: Ideas About Regression Testing," he shared his thoughts on regression testing and posed an interesting conundrum. Typically, regression testing (regardless of whether or not it is automated) is viewed as an activity that looks for issues that cause the quality of our products to regress. However, if "quality" is something that is fluid and decided by our users and their desires and needs, does a pass or fail in a regression testing phase truly tell us whether quality has regressed? Isn't that for the user to decide?

What Michael proposes is that the testing (or automated checking) we do isn't what determines whether there has been a regression in quality—it's our interpretation of the results that does. If we apply this thinking to automated regression checking, it demonstrates a symbiotic relationship between us as individuals and our automation.

Our automated checks act as change detectors, as Michael calls them, and when a change is detected, we determine whether that change has caused a reduction in quality.

Understanding automated checks as change detectors is important because it helps frame what we might want to automate. Rather than attempting to automate every path or permutation for an API endpoint, our goal is to use our automated checks as indicators that something has changed in the system, and ideally, we want to place those indicators in and around areas of the system that matter most to us. This helps us focus on what to automate, but how do we identify the areas that matter most to us?

6.1.3   *Letting risk be our guide*

Understanding this mindset of automated checks as change detectors helps us frame our thinking around what we want to check because we can build a coverage model that focuses on giving us feedback on the areas that we care about the most. Rather than using code coverage and requirements or automating legacy test cases, we can use risks as our guide as to what to automate first. For example, let's take the `booking` API. We might identify a series of risks, such as the following:

- *Unable to retrieve bookings*—We create a check that will send a request to determine whether we get a positive response back.
- *Booking payload isn't parsed correctly*—For this, we would create a check that sends a booking with the values we expect to be valid and assert whether a positive response or an error comes back.
- *Incorrect status code for deleting a booking*—We create a check that builds a booking and then, with the correct credentials, deletes it and confirms that the correct type of status code is returned.

Once these risks are identified, we can then begin to prioritize them in order of what we're most worried about. For example, we may feel inconsistent feedback is a risk we're less worried about than being unable to create a room. The order of the risks (and their proposed solutions) then becomes our to-do list of what checks to automate. By following this process, we identify and automate the change detectors that are most crucial to us first and ensure the automation we create is valuable to us.

> ### Unit checking and TaTTa
>
> Although we'll look at how we can create automated API checks, it would be foolish not to discuss unit checking as part of our API testing strategy. Automated API checks are certainly valuable, but if you have the capability to push your checks "lower," that is, make them unit checks, then you should. One technique I've developed to help identify whether something should be written at the API layer or the unit layer is to ask myself, am I *testing the API* or *testing through the API* (TaTTa, for short)? For example, if my focus is on risks around the correct status codes being returned when sending incorrect data, I may be *testing the API*. If I am testing a tax calculation, however, I may be *testing through the API*, meaning I am using the API as a gateway to code inside my API that might be better served with a unit check.

> **Activity**
>
> Pick one of the endpoints for the `booking` API in our API sandbox and write down a
> list of risks you think could affect that endpoint. Once you have your list, arrange them
> in priority order, and write out how you would check to ensure that that risk doesn't
> appear in the sandbox. We'll return to this list later on in the chapter.

6.2   Setting up a Web API automation tool

We've discussed the thinking and theory behind successful automation, but now let's
put it into practice. We're going to look at how to set up and implement automated
API checks by focusing on three risks:

- `GET /booking/` always returns the correct status code.
- `POST /booking/` always successfully creates a booking.
- `DELETE /booking/{id}` always deletes a booking.

Our first step is to get ourselves set up with the dependencies we need to build our
framework, followed by an overview of how we can structure our framework to ensure
we create well-written, valuable automation.

> **API checking model**
>
> Throughout the rest of this chapter, we will develop our API checks in Java. However,
> the underlying principles of how to arrange our API checking code can be applied
> across any language. So I encourage you to still read through how we go about auto-
> mating API checks to better understand how to arrange them in a way that makes
> them easy to read and maintain. Additionally, you can head to https://github.com/
> mwinteringham/api-framework/ to see how this pattern is used across different
> languages.

6.2.1   Dependencies

For our project, we're going to use Maven to handle our dependencies, so we'll start
by creating a new Maven project and adding in the following dependencies into our
POM.xml that make up our framework:

```
<dependencies>
    <dependency>
        <groupId>org.junit.jupiter</groupId>
        <artifactId>junit-jupiter</artifactId>
        <version>5.7.1</version>
    </dependency>
    <dependency>
        <groupId>io.rest-assured</groupId>
        <artifactId>rest-assured</artifactId>
        <version>4.3.3</version>
    </dependency>
```

```
    <dependency>
        <groupId>com.fasterxml.jackson.core</groupId>
        <artifactId>jackson-databind</artifactId>
        <version>2.12.2</version>
    </dependency>
    <dependency>
        <groupId>com.fasterxml.jackson.core</groupId>
        <artifactId>jackson-core</artifactId>
        <version>2.12.2</version>
    </dependency>
    <dependency>
        <groupId>com.fasterxml.jackson.datatype</groupId>
        <artifactId>jackson-datatype-jsr310</artifactId>
        <version>2.11.4</version>
    </dependency>
</dependencies>
```

With these dependencies added and imported, we now have everything we need to create a basic API automation framework. Let's take a quick tour through each of the dependencies to get a better understanding of how it contributes to the wider framework.

JUNIT

If you've done any sort of unit checking in Java, you are likely to be familiar with JUnit. However, if you're not or might be questioning its use in an API automation context, essentially, JUnit serves as the tool that will organize and execute our code.

Specifically, we'll use the `@Test` annotation to organize our checks, as well as the built-in assertion dependency to check response results.

REST ASSURED

REST Assured is responsible for creating and executing our HTTP requests and parsing HTTP responses. We can view this as the "engine" in the framework. Many Java dependencies exist that allow us to create HTTP requests and parse responses. We'll use REST Assured, but with our framework's structure, it's easy enough to replace REST Assured with another tool of choice such as Spring or java.net.http without impacting our automated checks.

That said, we're using REST Assured for its ease of use and its clarity when creating requests. You can learn more about REST Assured at https://rest-assured.io/.

JACKSON

Finally, we have Jackson. The three dependencies—`databind`, `core`, and `datatype-jsr310`—help us to convert POJOs (plain old Java objects) into JSON for our HTTP requests and back into usable objects when we receive JSON back in HTTP responses.

Other dependencies?

These five dependencies give us everything we need to get a basic API automation framework up and running. What you might want to consider once we've finished this chapter is how you could expand your framework. You might want to improve the reporting from the framework, expand the assertion approach to handle larger response bodies, or reduce boilerplate in your codebase. All of these options are available to us, but we need to walk before we can run.

6.2.2 Structuring our framework

A surefire way to fail with automation is to build an automation framework that is hard to maintain or to read. It's important to remember that our automation code is exactly that: code. We should use the same techniques and approaches for our automation code that we use for keeping our production code clean, readable, and maintainable. After building a lot of API automation and researching patterns for automation, such as the Page Object model in UI automation, I've found the structure for a framework shown in figure 6.3 to be the most effective.

Figure 6.3 A model that shows the relationships of the three core areas of an API checking framework

Let's break down each of these areas quickly to explain their role in the framework.

CHECKS

This is where we create and organize our checks, much like we would do in any automation framework. However, the goal in this part of the framework is to make our automated checks as easy to read as possible. Understanding the intent of an automated check is important. If you don't know what it does, how do you know whether it truly passed or failed?

We do this by deferring the actions of creating data and sending/receiving HTTP requests and responses to the other main sections of our framework and ensuring that any data or action that is asserted is carried out in this area. If we have well-named methods, objects, and assertions, it should be easier for others to understand what our check is focusing on.

With this in mind, we're going to create a new package titled `com.example.checks` where we will store our automated checks.

REQUESTS

A common pattern I've seen in frameworks is for maintainers of API automation frameworks to not abstract HTTP requests into their own area. This causes all sorts of headaches as the number of automated checks grow. Having to update a URL in over 1000+ checks is not an efficient use of our time.

So in the requests package, we organize our classes by the web API we are requesting. Each request will have its own methods that we then call in our checks area of the framework. This way, if we have to update a URL, we only have to change it in one place.

To establish this part of the framework, we will create an additional package named `com.example.requests`, and here, we will add our request classes as we build out our automated tests.

PAYLOADS

Many web APIs deal with complex models that are used for requests and responses, which results in a lot of POJO classes. The motivation for this area of the framework is to create a place to cleanly organize these classes based on whether they are used for request or response payloads, as well as to tidy them into their own areas, depending on which API you're requesting.

For this area of the framework, we will start by creating a package titled `com.example.payloads`. We then have the option to arrange our POJO classes within these packages by specific API, if so inclined.

With the tour of our framework's dependencies and organization complete, we should have a project setup that looks something like figure 6.4.

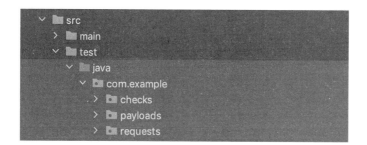

Figure 6.4   The project layout of an API checking framework taken from IntelliJ

6.3   *Creating automated API checks*

Now that we're set up, let's begin creating automated checks for our three risks.

6.3.1   *Automated check 1: A GET request*

For our first automated check, we're going to create a check that sends a GET request to https://automationintesting.online/booking/ and asserts that the status code we get back is a 200.

CREATE A BLANK CHECK

First, we need to create a class that will hold our checks. In the `com.example`
`.checks` package, create a class named `BookingApiIT`. Once created, we will create
our first blank check as follows:

```
public class BookingApiIT {

  @Test
  public void getBookingSummaryShouldReturn200(){

  }

}
```

If you're unfamiliar with JUnit, the `@Test` annotation informs JUnit (as well as your
IDE) that the method `getBookingShouldReturn200` is a check that can be run.
This gives us the bones of our check to run, but now we need something to run.

CREATE A GET REQUEST

With our check created, we add the ability to send and receive HTTP requests and
responses. We'll start this by creating a new class in `com.example.requests` that is
called `BookingApi`.

Before we add any code into the class, though, let's pause for a second and talk
very briefly about how we name classes within the requests package. The naming con-
vention is dependent on whether the test code is responsible for testing one or more
web APIs. The rule to go for is as follows:

- *Just one API*—Name the classes after the resources. For example, the Ghost CMS
  API is just one API with multiple resources (https://ghost.org/docs/content
  -api/), so we could arrange classes by resources such as posts, pages, and tags.
- *Multiple APIs*—Name the classes after each web API. For example, with restful-
  booker-platform, there are APIs such as `booking`, `auth`, `room`, and so on. Each
  of these APIs would have its own class.

I find this helps separate requests nicely and makes the code more readable.

With our `BookingApi` class created, we can now add the following code:

```
public class BookingApi {

    private static final String apiUrl =                              Declares the
        "https://automationintesting.online/booking/";                base URL

    public static Response getBookingSummary(){                      Sends the
        return given().get(apiUrl + "summary?roomid=1");             GET request
    }

}
```

The `apiUrl` ensures that if our base URL to `/booking/` needs replacing in the
future, it can be controlled from one location. Or, if we're working with multiple environments, this can be controlled via environmental variables.

The getBookingSummary method contains the code from REST Assured to send a request. As you can tell, the get() method is doing a lot of the heavy lifting for us. By providing the get() method with a URL, REST Assured creates everything required to send a basic GET request to our web API. The given() method doesn't actually do anything other than add readability to our automated test using the Given-When-Then approach. If you're not familiar with this syntax, don't worry too much—we will use it only where necessary.

Finally, once the request is complete, REST Assured will respond with a Response object that we can examine to learn how the web API responded to our request.

With the getBookingSummary method created, we can now add it to our check along with an assertion as follows:

```
@Test
public void getBookingSummaryShouldReturn200(){
    Response response = BookingApi.getBookingSummary();

    assertEquals(200, response.getStatusCode());
}
```

Now our check uses getBookingSummary to send a GET request to /booking/ and receives a Response object, which we extract the status code from using getStatusCode to assert whether it matches our expectation of it being a 200 status code.

If we run this now, we should see a pass and confirm it's feeding back the correct information; we can update the status code to a different number and watch the automated check fail.

6.3.2   *Automated check 2: A POST request*

For our next automated check, we are going to check that sending a POST to https://automationintesting.online/booking/ with a valid payload returns a 201 status code.

CREATE A NEW BLANK CHECK

We begin by adding a new check to the BookingApiIT class like so:

```
@Test
public void postBookingReturns201(){

}
```

CREATE A POJO

Before we send our POST request, we need to create the Booking payload we want to see created in the web API. To help remind us of what we need to create, here is an example of the JSON payload:

```
{
    "roomid": Int
    "firstname": String,
    "lastname": String,
    "depositpaid": Boolean,
    "bookingdates": {
        "checkin": Date,
```

```
        "checkout": Date
    },
    "additionalneeds": String
}
```

To create our payload, we're going to build a POJO that is structured in the same way as our JSON object and then create an instance of our POJO and send it to our request library.

First, we create two new classes in the `com.example.payloads` package named `Booking` and `BookingDates`. Then, with our classes created, we open our `Booking-Dates` class and add in the following:

```
public class BookingDates {                    Declares the variable
                                               as JsonProperty
    @JsonProperty           ◁──┐
    private LocalDate checkin;      ◁──┐ Declares the
    @JsonProperty                        │ variable
    private LocalDate checkout;     ◁──┘
                                               Default constructor
    public BookingDates() {}   ◁──┘ required by Jackson

    public BookingDates(LocalDate checkin, LocalDate checkout){
        this.checkin = checkin;
        this.checkout = checkout;   Custom constructor
    }                          ◁──┘ to build payload

    public LocalDate getCheckin() {
        return checkin;                Getter for
    }                          ◁────────┘ Jackson use

    public LocalDate getCheckout() {
        return checkout;
    }

}
```

Let's break down what's going on in this code as follows:

1 We declare our variables, ensuring that the name of each variable matches the name of the key in the JSON object. For example, we can see that the check-in date in our `Booking` object is labeled `checkin`, so that's what we name our variable. We also ensure that the data type of the variable matches the data type we want to use in the JSON object.

2 Next, we provide the annotation `@JsonProperty` above each of the variables. This enables the Jackson dependencies to know which variables are to be converted into key-value pairs when the POJO is transformed into a JSON object for our request.

3 We create two constructors—one that allows us to assign values to our variables and an empty one, which we will learn about when we create our next automated check.

4 Finally, we create getter methods that Jackson will use to retrieve the values assigned to each variable to use as the values in the JSON object.

With our `BookingDates` subobject created, we repeat the process with the main booking object by adding the following into the `Booking` class:

```java
@JsonIgnoreType
public class Booking {

    @JsonProperty
    private int roomid;
    @JsonProperty
    private String firstname;
    @JsonProperty
    private String lastname;
    @JsonProperty
    private boolean depositpaid;
    @JsonProperty
    private BookingDates bookingdates;
    @JsonProperty
    private String additionalneeds;

    // default constructor required by Jackson
    public Booking() {}

    public Booking(int roomid, String firstname, String lastname, boolean
     depositpaid, BookingDates bookingdates, String additionalneeds) {
        this.roomid = roomid;
        this.firstname = firstname;
        this.lastname = lastname;
        this.depositpaid = depositpaid;
        this.bookingdates = bookingdates;
        this.additionalneeds = additionalneeds;
    }

    public int getRoomid() {
        return roomid;
    }

    public String getFirstname() {
        return firstname;
    }

    public String getLastname() {
        return lastname;
    }

    public boolean isDepositpaid() {
        return depositpaid;
    }

    public BookingDates getBookingdates() {
        return bookingdates;
    }

    public String getAdditionalneeds() {
        return additionalneeds;
    }

}
```

As we can see, the pattern is the same. Create variables that match the keys found in the JSON object, add `@JsonProperty` to each of them, and create the required constructors and getters. We've also added `@JsonIgnoreType` at the top of the class, which will be used in the next check, so ensure it's added, but ignore it for now. Also, notice how we are using the `BookingDates` class for a `BookingDates` subobject. This is how we create complex JSON payloads by creating relationships between classes that match how JSON objects and subobjects relate to one another.

Finally, with our POJOs now created, we can build the payload we would like to send in our request by updating our check to

```
@Test
public void postBookingReturns201(){

    BookingDates dates = new BookingDates(
        LocalDate.of( 2021 , 1 , 1 ),
        LocalDate.of( 2021 , 1 , 3 )
    );

    Booking payload = new Booking(
        1,
        "Mark",
        "Winteringham",
        true,
        dates,
        "Breakfast"
    );
}
```

That gives us everything we need to create our payload in the most straightforward manner with Java. If we wanted to make this all look a bit clearer, we could use tools like Lombok to reduce the level of boilerplate that exists in the POJOs. Or you could take advantage of data builder patterns to create a more readable and abstract approach to creating your POJOs.

Reusing POJOs from production code?

For some, POJOS will be a familiar subject. POJOs are used widely across web API production code, which begs this question: Why can't I just use them rather than duplicate code? There is no right or wrong answer to this question, but there is a trade-off. Yes, reusing POJOs from your production code does save time, reducing the maintenance of keeping POJOs up to date. However, it does introduce the risk of false positives in your tests. Although uncommon, it is possible, when reusing production code, to introduce issues into our POJOs that won't be flagged when we run our tests. After all, if you've accidentally omitted an important part of your POJO or misnamed it, using the same model to create your test payload is going to create a POJO that is always accepted.

CREATING OUR REQUEST

Now that we have our payload, we can create our POST request in the `BookingApi` class, which looks like this:

```
public static Response postBooking(Booking payload) {
    return given()
            .contentType(ContentType.JSON)
            .body(payload)
            .when()
            .post(apiUrl);
}
```

Declares Content-Type header

Adds in request body

We've expanded our use of REST Assured to provide a content-type header using `contentType()` as well as passing our payload in using the `body()` method. Once again, we return a `Response` object after the request is complete.

With our request code in place, we can update our check to now make a request as follows:

```
@Test
public void postBookingReturns201(){

    BookingDates dates = new BookingDates(
        LocalDate.of( 2021 , 1 , 1 ),
        LocalDate.of( 2021 , 1 , 3 )
    );

    Booking payload = new Booking(
        1,
        "Mark",
        "Winteringham",
        true,
        dates,
        "Breakfast"
    );

    Response response = BookingApi.postBooking(payload);
}
```

ASSERT THE RESPONSE

All that's left to do is add our assertion at the end to check whether the status code returned is 201, as shown here:

```
@Test
public void postBookingReturns201(){

    BookingDates dates = new BookingDates(
        LocalDate.of( 2021 , 1 , 1 ),
        LocalDate.of( 2021 , 1 , 3 )
    );

    Booking payload = new Booking(
        1,
        "Mark",
        "Winteringham",
```

```
        true,
        dates,
        "Breakfast"
    );

    Response response = BookingApi.postBooking(payload);

    assertEquals(201, response.getStatusCode());
}
```

We could, of course, assert on other aspects of the response back from our web API, such as checking to see whether the response body contains expected values. However, that requires us to do some additional work to parse the response body—something we'll look at in the final automated check.

6.3.3 Automated check 3: Combining requests

For our final check, we're going to look at deleting a booking, which requires a few steps:

1 Create a booking.
2 Get an authentication token to permit us to delete a booking.
3 Use the token and the booking ID to delete the booking.

To achieve this, we'll need to be able to not only create request payloads but parse the response body payloads for future use.

CREATING OUR INITIAL CHECK

Let's begin by creating a new check inside `BookingApiIT` like so:

```
@Test
public void deleteBookingReturns202(){

    BookingDates dates = new BookingDates(
        LocalDate.of( 2021 , 2 , 1 ),
        LocalDate.of( 2021 , 2 , 3 )
    );

    Booking payload = new Booking(
        1,
        "Mark",
        "Winteringham",
        true,
        dates,
        "Breakfast"
    );
}
```

As mentioned in step 1 of this automated check, we need to create a booking that will ultimately be deleted. We've created our check and added in the initial work to create the payload for the booking request that uses the POJOs and request methods we created in the previous check.

CREATE A POJO TO PARSE OUR RESPONSE

To delete our booking, we're going to need the ID of the booking to pass to our delete request. If we look at the response body for a successfully created booking, we can see it comes back with a booking ID:

```
{
    "bookingid": 1,
    "booking": {
        "roomid": 1
        "firstname": "Jim",
        "lastname": "Brown",
        "depositpaid": true,
        "bookingdates": {
            "checkin": "2018-01-01",
            "checkout": "2019-01-01"
        },
        "additionalneeds": "Breakfast"
    }
}
```

This means we're going to have to parse the response body from JSON into a POJO that we can then query to retrieve the booking ID. Fortunately, most of the work has been done for us because the object under `booking` is the same model as the one we used for creating our request payload. This means all we need to do is create a new class called `BookingResponse` in `com.example.payloads` and add the following:

```
public class BookingResponse {

    @JsonProperty
    private int bookingid;
    @JsonProperty
    private Booking booking;

    public int getBookingid() {
        return bookingid;
    }

    public Booking getBooking() {
        return booking;
    }

}
```

Just like with the other POJOs, we create our variables to match the keys in the JSON object and assign the correct data types to them—see how we're reusing the `Booking` class for this? We also add getters so that we can extract the values we need at a later date.

With our `BookingResponse` POJO complete, we can now update our test to the following:

```
@Test
public void deleteBookingReturns202(){
```

```
BookingDates dates = new BookingDates(
    LocalDate.of( 2021 , 2 , 1 ),
    LocalDate.of( 2021 , 2 , 3 )
);

Booking payload = new Booking(
    1,
    "Mark",
    "Winteringham",
    true,
    dates,
    "Breakfast"
);

Response bookingResponse = BookingApi.postBooking(payload);
BookingResponse createdBookingResponse =
 bookingResponse.as(BookingResponse.class);
}
```

Notice the final line of code. We're taking the `Response` object from `postBooking` and calling the `.as()` method by providing it with the `BookingResponse` class structure. Essentially, we're asking REST Assured to map the values of the JSON response body to the `BookingResponse` class and create a new `BookingResponse` object. If our POJO and JSON response body align, the values from each entry in the JSON response body will be stored in each of our object's variables for later use.

With that done, we now have an object with the booking response data required for our deletion later in the check.

What's with the blank constructors in Booking and BookingDates?

You'll remember that earlier we had to add in blank constructors for the `Booking` and `BookingDates` classes, but we haven't added in one for `BookingResponse`. Why is that? When we receive an HTTP response with a JSON body to parse, it comes back as a plain string, so we need to convert that JSON into an object that we can use. To do this, we use Jackson and REST Assured to trigger a series of steps:

- Create a new empty object based on the class provided (in our example, it's `BookingResponse.class`).
- With the empty object created, iterate over each of the keys in the JSON object, and using the metadata taken from `@JsonProperty` above each variable, find the correct variable in our object to store the matching value.

So to successfully execute this process, we need the ability to create an empty object, which Jackson can do for us automatically, provided we don't add in custom constructors. This is why `Booking` and `BookingDates` require empty constructors to be explicitly created. If they were missing, Jackson and REST Assured would attempt to use the custom constructor that contains parameters and ultimately would fail.

(continued)

I found this all to be quite confusing when I first started working with API automation. One way to help you get your head around this concept is by going into either `Booking` or `BookingDates` and trying to delete the empty constructor and run the check. Doing so will likely result in an error like this:

```
com.fasterxml.jackson.databind.exc.InvalidDefinitionException: Cannot
construct instance of `com.example.payloads.Booking` (no Creators, like
default constructor, exist)....
```

The main thing to remember if you see an error like this in the future is that it's likely that you need to explicitly create an empty constructor in your POJO.

DO THE SAME FOR AUTH

We've created our booking that we will ultimately delete, but we still need to authorize ourselves so that our delete request can be processed. To do this, we're going to need an Auth payload that can allow us to create and receive tokens that we send to and receive from the `auth` API. We need to create two new POJOS in `com.example` `.payloads`. The first is Auth, which we'll use to create our payload requests like so:

```java
public class Auth {

    @JsonProperty
    private String username;
    @JsonProperty
    private String password;

    public String getUsername() {
        return username;
    }

    public String getPassword() {
        return password;
    }

    public Auth(String username, String password) {
        this.username = username;
        this.password = password;
    }

}
```

CREATE REQUESTS

With our POJOs created, our next step is to create the necessary code to send a request to `/auth/login`. Because this is a new API that we're sending a request to, we're going to create a new class named `AuthApi`. However, before we do that, we're going to move some details from `BookingApi` into a class of its own that can be shared across all our `*Request` classes.

In `com.example.requests`, we'll create a new class called `BaseApi` and add in the following:

```
public class BaseApi {

    protected static final String baseUrl =
    "https://automationintesting.online/";

}
```

With a `BaseApi` created that is responsible for managing the `baseUrl` of all our requests, we can then update `BookingApi` to use `BaseAPI` as follows:

```
public class BookingApi extends BaseApi {

    private static final String apiUrl = baseUrl + "booking/";
```

Then we'll create our `AuthApi` class and add the following:

```
public class AuthApi extends BaseApi {

    private static final String apiUrl = baseUrl + "auth/";

    public static Response postAuth(Auth payload){
        return given()
                .contentType(ContentType.JSON)
                .body(payload)
                .when()
                .post(apiUrl + "login");
    }

}
```

TIE IT ALL TOGETHER AND ASSERT

We now have everything we need to update our automated check to get our authentication token for future requests, as shown here:

```
@Test
public void deleteBookingReturns202(){

    BookingDates dates = new BookingDates(
        LocalDate.of( 2021 , 2 , 1 ),
        LocalDate.of( 2021 , 2 , 3 )
    );

    Booking payload = new Booking(
        1,
        "Mark",
        "Winteringham",
        true,
        dates,
        "Breakfast"
    );

    Response bookingResponse = BookingApi.postBooking(payload);
    BookingResponse createdBookingResponse =
    bookingResponse.as(BookingResponse.class);
```

```
Auth auth = new Auth("admin", "password123");

Response authResponse = AuthApi.postAuth(auth);
    String authToken = authResponse.getCookie("token");
}
```

With our code in place to create a booking for deletion and to get an authorization token, we can finish up the automated check to delete our booking and assert the response. First, let's create our method that will send our delete request in Booking-Api:

```
public static Response deleteBooking(int id, String tokenValue) {

    return given()
            .header("Cookie", "token=" + tokenValue)
            .delete(apiUrl + Integer.toString(id));
}
```

Then we update our check to delete our booking and assert the status code response as follows:

```
@Test
public void deleteBookingReturns202(){

    BookingDates dates = new BookingDates(
        LocalDate.of( 2021 , 2 , 1 ),
        LocalDate.of( 2021 , 2 , 3 )
    );

    Booking payload = new Booking(
        1,
        "Mark",
        "Winteringham",
        true,
        dates,
        "Breakfast"
    );

    Response bookingResponse = BookingApi.postBooking(payload);
    BookingResponse createdBookingResponse =
     bookingResponse.as(BookingResponse.class);

    Auth auth = new Auth("admin", "password");

    Response authResponse = AuthApi.postAuth(auth);
        String authToken = authResponse.getCookie("token");

    Response deleteResponse = BookingApi.deleteBooking(
            createdBookingResponse.getBookingid(),
            authToken);

    assertEquals(202, deleteResponse.getStatusCode());
}
```

That completes our final automated check. This example automated check demonstrates that we can extract values from HTTP response bodies for use in other requests or for asserting against.

Automating with GraphQL

Because GraphQL is normally served over HTTP, we're in the fortunate position of being able to use the same toolset for automating a GraphQL API as a REST API. The difference between the two is how you create your HTTP request. For example, if you want to send a query such as the following

```
query Character {
  character(id: 1) {
    name
    created
  }
}
```

you simply need to create a POJO that would represent this structure and send it to REST Assured in the same way as we sent payloads in the examples we created earlier. To learn more about this, the folks at Applitools have created a handy blog on how to use REST Assured with GraphQL (http://mng.bz/z5J1).

Activity

With your automation framework now established, go back to the list of risks and checks you identified, pick the top one off the list, and attempt to automate it. To help build up your familiarity and skill with this approach, try to go through each identified check in your list and automate them all.

6.3.4   *Running your automated tests as integration tests*

Now that we have our automated checks in place, how do we run them as part of the build process?

As you'll recall, we named the class that contains our automated checks `Booking-ApiIT`. The addition of `IT` at the end of the class helps us to distinguish our automated checks from any unit checks we may have created to check individual components within our web API. This helps us to cleanly separate the concerns and intents of our automated checks, but it does mean that if we were to run `mvn clean install` on this project right now, our automated checks wouldn't run. This is because when maven goes through its `test` phase, it looks for classes that have the word `Test` at the end and ignores any other files. That's a problem because our files end with `IT`.

We need to update our maven project to recognize our automated checks as part of the build process, which we can do by adding the `maven-failsafe-plugin` to our `pom.xml` as follows:

```
<build>
    <plugins>
        <plugin>
            <groupId>org.apache.maven.plugins</groupId>
            <artifactId>maven-failsafe-plugin</artifactId>
            <version>2.22.2</version>
            <executions>
                <execution>
                    <goals>
                        <goal>integration-test</goal>
                        <goal>verify</goal>
                    </goals>
                    <configuration>
                        <includes>
                            <include>**/*IT</include>
                        </includes>
                    </configuration>
                </execution>
            </executions>
        </plugin>
    </plugins>
</build>
```

The plugin enables us to hook the running of our automated checks into the `integration-test` or `verify` goals in Maven by adding those goals into the executions section of the plugin. The `<include>**/*IT</include>` uses wild-cards to look up any files that end in `IT` to run, such as our `BookingApiIT` class.

With this in place, running `mvn clean verify` will now execute our automated checks, meaning we can add our automated checks project to our pipeline and run `mvn clean verify` against our environment under test. And with that, we now have a series of automated tests that we can run regularly, either locally or as part of a continuous integration process.

6.4 *Utilizing automation in our strategy*

As we've discussed how to create automated checks within this chapter, it has become apparent that to successfully implement them, we require some preexisting knowledge of the system. Unlike other testing activities, which are focused on learning new information, the automation we've learned about in this chapter is focused on confirming what we already know is still true as new iterations of the product appear. If we go back to our testing model from chapter 1, we can see that this activity focuses on the areas in which our knowledge of what we want to build (imagination) and what we've built (implementation) overlap, as shown in figure 6.5.

This is an important activity to have in our strategy. As the product grows, we not only have to test the newly added features and fixes, but we also need to confirm that our expectations of how the system worked in the past are still true. But as we learned, there is a difference between what our automation tools tell us about our system and what we as individuals observe. A successful strategy balances the use of automation to help support us and warn us of potential changes so that we can utilize other testing activities (such as exploratory testing) to learn more.

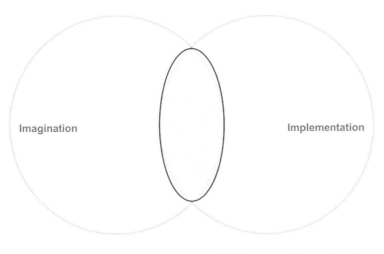

Figure 6.5   A demonstration of how automation focuses on the overlap of imagination and implementation, that is, what we currently know about our system, within a test strategy model

Summary

- Automation sacrifices feedback quality for speed and efficiency.
- Using automation in a regression checking context means building automated checks that serve as change detectors.
- Change detectors tell us whether something has changed in a system that we need to react to.
- We can identify and prioritize change detectors based on risks we care about.
- We can build our own API checking frameworks using JUnit, REST Assured, and Jackson.
- To help keep our code DRY ("don't repeat yourself") and maintainable, we organize it into three distinct sections: tests, requests, and payloads.
- We can use Java to build HTTP requests and parse the results to assert on changes within our APIs.
- The `maven-failsafe-plugin` can be used to execute automated API checks as part of a build pipeline.
- We can use automation in balance with other testing activities to support us.

Establishing and implementing a testing strategy

This chapter covers

- How to prioritize and implement specific actions as part of our strategy
- Why different strategies are required for different contexts
- Formulating a plan based on a strategy
- Analyzing a working context to create a successful plan

There is a saying that nearly every tester has said at some point in their career: you can't test everything. Constraints such as budgets, deadlines, complexity, skillsets, and more can impact the amount of time we have to test and to learn. There is never enough time to test. To counter this, we need to be strategic about what we test and what we don't.

Throughout part 2 of this book, we've explored a range of different testing activities that focus on different areas of the software development life cycle and on different types of risks, but our discussions around putting together a testing strategy have been abstract. How do we determine what testing activities take priority and what steps we need to take to execute our strategy successfully? What works for one project might not work for another; therefore, in this chapter, we'll explore why there is no one-size-fits-all strategy and the steps we need to take to identify our test strategy and begin implementing it.

7.1 Establishing a strategy for our context

Before we look at how we can formalize our strategy and determine the next steps in implementing it, let's first recap what we've learned so far. We've explored two models around testing strategy. The first is our model of the purpose of testing, which demonstrates that we want to test the imagination (what we want to build) and the implementation (what we have built) and that the more we learn in both areas, the more these two sections begin to overlap. This can be represented in a visual model, like the one in figure 7.1.

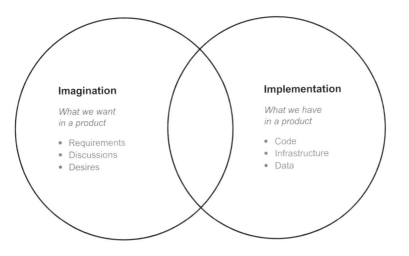

Figure 7.1   A recap of the test strategy model with the imagination/implementation model for thinking about testing

As we've explored different testing activities in previous chapters, we've also seen how different activities focus on different areas of the imagination/implementation model. We've seen that testing API designs digs deeper into the imagination side of our work, and exploratory testing expands what we can learn about what we've implemented. That automation can help us confirm that what we already know about our product is still true as it changes. This can be summarized by adding these activities to their respective areas of the imagination/implementation model, as shown in figure 7.2.

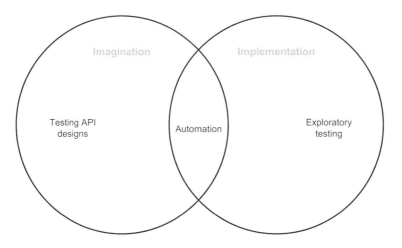

Figure 7.2   The imagination/implementation model, complete with respective testing activities

This, of course, is not a comprehensive list of every testing activity available to us. But it helps us to appreciate that different testing activities reveal different information and focus on different risks. We'll look at more testing activities in part 3 of this book, but with just these three activities, we can begin to see the challenge of determining what to do in our testing strategy and when.

7.1.1   *Identifying what's a priority*

As said before, although it might be desirable to say, "Let's do all of it!", the reality of our situation will almost certainly mean that it's unsustainable to adopt every testing activity at once. This is why a strategy can help. It helps us to identify what opportunities are available to us, which should take priority, and what to plan for in the short- and medium-term for our testing. How do we determine what takes priority? This is where the second model we learned about, which explores quality characteristics and risks, can help.

To briefly summarize, in chapter 3, we looked at a model that demonstrated the initial steps we need to take before picking and choosing testing activities, including the following:

- Defining what quality characteristics matter to our users and business
- Identifying risks that could impact those quality characteristics

This was summarized in a model that demonstrated quality characteristics and risks, as shown in figure 7.3.

The model was used in chapter 3 as a visual demonstration of how identifying each risk is a stepping stone toward helping our teams improve and maintain the quality of our products. It's these risks that help guide us in determining what testing we want to

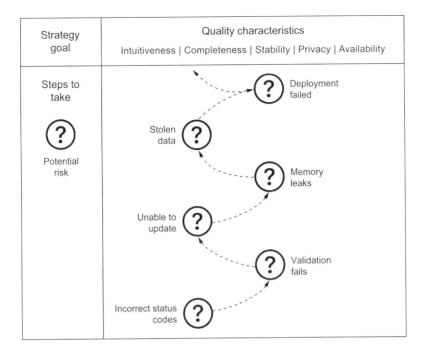

Figure 7.3   A recap of the quality characteristics and risks model that shows that exploring risks are steps toward our strategies goal

do and what priority it takes. For example, if we were to stretch the analogy of the steps a bit further, we could say the first risk in the stepping stones of our model is the one that takes priority:

Incorrect status codes or responses are sent on successful requests.

If this is the risk we're most concerned about, then an activity such as testing API designs might become a priority in our strategy.

Different risks will indicate what testing activities we should do. It takes skill and practice to identify whether a risk might manifest as a result of a misunderstanding within the imagination side of our model or as an unexpected side effect that exists within our codebase within the implementation side. But being able to look at a specific risk and understand what types of testing activities will work best to mitigate them will set us on the right path toward selecting the most effective testing approach.

For example, let's return to our list of risks for our sandbox API and pick the top three risks that we're concerned about:

1 Incorrect status codes or responses are sent on successful requests.
2 Validation on APIs doesn't work as expected.
3 Admin is unable to update the look and feel of the guest pages.

We could analyze these risks and determine what testing activities we want to implement, resulting in a testing strategy model like the one shown in figure 7.4.

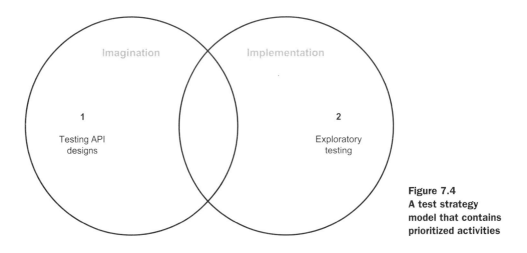

**Figure 7.4
A test strategy
model that contains
prioritized activities**

Notice how we've labeled the activities in priority order. The activity "Testing API designs" is labeled as the first activity to focus on because it can help us mitigate the highest priority risk, followed by exploratory testing, which can help us mitigate the other risks in the priority list. It's this pattern of using quality to guide what testing we can do that helps us to identify and prioritize what we want to carry out in our testing strategy.

7.1.2   *Different strategies for different contexts*

The pattern of using our understanding of quality to guide our testing can be summarized in the model shown in figure 7.5.

**Figure 7.5   A model demonstrating
the relationship between quality,
risk, and our testing activities**

By following this pattern, we not only have a clear path to take but also a means to establish a strategy that reacts to what our users want and to our working context.

You learned in chapter 3 that quality is a fluid concept and can mean many different things to different people. Quality can be affected by what type of industry it is part of (e.g., health care versus e-commerce) or the domain of our product, such as the Internet of Things or Software as a Service. These differences will have an impact on what quality means to our users and to us.

For example, if we were to consider a different project from our API sandbox project, such as a stocks- and shares-buying platform, we would soon discover that the quality characteristics differ from our API sandbox example. For example, they might include

- Accuracy
- Responsiveness
- Auditability

These quality characteristics will result in a different range of risks to consider, including the following:

- The number of stocks or shares purchased is too low or too high.
- Laws and regulations are broken due to incorrect details of purchases and sales found in audit logs.
- The number of stocks or shares isn't purchased in a timely manner, meaning someone else buys them before we can.

These risks might result in a strategy that has a different priority or focus, as captured in figure 7.6.

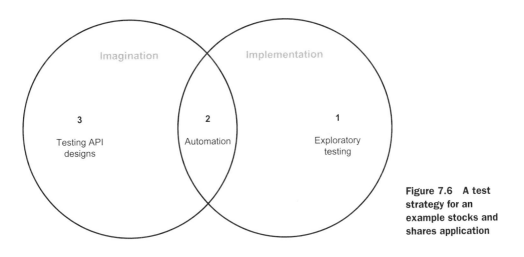

Figure 7.6   A test strategy for an example stocks and shares application

This example is an oversimplification of a hypothetical project, but it demonstrates that by following the same pattern of identifying quality characteristics, then risks, and then testing activities, we can create the right testing strategy for our product and team's needs.

7.2   Turning a testing strategy into a testing plan

Establishing a strategy maps the path we intend to take at any given time, but it lacks detail. It shows us the vision for our testing, but if we are actually to achieve it, we need a plan. Taking the time to plan out the details of how we intend to implement, execute, and reflect on our testing strategy is essential because the vision for our testing will almost always come into immediate conflict with the reality of our situation as soon as we begin. We might want to create a new automation framework but realize we lack the skills as a team to develop it. Or we might want to start facilitating API design testing sessions, but our team is spread across too many different time zones.

By taking the time to put together a plan, we can identify the constraints that exist within our context and use that information to help us plan out detailed tasks for how we intend to implement our testing strategy successfully. To do this, we need to ensure that during our planning we do the following:

- *Identify what constraints we have on our testing*—The success of a testing strategy is going to be based on our ability to test in a given context. This is why, before we start to put together our plan, analyzing the testability of our context is important. There is no point in trying to implement a specific testing activity if we don't know how easy or hard it is to do our testing in a given context, such as attempting to test API designs when the team works remotely and there are no formal API design sessions.
- *Organize and communicate our plan*—By planning out what we want to achieve with our testing, we have the opportunity to communicate how we're going to implement it. This means striking a balance and sharing the correct amount of detail for our plan.
- *Plan iteratively and in small chunks*—Trying to implement an entire testing strategy at once is difficult to execute and monitor. Instead, planning to implement specific activities allows us to create a manageable plan that requires less upfront investment, makes it easier to track whether it's working, and if it's not, enables us to react appropriately.
- *Take time to reflect and react*—Our plans will not always go the way we want them to, and as we progress, we learn more about our working context, meaning we have to be aware of issues as they arise and be willing to adapt to overcome them.

Let's take some time to go through each of these points and see how they can help us turn the vision of our testing strategy into a clear plan for our teams to carry out.

7.2.1   Understanding your context's testability

When discussing testability, we're referring to anything that impacts our ability to test—ranging from the product we're testing to the individuals involved in our project. Each aspect of testability can influence our testing by either making it harder or easier to carry out a specific testing activity. By assessing the testability of a context, we can use that knowledge to help us to promote and leverage the positive influences of our testability and reduce the negative influences or eliminate them entirely.

The first step toward assessing testability is to understand what exactly can affect it. Fortunately, we have some excellent sources on testability that can help us, such as the 10 Ps of Testability that were created by Rob Meaney and Ash Winter. Rob and Ash have explored the topic of testability deeply and have formalized the different influences on testability into a model, which can be seen in figure 7.7.

The 10 Ps of Testability

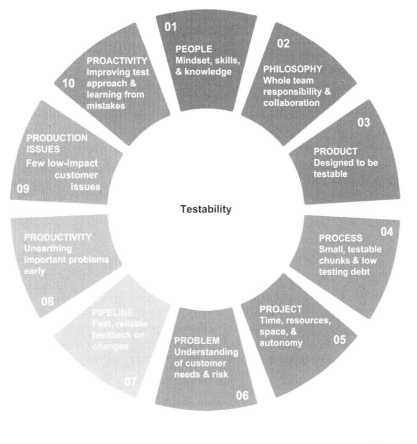

© 2019 Robert Meaney
🐦 @robmeaney

Figure 7.7 The 10 Ps of Testability model created by Rob Meaney and Ash Winter

Rob and Ash created the model as part of their book, *Team Guide to Software Testability* (https://leanpub.com/softwaretestability), which explores testability in detail. To help us get started, we can use their 10 Ps model as a place to kickstart our analysis by learning what each "P" stands for and what useful details we can learn, as described next:

- *People*—How we test is impacted by our skills, knowledge, and mindset around testing. If we have limited testing skills as individuals, then our own ability to test is limited. Therefore, when planning our testing, we need to take into account how hard or easy it is for our team members to carry out the specific testing activities we care about.

- *Philosophy*—Although "People" focuses on an individual's abilities and how they impact testing, philosophy is focused on the beliefs and attitudes of a team as a whole. For example, if a team has little buy-in into a quality mindset and the value of testing, it will make implementing a testing strategy as a whole difficult.

- *Product*—How our products are built and the technologies we use can also have a huge influence on our ability to test. A product that is hard to deploy, lacks access, or is constantly crashing will impact how easy it is to implement testing tools and disrupt our testing. When planning our testing activities, we should ensure our products are as amenable to our testing as possible.

- *Process*—Does our team try to deliver work in small, manageable chunks of work, or is everything done in large releases? The process by which we deliver our work can also impact our testing. If releases are done rarely and contain a large number of changes, this can affect the maintenance of automation, result in a frantic rush to catch up on testing, and make it hard to identify all the priority risks to test for.

- *Project*—The length and funding of a project will also play a big part in how we put a plan together. If our project deadlines are short, we might not have time to implement specific testing activities. If we require training to achieve other testing activities (as identified in "People"), will we have the budget and time to train team members?

- *Problem*—This relates to our understanding of the problem our software is trying to solve. We can further this by also understanding how our users interact with our system. If our knowledge of either of these areas of information is lacking, it will mean we are likely to have gaps in our testing.

- *Pipeline*—If we're to implement certain testing activities such as automation, where will the activity be carried in the pipeline as our product is built and deployed to production? Do we have a pipeline at all? Knowing the pipeline through which our product goes can help us to plan when and where we want our testing to be done.

- *Productivity*—This relates to how productive we are as a team in attempting to discover issues. What makes productivity interesting is how fluid it can be. There may be long-term impacts on productivity, such as the culture of an organization, but also short-term impacts such as illness, volume of meetings, and mental health. Although we can't plan for all of these, knowing what might impact our plans in the future will help us work out how to resolve these issues up front or plan around them.

- *Production issues*—If we don't have many production issues to deal with, this means we might have more time to focus our testing efforts elsewhere (or conversely, it might imply we have poor feedback loops). Equally, when we do find production issues, if we're not in a good place to resolve them quickly, then our opportunities to test might be affected. Understanding how often production issues occur and how we deal with them can allow us to establish what time is available to us to test.

- *Proactivity*—How open as a team are we to improving our testing on a regular basis? What opportunities are available to us to reflect and improve? Feedback and reflection are vital to measuring how successful our strategy and plans are. Will there be opportunities to take advantage of, or will we need to implement our own?

Each of the entries in the 10 Ps model offers us an opportunity to learn more about what is helping or hindering our testing. This is useful because the issues that are impacting our testability might not necessarily be obvious at first glance. For example, I once worked on a project in which we had issues with establishing a test environment. This issue could be attributed to the "Pipeline" part of the 10 Ps model. But after further investigation and conversations, we discovered the issue was that two high-level executives in the company were competing for next year's budget. They were deliberately disrupting the work of each other's departments so they could secure a higher budget for the next year, meaning the issue sat more under the "Philosophy" category.

Not all testability issues are this extreme, but this highlights how analyzing the testability of a context can help us to identify potential roadblocks and address them if required. These details can be added to our plans in terms of actions to resolve issues. For example, we would like to adopt a new automation tool, but our testability analysis shows the team has limited experience in implementing automation or with the tool in question. We can factor that knowledge into our plans and attempt to address the issue with training or securing time to familiarize ourselves with said tooling.

Alternative models of testability

Rob and Ash's 10 Ps of Testability is certainly not the only model that has been created to help teams explore their own testability. Other notable models include the Heuristics of Software Testability by James Bach (http://mng.bz/KOAX) and the Dimensions of Testability by Maria Kedemo and Ben Kelly (http://mng.bz/9V7j). Exploring each model can be beneficial because although they share some similarities, the way each model represents testability can help us trigger more questioning and understanding of our own testability.

Understanding our testability not only helps us to manage problems that can hinder our testing but can also help us to reprioritize and refocus. If, after discovering that our context's testability is low and that the testing activities we want to implement as part of our test strategy will require considerable investment to make them successful, we might want to reconsider. We can assess the balance of the cost of the work against the risks identified and ask ourselves whether other risks are quicker and easier to address. This doesn't mean abandoning our initial plans but approaching our strategy with an understanding that some streams of work might require long-term investment so that we don't end up putting all our eggs into one basket (or plan) only to see them fail and have to return back to square one.

7.2.2   *Organizing and documenting a plan*

Traditionally, test plan documents have been large, detailed documents that try to capture every detail that is to be carried out exhaustively. Although it's good to be thorough, the result is dense, hard-to-decipher documents that are hard to maintain in the face of inevitable change. For some, it can feel like this is a lot of work for little reward, so it's no surprise to see that a trend has appeared in which teams simply abandon test plans, citing the agile manifesto principle:

> Working software over comprehensive documentation

Although this principle is sometimes misinterpreted as a call to action to abandon all documentation, in fact, it is promoting a more sober, value-driven approach to documentation. It's OK to have some documentation as long as it enables us as individuals and teams to deliver working software first. This mindset can and should be applied to our test documentation. It is possible to strike a balance between capturing and communicating the right amount of information for a test plan without it becoming over-saturated with detail or too vague. This is something that Lisa Crispin and Janet Gregory advocate for in their book, *Agile Testing: A Practical Guide for Testers and Agile Teams* (Addison-Wesley Professional, 2008). They write:

> *"Consider a lightweight test plan that covers the necessities but not any extras."*

Lisa and Janet propose the idea of building a test plan that addresses the information we require and keeping it lightweight, suggesting that a test plan can be captured in just one page. This idea of the one-page test plan has been further expanded upon by Claire Reckless in her excellent article "The One-Page Test Plan" (http://mgn.bz/jAoa), which also captures the issue of larger test plans neatly:

> *Present a very busy manager with a document spanning many pages, packed with information, which might require an hour or more to read, and they may never get time to look at it. Present them with a short document where they can get a view of the testing planned for a project, and they might be more likely to take a look.*

Claire explores a range of different approaches to create a short and simple plan that communicates the required details and nothing more, ranging from simple one-page Word documents to dashboards. Regardless of the format, the main goal is always to create a plan that clearly states our intention to our team. Or as Lisa and Janet put it

> *Whatever type of test plan your organization uses, make it yours. Use it in a way that benefits your team, and make sure you meet your customer's needs.*

If we want to create a test plan that works for us and isn't overly complicated, what should we place in it? Let's consider some details we can add using the example of encouraging our team to adopt the activity "testing API designs":

- *Introduction*—The introduction will share details of what the test plan is about and what it is covering. For our example, we can state in this section that this is a test plan for implementing a team-based approach to testing web API designs.
- *Risks*—These are the risks that could impact our plans, which might have been identified as we assessed the testability of our context. In our example, we might want to raise risks around a team's unfamiliarity with collaborative sessions or that a remote team may struggle to connect.
- *Assumptions*—Similar to risks, our analysis of our testability may highlight assumptions we have to make about how well we can test. Therefore, adding these to our plan can communicate them clearly to see whether they are valid assumptions and keep them in our mind when executing our plans. For example, we could make an assumption that our team are already having informal conversations around API designs that we can take advantage of.
- *Tools*—Simply put, what tools do we want to use as part of our plan? For example, we discussed in chapter 4 the use of Swagger to document APIs, so we might list Swagger tooling here.
- *Resources*—Any additional resources—perhaps how much an individual's or the team's time will be required to implement a plan, or maybe training or budgetary requirements—could also be captured in a plan. For our plan, we might want to consider some coaching or training from an outside source to help us adopt a new testing approach like testing API designs.
- *Scope*—Here, we can share what is in or out of scope in what our plan covers. Making these details clear can help us to clearly communicate what we hope to achieve, as well as capture other areas of testing that need to be considered in the future. For example, we might say that the testing of web APIs we design and not APIs we depend on is in scope.

We might consider many other options, and we can add all these details or only select items. Our testability analysis might help us to identify what is best to communicate to others so they can understand our intentions clearly and help us implement them.

7.2.3   Executing and reflecting on a plan

When discussing strategies and plans, it's almost cliché to quote Robert Burns, but one of his most famous quotes reminds us of an important point in our planning:

> *The best-laid plans of mice and men often go awry.*

To repeat the point at the start of this chapter, we can't test everything. The same can be said for planning our testing; we can't plan for every eventuality. Analyzing the testability of our context is time-consuming, meaning we won't necessarily have enough time to reveal everything impacting us up front. Contexts change, budgets increase or decrease, project deadlines are pushed forward and backward, team members leave, and new ones join. All of these events will affect our plans, so it's important to execute and reflect on our plans in a way that allows us to identify issues and react to them quickly.

EXECUTION

When executing our plans, we can take a leaf out of modern software development practices by breaking up our work into small, manageable tasks. Rather than attempting to adopt a new testing activity wholesale with a full-blown process for running it, it's better to take an agile mindset. By trying short, small experiments, we can test out whether our new ideas and approaches are successful and then consider the next step to take to establish them further.

For example, we learned in the testing API design chapter that getting a team together to collaboratively discuss how our APIs work can be an opportunity to test ideas and clarify assumptions. Attempting to get a whole team to attend a formal meeting in which we want people to start talking design might be difficult to organize and could be met with open hostility if the session doesn't go well (speaking from experience). Instead, taking smaller steps would give us time to ease others into a new approach and react to any changes or resistance. This might include tasks such as the following:

1 Inform the team of our intentions to begin testing API designs, and survey the team to see if there is interest.
2 Begin with an informal session with interested parties, communicating that this is an experiment, and see how it goes.
3 Reflect on the session, tweak accordingly, and attempt another.
4 Share successes with the team, attempt to make the sessions part of the regular process, and invite others to join.

Each step may require a few iterations and perhaps glosses over the complexities of influencing change within a team. However, it does demonstrate that we have an opportunity after each task to reflect and replan. If, at step one, no one is interested in collaborating, then perhaps a different approach is required. The key is that we learn and adapt as quickly as possible to ensure the success of our plans.

REFLECTION

Taking smaller steps to implement a plan is all for naught if we don't take the time to reflect on the progress of our plans and how they are working in the real world. This means establishing mechanisms or taking advantage of existing ones that allow us to assess our work so far and change our course if required.

Retrospectives are an excellent example of a place to discuss what we want to achieve in the coming days or weeks with our testing, as well as an opportunity to measure how our work is progressing. If you recall, our testing goal is to support our team's efforts in improving the quality of our product. Having our team in one place to discuss how things are going is an excellent opportunity to survey the team and learn how our plans are helping them. We can also use this time informally to assess our feelings on the quality of our product. Has it improved? Do we feel, anecdotally, that the changes to our test strategy and plans have contributed to that improvement?

Adopting experimentation models, such as Claudio Perrone's "Popcorn Flow" model (https://agilesensei.com/popcornflow/), can also allow us to take a structured process to introduce ideas, measure them, and learn from them using a lean mind-set. Approaches like these, however, do require some level of investment and buy-in from the team for them to become comfortable with regular experimentation and reflection.

Finally, just having conversations can bear useful reflections. Sometimes testing is not communicated about clearly, which leads to a misunderstanding of its complexity and value. By clearly demonstrating to others what we're doing in our testing and asking for feedback, they can equally share the value and help us to understand better how we can help team members.

7.2.4 *Evolving our strategy*

By following the steps of assessing testability, organizing our plan, executing it, and then finally reflecting on our progress, we can begin to see the vision of testing strategy become real. However, as our work changes over time, so do the risks that affect it. That's why our strategy and the resulting plans have to adapt and evolve constantly over time. As we regularly reflect on what quality means to our users and the risks related to those ideas, the priority of what testing we do when will change. Whether it's a new testing activity we're establishing or a preexisting one, following this pattern helps us identify where to focus our energy at a given time and where to hold back until it is required.

Summary

- We can use the two models of implementation/imagination and quality characteristics/risks together to help guide us in our testing strategy.
- The risks we identify can be mitigated by different testing activities; the higher the priority of the risk, the greater reason to carry out that testing activity.
- The pattern for establishing a strategy can be summarized as identifying quality characteristics, analyzing risks that affect quality, and selecting activities that help mitigate risks.
- A testing strategy helps us establish the vision for our testing, but we require a plan or plans to ensure that vision is met.
- The success of our plans and strategy will be influenced by our testability or ability to test in a given context.
- We can use the testability model 10 Ps by Rob Meaney and Ash Winter to help us analyze different aspects of a context to discover testability issues.
- Understanding testability helps us to create a better plan of action and reprioritize if there are complex issues to resolve.

- A test plan doesn't need to be a complex document that details everything. A one-page test plan with details we require can help communicate our intentions clearly.

- When executing our plans, starting with small manageable tasks that iteratively introduce activities can help us to reflect on and react to issues.

- Ceremonies, such as retrospectives, and experiment models, like Popcorn Flow, can facilitate opportunities to reflect on how our plans are going.

Part 3

Expanding our test strategy

The testing activities we've discussed so far are essential parts of a testing strategy, but they are by no means the only opportunities available to us. Activities such as performance and security testing are sometimes considered things we can do at the end of a project. But as we'll learn, these activities can and should be baked into a test strategy as early as we can reasonably action them. Not only can they expand our understanding of how our web APIs work and how others interact with them in production, but they are also exciting and innovative ways to expand our testing further.

We'll learn a range of different ways to expand our testing strategy by first discovering ways to advance our automation with a myriad of tools and techniques in chapter 8. We'll then discuss how contract testing can help extend our automation further and help teams to collaborate around API design in chapter 9. Next, we'll discuss performance testing in chapter 10 and how we can begin planning and implementing this activity much earlier in a testing strategy than commonly thought. Chapter 11 will discuss how we can bake a security testing mindset into a range of activities we've already learned about such as modeling, exploratory testing, and automation. We'll then conclude this part and the book by discovering how testing in production and site reliability engineering practices can help expand our testing strategy further into our live environments.

Advanced web
API automation

This chapter covers

- Using automation to guide delivery
- Improving automation stability with mocks
- Considerations when adding automated checks to a build pipeline

As web API technology has advanced, so have the tools for supporting our automation. In chapter 6, we discovered how to build automated checks for APIs that can help indicate potential issues for further investigation, but there is much more we can do. Therefore, in this chapter, we'll build on our knowledge of automating API checks and explore how we can take our automation further to help us in different ways. To do this, each section in this chapter will explore a way in which we can get more out of our automation, such as by

- Guiding our delivery with automated acceptance testing
- Reducing false positives in our automation with the use of mocks
- Using property-based testing to discover unexpected issues

Assumptions and supporting codebase

Some of the activities in this chapter are based on automated checks created in chapter 6. It is assumed that you have been through chapter 6 and have created your own code that can now be updated. If you haven't, I encourage you to read through chapter 6 before continuing. Alternatively, you can grab a copy of the codebase for the supporting repository here: http://mng.bz/WMjg.

8.1   *Acceptance test-driven development*

As we've explored in previous chapters, different testing activities help us mitigate different risks, which is no different when it comes to automating API checks. The automated API checks that we've created so far have focused on risks we've identified that are based on our knowledge of the system—for example, what if we don't get the correct status code back, or what if we change something in the system that causes the wrong status code to come back? These fall under the umbrella of what we can call "regression risks," which focus on how the system may change in a way that is undesirable as we add new features and modify our system code.

However, the tools at our disposal can also help us mitigate risks around delivering the wrong thing. This is subtly different from our regression risks because its focus isn't on how the system can go wrong but how we as teams can misunderstand what needs to be delivered. This is what acceptance test-driven development can help mitigate.

By adopting an acceptance test-driven development approach (ATDD), we can leverage the same model as test-driven development (TDD), which follows:

1   Create a failing automated check.
2   Write some production code.
3   Refactor our code with confidence.

The difference between TDD and ATDD is that the expectations of the automated check come from a conversation with the business about what they want an API to do. ATDD checks tend to be more high level, focused on business behavior, than the expectations we set when working in the TDD space, which focuses on individual pieces of logic at a given time.

With ATDD, we start with a conversation with the business and produce a captured example like this for automation:

- Feature: Booking reports
- Scenario: User requests total earnings of all bookings
  - Given I have multiple bookings
  - When I ask for a report on my total earnings
  - Then I will receive a total amount based on all my bookings

This scenario, which is written using a language known as Gherkin (Given-When-Then), can be used by certain automation tools to create a failing automated check. It fails because the production code that we are checking doesn't exist. But once we write enough production code to make the check pass, we have feedback that our work is done and that we've built what the business wants and avoided any potential scope creep.

8.1.1 Setting up an automated acceptance testing framework

For this activity, we'll create a new Maven project, this time with an expanded dependency list to include new libraries to create automated acceptance checks, as shown next:

```
<dependencies>
    <dependency>
        <groupId>org.junit.jupiter</groupId>
        <artifactId>junit-jupiter</artifactId>
        <version>5.7.1</version>
    </dependency>
    <dependency>
        <groupId>io.rest-assured</groupId>
        <artifactId>rest-assured</artifactId>
        <version>4.3.3</version>
    </dependency>
    <dependency>
        <groupId>com.fasterxml.jackson.core</groupId>
        <artifactId>jackson-databind</artifactId>
        <version>2.12.2</version>
    </dependency>
    <dependency>
        <groupId>com.fasterxml.jackson.core</groupId>
        <artifactId>jackson-core</artifactId>
        <version>2.12.2</version>
    </dependency>
    <dependency>
        <groupId>io.cucumber</groupId>
        <artifactId>cucumber-java</artifactId>
        <version>6.11.0</version>
    </dependency>
    <dependency>
        <groupId>io.cucumber</groupId>
        <artifactId>cucumber-junit</artifactId>
        <version>6.11.0</version>
    </dependency>
</dependencies>
```

In addition to the libraries we used in the previous chapter, we've added two libraries from Cucumber. This enables us to create a relationship between our example scenarios and our automation code. For example, when the step "Given I have multiple bookings" is run by Cucumber, it will trigger automation code to create multiple bookings. To get started, we're going to create a similar framework setup to the one we created earlier with the following packages in the test folder:

- `requests`
- `payloads`
- `stepdefinitions`

And in `com.example`, we're going to create a new class called `RunCukesTest`, which contains the following:

```
@RunWith(Cucumber.class)
@CucumberOptions(
    features = {"src/test/resources"}
)

public class RunCukesTest {
}
```

Finally, we need to add our example scenario into our framework by creating a new file called `BookingReports.feature` in the resources folder, like so:

```
Feature: Booking reports

  Scenario: User requests total earnings of all bookings
    Given I have multiple bookings
    When I ask for a report on my total earnings
    Then I will receive a total amount based on all my bookings
```

This means that when we run `mvn clean test`, we get the following feedback:

```
io.cucumber.junit.UndefinedStepException: The step "I have multiple bookings"
    is undefined. You can implement it using the snippet(s) below:

@Given("I have multiple bookings")
public void i_have_multiple_bookings() {
    // Write code here that turns the phrase above into concrete actions
    throw new io.cucumber.java.PendingException();
}
```

This happens because the `RunCukesTest` class connects JUnit and our feature files together, enabling Cucumber to run our `BookingReports.feature` file as a test. The output we're getting shows an `UndefinedStepException` because as Cucumber runs our feature file, it's looking for "step definitions" that match the step in the check we're running. We'll look at this more in a minute, but for now, this confirms that we are set up and ready to create our failing automated check.

8.1.2 *Creating our failing automated check*

Now that we have everything set up, we can begin automating by creating a new class in the `com.example.stepdefs` package named `BookingReportsStepDefs` with the following code:

```
public class BookingReportsStepDefs {

    @Given("I have multiple bookings")
    public void i_have_multiple_bookings() {
        // Write code here that turns the phrase above into concrete actions
        throw new io.cucumber.java.PendingException();
    }
```

```
@When("I ask for a report on my total earnings")
public void i_ask_for_a_report_on_my_total_earnings() {
    // Write code here that turns the phrase above into concrete actions
    throw new io.cucumber.java.PendingException();
}

@Then("I will receive a total amount based on all my bookings")
public void i_will_receive_a_total_amount_based_on_all_my_bookings() {
    // Write code here that turns the phrase above into concrete actions
    throw new io.cucumber.java.PendingException();
}

}
```

Notice that each method has an annotation attached to it in which a phrase is being passed in as a parameter. If we look at the first annotation

```
@Given("I have multiple bookings") "
```

we can see that this matches the first line of our example scenario in the `Booking-Reports.feature` file, shown here:

```
Given I have multiple bookings
```

This is what the Cucumber library allows us to do: take scenarios that have been written in plain English in collaboration with the business and tie each step to a specific block of automation code we would like to run. This is where the term *step definition* comes from—we're defining what will specifically be run for each step to help us check whether we're building the right thing. At the moment, though, if we were to run this code, we would simply return a `PendingException`, so we need to enter our automation code to create our failing automated check.

With this in mind, let's start with the first step, the creation of multiple bookings. First, let's update the first step definition to contain the code to create our bookings:

```
@Given("I have multiple bookings")
public void i_have_multiple_bookings() {
    BookingDates dates = new BookingDates(
            LocalDate.of(2021,01, 01),
            LocalDate.of(2021,03, 01)
    );

    Booking payloadOne = new Booking(
            "Mark",
            "Winteringham",
            200,
            true,
            dates,
            "Breakfast"
    );
```

```
    Booking payloadTwo = new Booking(
            "Mark",
            "Winteringham",
            200,
            true,
            dates,
            "Breakfast"
    );

    BookingApi.postBooking(payloadOne);
    BookingApi.postBooking(payloadTwo);
}
```

This is supported by creating the following POJOs in com.example.payloads. First, we'll create a BookingDates class and add the following:

```
public class BookingDates {

    @JsonProperty
    private LocalDate checkin;
    @JsonProperty
    private LocalDate checkout;

    public BookingDates(LocalDate checkin, LocalDate checkout){
        this.checkin = checkin;
        this.checkout = checkout;
    }
}
```

Then we'll create a Booking class and add-in:

```
public class Booking {

    @JsonProperty
    private String firstname;
    @JsonProperty
    private String lastname;
    @JsonProperty
    private int totalprice;
    @JsonProperty
    private boolean depositpaid;
    @JsonProperty
    private BookingDates bookingdates;
    @JsonProperty
    private String additionalneeds;

    public Booking(String firstname, String lastname, int totalprice, boolean
      depositpaid, BookingDates bookingdates, String additionalneeds) {
        this.firstname = firstname;
        this.lastname = lastname;
        this.totalprice = totalprice;
        this.depositpaid = depositpaid;
        this.bookingdates = bookingdates;
        this.additionalneeds = additionalneeds;
    }

}
```

And finally, we'll create the code necessary to send our request in `com.example`
`.requests` in a class called `BookingApi`:

```
public class BookingApi {

    private static final String apiUrl = "http://localhost:3000/booking/";

    public static Response postBooking(Booking payload) {
        return given()
                .contentType(ContentType.JSON)
                .body(payload)
                .when()
                .post(apiUrl);
    }

}
```

With this in place, if we were to run our automated acceptance check again using `mvn`
`clean test`, we'll see that the first step of the scenario now runs, but the second step
returns a `PendingException`. So let's complete the other two-step definitions to create our failing automated check, like so:

```
private Response totalResponse;

@When("I ask for a report on my total earnings")
public void i_ask_for_a_report_on_my_total_earnings() {
    totalResponse = BookingApi.getTotal();
}

@Then("I will receive a total amount based on all my bookings")
public void i_will_receive_a_total_amount_based_on_all_my_bookings() {
    int total = totalResponse.as(Total.class).getTotal();

    assertEquals(total, 400);
}
```

To get this code working, we will need to create a new class in `com.example.pay-`
`loads` named `Total` with the following code:

```
public class Total {

    @JsonProperty
    private int total;

    public int getTotal() {
        return total;
    }

}
```

We also need a new method in the `BookingApi` class to send the request to the total
endpoint:

```
public static Response getTotal() {
    return given()
            .get(apiUrl + "report");
}
```

With our code in place, that gives us everything we need to run a failing automated check to code against, as we see when we run `mvn clean test` and we get a `java.net .ConnectException: Operation timed out` error.

8.1.3   *Getting our automated check to pass*

With a failing check in place, the next step would be to create the necessary production code to make the automated check pass. Depending on our role, we might be responsible for creating the production code, or it could be passed onto a team member who would do the work.

Once the production code is complete and the check is passing, we have clear feedback that we have delivered the *what* we've been asked to build. We then have the option to either refactor our production code, while ensuring that our checks don't break, or move onto the next scenario that requires delivery.

Additionally, once we have gotten our automated acceptance check to pass, we now have the opportunity to add it to our other automated checks to run as part of our build pipeline. This enables us to build a suite of automated checks that can provide feedback to our team if any changes to the system cause it to no longer deliver the functionality the business expects.

8.1.4   *Beware of traps*

It's worth reiterating here that the acceptance test-driven design approach differs from any other automated API testing activities because the focus is on *the risk of not delivering the right thing*. The goal with ATDD is not to exhaustively check every risk or every combination of values an API can take, nor is it to replace TDD (they work side by side). It's to capture what the business wants and use it as a guide to keep us honest in our delivery.

That said, staying honest with an approach like this takes time, maturity in a team, and regular reflection. It's easy to fall into the trap of trying to use the ATDD approach to check everything. Before we conclude this section, I want to share a few antipatterns that teams fall into with ATDD that we should keep an eye on.

GOING ALONE

The key to success with ATDD isn't really in the automation but in the conversations had before capturing your scenarios. It's important that our team meets regularly to discuss new features and capture scenarios that describe those features in a collaborative manner.

The goal of collaborative conversations is to dispel any miscommunication or misunderstandings before work begins, so our team can deliver the right thing the first time. If the whole team agrees with what the scenarios describe, we can automate them with confidence, knowing that when they pass, the team has delivered what was requested.

The trap here is when one person starts writing the scenarios by themselves. It may be another member of the team; it may be you. The problem is that if we've missed the conversation part of this process, we risk codifying our own misunderstandings of what needs to be delivered. Then, although our automated acceptance checks have passed, the work we've done doesn't match the businesses expectations, which will result in that awful rework we all hate so much.

TRYING TO AUTOMATE EVERYTHING

Getting people in the room is a good start, but it's important to keep focused. The goal is to capture scenarios that describe the core business features we are being asked to deliver. Sometimes this might involve capturing negative scenarios about how we handle business validation. However, we don't want to capture every way in which a feature might go wrong.

Remember, the focus is on risks around *delivering the right thing the first time*, not writing automated checks for every eventuality. Failure to do so may result in a list of scenarios that no longer capture the essence of business expectations and generate a lot of code that has little value and requires more maintenance.

8.2   *Web API mocking*

One of the biggest challenges when working with automation is reducing the number of false positives we get from our automation. Sometimes known as "flaky tests," these issues stem from a range of issues with the products we're automating. Two of the more common issues are state management and/or complex dependencies between the web API we're testing and other APIs within our platform.

To demonstrate this, let's return to the following automated check we created in chapter 6 that would create a booking, log in as an administrator, and then delete the booking:

```
@Test
public void deleteBookingReturns202(){

    BookingDates dates = new BookingDates(
        LocalDate.of( 2021 , 1 , 1 ),
        LocalDate.of( 2021 , 1 , 3 )
    );

    Booking payload = new Booking(
        1,
        "Mark",
        "Winteringham",
        true,
        dates,
        "Breakfast"
    );

    Response bookingResponse = BookingApi.postBooking(payload);
    BookingResponse createdBookingResponse =
     bookingResponse.as(BookingResponse.class);

    Auth auth = new Auth("admin", "password");

    AuthResponse authResponse = AuthApi.postAuth(auth).as(AuthResponse.class);
```

```
Response deleteResponse = BookingApi.deleteBooking(
        createdBookingResponse.getBookingid(),
        authResponse.getToken());

    assertEquals(202, deleteResponse.getStatusCode());
}
```

The problem arises with the fact that although the check is focused on the `booking` API, it relies on a working `auth` API to ensure that we are able to authorize our delete request. This can be summarized in the dependency model shown in figure 8.1.

Figure 8.1   booking API sends a token to auth API and gets a positive response

The success of the delete booking process is dependent on the `auth` API, which means any issues with the `auth` will result in a failure that isn't necessarily related to the `booking` API, whether it's incorrectly configured user accounts, errors in the `auth` API, or connectivity issues between each API. It could result in a persistently failing check that requires maintenance and debugging, which can degrade trust in the check itself.

Fortunately, we can remove the impact of these issues with the use of web API mocking libraries that help us both isolate our web API under test as well as control the flow of information coming into it, as demonstrated in figure 8.2.

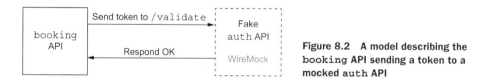

Figure 8.2   A model describing the booking API sending a token to a mocked auth API

With a mocked web API in place, we are able to set out which requests it should receive and in what format, as well as what information is sent back. To better understand how a mocked web API works, let's take a look at how we can update our existing check using the mocking tool WireMock.

8.2.1   *Getting set up*

Before we jump in to using a mock, we need to take a few steps to get ourselves ready.

SETTING UP THE BOOKING API

To have our automation run successfully, we will require a locally running version of the `booking` API to send our requests to. We'll also need to ensure that nothing else is listening on port 3004, because our fake `auth` API will be set up to use the port. For this activity, you can download a standalone copy of the `booking` API from the chapter 8 folder in the api-strategy-book-resources repository (http://mng.bz/827K). Either download or clone the repository and load the chapter-8 module into your IDE. You can then use your IDE to build and run the `booking` API by running the `main` method in the `BookingApplication` class.

SETTING UP OUR NEW AUTOMATION CODE

First, we establish everything we need to implement our mock, starting with our new example check. To do this, add a new check to your `BookingApiIT` class like so:

```
@Test
public void deleteBookingReturns202WithMocks(){
    BookingDates dates = new BookingDates(
            LocalDate.of( 2021 , 2 , 1 ),
            LocalDate.of( 2021 , 2 , 3 )
    );

    Booking payload = new Booking(
            1,
            "Mark",
            "Winteringham",
            true,
            dates,
            "Breakfast"
    );

    Response bookingResponse = BookingApi.postBooking(payload);
    BookingResponse createdBookingResponse =
     bookingResponse.as(BookingResponse.class);

    Response deleteResponse = BookingApi.deleteBooking(
            createdBookingResponse.getBookingid(),
            "abc123");

    assertEquals(202, deleteResponse.getStatusCode());
}
```

Notice that we've removed the calls to the `auth` API and added in a hardcoded value for the cookie we want to send for `deleteBooking`. If we were to run this right now, it would likely fail because `abc123` isn't a valid token. However, we'll rectify this by adding our mocked API into the check.

The mocking library we'll use is WireMock, which enables us to programmatically create mocks within our codebase. WireMock comes with a range of features that we can take advantage of. For our example, we'll use the stubbing features to establish a fake `auth` API with a `/validate` endpoint that will always respond with an OK if the correct fake token is sent to it. You can learn more about the other features of WireMock at https://wiremock.org/.

To add WireMock, we'll drop the WireMock dependency into our POM.xml file like this:

```
<dependency>
    <groupId>com.github.tomakehurst</groupId>
    <artifactId>wiremock-jre8</artifactId>
    <version>2.30.1</version>
    <scope>test</scope>
</dependency>
```

8.2.2 Building our mocked check

With our APIs now set up and our code in place, let's begin to update our check so that it makes use of WireMock for the `auth` API.

UPDATE THE BOOKINGAPI APIURL

Because we're now working against a local deployment of restful-booker-platform, our first step is to update the `apiUrl` in the `BookingAPI` class to the following:

```
private static final String apiUrl = "http://localhost:3000/booking/";
```

The change means we'll now send requests to our `localhost` instance rather than the instance on `automationintesting.online`.

SETUP WIREMOCK

Now we're ready to set up WireMock to take the form of the `auth` API. This requires us to add the following code:

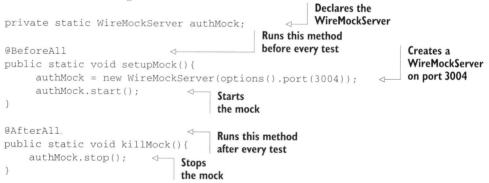

With this code in place, we now have a mock server that is listening on port 3004 to take requests. At this point, the mock server doesn't have any endpoints set up within it, so our next step is to create the mocked endpoint.

CREATE A MOCKED ENDPOINT

To create the endpoint, we need to add the following code into our check:

```
authMock.stubFor(post("/auth/validate")
            .withRequestBody(equalToJson("{ \"token\": \"abc123\" }"))
            .willReturn(aResponse().withStatus(200)));
```

Let's look through each step to better understand what is going on:

1 We call `authMock` that was created in the `@BeforeAll` hook before the check began.

2 To create our mocked endpoint, we call `stubFor` and add the configuration details for the endpoint within it as a parameter.

3 The `post()` method declares that the endpoint is a POST endpoint listening on the `/auth/validate` path.

4 `withRequestBody()` allows us to set conditions about what structure and data the request body contains. For this example, we're saying that the request body must match a JSON object of `{"token": "abc123"}`. Notice that the value matches the `abc123` we've set for `deleteBooking()`.

5 The `willReturn` method allows us to state what response is given if the request matches all our expectations within our mocked endpoint. For this example, we only require a 200 status code, which we set with `aResponse().withStatus(200)`.

This establishes our mocked endpoint and completes our check, resulting in the following completed check:

```
@Test
public void deleteBookingReturns202(){
    authMock.stubFor(post("/auth/validate")
            .withRequestBody(equalToJson("{ \"token\": \"abc123\" }"))
            .willReturn(aResponse().withStatus(200)));

    BookingDates dates = new BookingDates(
            LocalDate.of( 2021 , 2 , 1 ),
            LocalDate.of( 2021 , 2 , 3 )
    );

    Booking payload = new Booking(
            1,
            "Mark",
            "Winteringham",
            true,
            dates,
            "Breakfast"
    );

    Response bookingResponse = BookingApi.postBooking(payload);
    BookingResponse createdBookingResponse =
     bookingResponse.as(BookingResponse.class);

    Response deleteResponse = BookingApi.deleteBooking(
            createdBookingResponse.getBookingid(),
            "abc123");

    assertEquals(202, deleteResponse.getStatusCode());
}
```

Now when the check runs, it will send a DELETE request to `/booking/{id}`, which in turn takes the token from the request cookie and sends that on to the mocked API. As long as the token value matches `abc123`, when sent to the mock, it will return a positive message. Otherwise, it will fail and cause the check to fail.

With this established, we now have more control over how the `booking` API's dependencies behave, and if we run into any issues, we'll be more confident that they lie with the `booking` API.

8.3   *Running as part of a pipeline*

Throughout this chapter, we've looked at innovative ways in which we can use tools and libraries to help guide our work as well as improve their stability and feedback. But the time will come when we want to run our automation as part of a pipeline that builds, checks, and deploys our work. So far, we've done most of our work within an IDE against either deployed instances of web APIs or running local versions of web APIs before running our checks. Although this is fine for developing our automation, what do we do when we run our checks in the pipeline?

Unlike unit checking, web API automation requires that a web API is up and running. And what's more, if our checks are being run as part of a wider pipeline, we should be aware that we need to get them up and running in an environment such as a Continuous Integration (CI) build box that differs from our own local environment. To achieve this, we're very likely going to need to implement some sort of tool, library, or script, but what approach we implement and how we do so depends on how our codebase is organized, the tools we use for our pipelines, and much more.

To demonstrate this, let's look at two different scenarios in which we could set up our automated checks to run. One scenario assumes that our automation is integrated with our production codebase, and the other assumes that our automation is in a separate location.

8.3.1   *Integrated with codebase*

Although not every situation allows us to have our automation code stored within the same project as our production codebase, it is certainly recommended. Not only do you have the ability to get faster feedback by running automated checks as part of the build process for a project (think of the test and integrated-test phases of a Maven build process), but it also gives us greater access and control over setting up our web APIs to begin running our checks against.

PROGRAMMATICALLY STARTING UP

For example, this is reflected in the testing tool sets that are offered as part of the Spring Boot libraries. Because the web APIs we're working with are part of a mature project that offers the necessary framework and tooling to create a Java web API, we have the opportunity to use a tool like `spring-boot-starter-test` to programmatically turn on our web API.

To take advantage of this library, let's look at expanding our mock example from the previous section so that we no longer need to "turn on" the `booking` API ourselves. First, we start by adding the necessary dependency to our pom.xml as follows:

```
<dependency>
    <groupId>org.springframework.boot</groupId>
    <artifactId>spring-boot-starter-test</artifactId>
    <version>2.5.4</version>
</dependency>
```

With `spring-boot-starter-test` in place, we now can add the following annotations to the top of our `BookingApiIT` class:

```
@ExtendWith(SpringExtension.class)
@SpringBootTest(webEnvironment = SpringBootTest.WebEnvironment.DEFINED_PORT,
    classes = BookingApplication.class)
@ActiveProfiles("dev")
public class BookingApiIT {
```

Let's take a second to look at each annotation and see what they're doing to help us start up our web API through our code:

1. `@ExtendWith(SpringExtension.class)` is used to connect Junit5 with Spring to allow us to pass details from our Junit class to our web API, which we do on the next line.

2. Next we use `@SpringBootTest` to configure how to start up our `booking` API. As we can see, we're providing two parameters: `webEnvironment = SpringBootTest.WebEnvironment.DEFINED_PORT`, which informs `SpringBootTest` to load the defined port from our .properties file, and then `classes = BookingApplication.class`, which tells `SpringBootTest` which class contains the `SpringApplication.run()` method that is used to start up our web API.

3. The `@ActiveProfiles("dev")` allows us to set which .properties file we want our web API to load up with. This is useful when we have different property files that configure a web API to be in a "production" or "test" mode (such as increasing or decreasing logging, depending on what state we want). By sending the parameter `dev`, we're loading the application-dev.properties file into the API.

With this code in place, we're now ready to run the `deleteBookingReturns202()` check in our class. Assuming the `booking` API is already off, now, when we run the check, we can see details of the API starting up in our log.

INCORPORATING INTO A PIPELINE

With `spring-boot-starter-test` taking care of the setup for our web API for automation, the process of incorporating our work into a pipeline is quite straightforward. Assuming we have a fail-safe plugin installed in our pom.xml (as shown next as a recap), we should be able to run `mvn clean install` and see `BookingApiIT` run with the `booking` web API starting up:

```
<build>
    <plugins>
        <plugin>
            <groupId>org.apache.maven.plugins</groupId>
            <artifactId>maven-failsafe-plugin</artifactId>
            <version>2.22.2</version>
            <executions>
                <execution>
                    <goals>
                        <goal>integration-test</goal>
                        <goal>verify</goal>
                    </goals>
                    <configuration>
                        <includes>
                            <include>**/*IT</include>
                        </includes>
                    </configuration>
                </execution>
            </executions>
        </plugin>
    </plugins>
</build>
```

With the running of the web API now integrated as part of our Maven build process, it's a simple case of setting up whatever CI tooling we're using to run `mvn clean install`.

8.3.2 Separate to codebase

Although it is always beneficial to have your production and automation code under one project, not every context allows such a setup. It may be that organizational structures such as siloed teams based on roles could mean completed work is passed "over the fence" to another team with little collaboration. Or we might have to deal with software that is architected in a way that means our codebase might already be compiled (e.g., when extending preexisting platforms). Still, regardless of the reason, it shouldn't deter us from attempting to integrate our work into a pipeline.

We can set up our web APIs programmatically, but this does require extra work. Let's return to our `booking` API example and imagine this time that we're working with a version of the web API that has been compiled as a JAR file. We will need to handle two things:

- Turning on the `booking` web API
- Waiting until the `booking` web API is ready to receive requests

Fortunately, the first step can be handled easily enough by taking advantage of existing code or scripts that are used as part of the deployment for a system. This might be something as simple as running a basic command line to run a JAR file, such as `java -jar example.jar`, or it could mean taking advantage of tools such as Docker to run an image containing our web API (which is beyond the scope of this book).

The more complex part is ensuring that our automation isn't run until the web API is able to receive requests; otherwise, we start receiving false positives from our automation. In these situations, we will likely need to either find a tool or create some code that will block a pipeline for a certain amount of time before allowing the automation to begin once the web API is ready.

There are many ways in which we could approach this. For example, we could build a utility tool that is used as part of our pipeline (like the monitor app I created in NodeJS for restful-booker-platform—http://mng.bz/E0Rq). Or we could extend our automation framework with preflight checks that verify that the web APIs are ready to receive requests, as demonstrated in this `before` hook that we could add to `BookingApiIT`:

```
private static void waitForApi(String url, int timeoutLimit) throws
    InterruptedException {
    while(true){
        if(timeoutLimit == 0){
            fail("Unable to connect to Web API");
        }

        try{
            Response response = given().get(url);

            if(response.statusCode() != 200){
                timeoutLimit--;
                Thread.sleep(1000);
            } else {
                break;
            }
        } catch(Exception exception){
            timeoutLimit--;
            Thread.sleep(1000);
        }
    }
}
```

The `waitForAPI` method takes the parameters `url` and `timeoutLimit`, which are used to send a request to our endpoint of choice. If the request fails due to a connection error, or if the response doesn't come back with a 200 status code, then the method counts down the `timeoutLimit` and waits for a second before sending the request again. The method can resolve in one of two ways:

1 The `timeoutLimit` reaches 0, and a `fail` assertion is thrown to indicate an issue.

2 A 200 response is received, and the `while` loop is broken, meaning the automated checking can begin.

With this code in place, we can then call the method in our `@BeforeAll` hook:

```
waitForApi("http://localhost:3000/booking/actuator/health", 20);
```

Our @BeforeAll will now check to see whether the booking API is up and running every second for 20 seconds. If the web API is not up by then, the checks will fail with a clear message that the API is unavailable.

It's worth reiterating that this is just a demonstration of one of the many ways in which we can use tools and/or libraries to get our web APIs up and running. The key takeaway should be the fact that something similar to this behavior will be required in any API automation framework that isn't able to easily turn on web APIs.

This approach may feel uncomfortable for some because it creates more code to maintain and more potential points of failure. That's why it's sometimes worth taking a step back to see whether we can make changes in our context that allow our production and automation code to be closely aligned, because this may save time in the future for everyone.

Summary

- We can use automated acceptance testing to help mitigate risks around delivering the right features at the right time.
- We can use tools like Cucumber to capture Gherkin scenarios that are then tied to failing automation. We can then create production code to make the scenario pass.
- Complex situations in which a web API under test is dependent on other web APIs can result in flakiness in our checks.
- By replacing the dependent web APIs with tools such as WireMock, we can control what information is being sent to the web API under test and reduce flakiness.
- Our web APIs need to be up and running when using automation, which is something we can do programmatically.
- If our automated checks are stored in the same project as our production codebase, we can take advantage of various tools and libraries to run our APIs, such as spring-boot-starter-test.
- If our automated checks live separately from our production code, we will need to employ tools or libraries to get our web API up and running before our checks can be run.

Contract testing

Imagine a situation in which you and your team are part of a larger organization, and you are responsible for a subset of web APIs in a wider API platform. Your team has worked hard to establish some robust testing activities, and you're about to release a new feature. The conversations before development began were productive, the exploratory testing sessions revealed lots of information, and all the automated checks are green as part of the build pipeline. You deploy the APIs only to discover that as soon as the deployment is complete, the platform falls over, and it's returning errors—something has gone wrong.

A frantic debugging session begins, and you discover that while your team was busy working on new features, another team responsible for an API you depend on changed its endpoints, and your APIs are unable to speak to one another anymore. Although the issue can be resolved by simply updating the API code with the latest

151

changes to our dependent APIs, the question remains, who is responsible for ensuring this type of issue doesn't occur again? Is it your team's responsibility to keep everyone apprised of any changes, or is the team you're dependent on responsible for informing you of changes? This is what contract testing aims to resolve.

9.1   *What contract testing is and how can it help*

Contract testing can be seen as a programmatic solution to a communication problem. Ideally, we want to encourage teams to communicate changes and requirements with one another when building integrations between APIs. However, the reality may be different. A range of factors might make it hard to easily communicate with one another, such as organizational or cultural issues that discourage teams from sharing, teams being located in different offices or countries, or a level of complexity in our platforms that makes it hard for us to see who we are impacting with our changes. Contract testing seeks to resolve or at least lessen the impact of these contributing factors by using automation frameworks to help clearly establish what integrations exist between APIs and alert us if there are breaking changes. The best way to explain how contract testing works is by representing it as a visual model, as shown in figure 9.1.

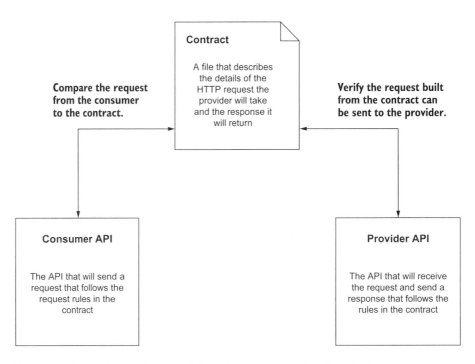

Figure 9.1   A model describing the relationship and process of contract testing

Essentially, contract testing can be broken down into the following three key components:

- *The contract*—A representation of the rules that have been set out for an HTTP request and HTTP response
- *The consumer*—One or more APIs that are using the contract to consume information from a different web API
- *The provider*—The API that uses the contract to "provide" data to different web APIs

As we learned earlier, to ensure that both the consumer and provider are integrated, the contract must be adhered to on both sides. If the consumer starts sending different data or the provider changes what data it accepts, then the integration fails. Therefore, a contract is stored separately from both the consumer and provider APIs and can be used at any point to validate that either API is still adhering to the contract.

For example, let's say we have a contract that sets out the following rules as represented as an HTTP request:

```
POST /auth/validate HTTP/1.1
Host: example.com
Content-Type: application/json

{
    "token" : "abc"
}
```

In addition to this, the contract also dictates that a response of 200 is sent back. We can implement the following tools that will use the contract as a means to validate that each API is conforming to the contract:

- For the consumer API, we validate that the HTTP request that comes from the consumer API matches all the rules set within a contract, either by intercepting the HTTP request and comparing it to the contract or by building a mock using the rules from a contract.
- For the provider API, we can build and send an HTTP request using the rules set in the contract and confirm that the expected status code is returned.

The idea behind doing this is that if either the consumer or provider APIs change, that means they no longer conform to the contract, resulting in two options for us:

- Roll back the change to conform to the contract.
- Update the contract.

If option two is selected and the contract is changed, when the other API in the relationship goes to run the contract test at a later time, it will fail. This acts as an indication that the contract between the APIs has changed and an update is required.

9.2   *Setting up a contract testing framework*

To help us learn how to implement contract testing, let's look at the integration between the booking API and the message API, which is demonstrated in figure 9.2.

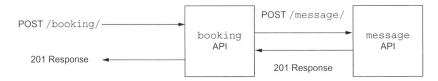

Figure 9.2   A model describing the relationship between the booking and message APIs

As we can see, the booking API is a consumer of the endpoint POST /message that the message API is the provider of. This means we first need to create a consumer contract test for the booking API before taking the results of that test to create a provider contract test for message.

Practice codebase

Throughout this activity, we'll add our contract tests into our API's codebase. A sample copy of the booking and message APIs has been added to the supporting code repository for this book that can be used to follow along, which can be found in the chapter 9 folder: http://mng.bz/DD8y. These sample APIs contain all the supporting production and test code we need to create our contract tests as well as completed versions of each contract test for reference. Before we progress, make sure you have a copy of the codebase loaded into your IDE. It is also assumed that you either have some experience with implementing API automation or have read chapter 6 of this book.

9.2.1   *Introducing Pact*

For our contract test implementation, we'll predominantly rely on the Pact tool set created by the Pact Foundation. What makes Pact a useful tool for contract testing is that it is, in fact, a series of tools that serves both consumer and provider APIs, supports most popular languages, and offers us the ability to store the resulting contracts that are shared between APIs. For example, in this activity, we'll use the following:

- Pact consumer library for the booking API
- Pact provider library for the message API
- Pact Broker for storing our contracts and API relationships

How these libraries work together can best be summarized by applying them to our original contract testing model as shown in figure 9.3, or, alternatively, you can learn more about Pact via their documentation at https://docs.pact.io.

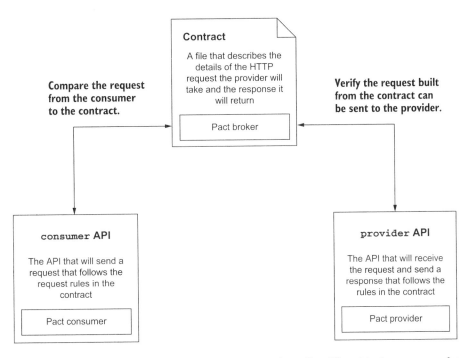

Figure 9.3 An expanded model of a contract test that shows the different tools we can use for each part of the contract testing process

First, we start by creating our consumer contract test for our booking API that, once successfully built, will create a Pact. A Pact is a JSON file that describes the rules for the HTTP request and HTTP response that consumers and providers use to integrate with one another. This will include details such as what URI it uses, what type of request body it takes, what headers to expect, and so on. Once this Pact is created, it can then be published to the Pact Broker, which stores the Pact for us to review and retrieve at a later date. With the Pact stored within the Pact Broker, we create a test in the message API that will pull down the Pact from the Pact Broker and use it to verify that the message API matches the rules within the Pact file. If it does, the provider will inform the Pact Broker that the Pact has been verified.

It can seem like a lot to take in when first establishing Pact in our codebase, but let's take it one step at a time by first implementing our consumer contract test.

9.3 *Building a consumer contract test*

As mentioned earlier, Pact has a range of tools to integrate with different languages and testing libraries. If we're using relatively common testing tools and API libraries, Pact will have the tooling to support them. Throughout all our automation activities, we've used JUnit5 as our test runner, so for our Pact consumer testing library, we'll use the JUnit5 support library by adding the following library to our pom.xml:

```
<dependency>
    <groupId>au.com.dius.pact.consumer</groupId>
    <artifactId>junit5</artifactId>
    <version>4.2.10</version>
</dependency>
```

9.3.1 *Adding Pact to our class*

With our library in place, we can now begin to establish our consumer test by creating a new class in the `example.com` called `BookingMessageContractIT`. With our class created, we add the following annotations:

```
@ExtendWith(PactConsumerTestExt.class)
@PactTestFor(providerName = "Message API", port = "3006")

@ExtendWith(SpringExtension.class)
@SpringBootTest(webEnvironment = SpringBootTest.WebEnvironment.DEFINED_PORT,
    classes = BookingApplication.class)
@ActiveProfiles("dev")
public class BookingMessageContractIT {

}
```

The `SpringExtension`, `SpringBootTest`, and `ActiveProfile` annotations, which we explored in chapter 8, are responsible for programmatically turning on the booking API before we run our automation. The other annotations, however, are new and described next:

- `@ExtendWith(PactConsumerTestExt.class)` allows JUnit to connect to Pact's features.
- `@PactTestFor` lets us establish the details of the provider API that the booking API relies upon. In this case, because our booking API relies on the message API, we name the provider as `Message API` and define what port we expect the provider to be listening on.

9.3.2 *Building the consumer check*

In chapter 8, we also looked at how we can use mocks as a means to mimic APIs we're dependent on by establishing a mocked API with all the details it requires to simulate a real API endpoint. When creating a consumer check, we follow that same mocking pattern using Pact to create our mock and define our Pact, or contract, between our two APIs. To do this, we add in the following code:

```
@Pact(consumer="Booking API", provider="Message API")
public RequestResponsePact createPact(PactDslWithProvider builder) {
    MessagePayload message = new MessagePayload(
            "Mark Winteringham",
            "test@example.com",
            "012456789156",
            "You have a new booking!",
            "You have a new booking from Mark Winteringham. They have booked
            a room for the following dates: 2021-01-01 to 2021-01-03");
```

```
    return builder
            .uponReceiving("Message")
            .path("/message/")
            .method("POST")
            .body(message.toString())
            .willRespondWith()
            .status(201)
            .toPact();
}
```

First, we declare the Pact we're creating by using the `@Pact` annotation like so:

```
@Pact(consumer="Booking API", provider="Message API")
```

This annotation defines the relationship between our consumer, the `booking API`, and the provider, the `message API`. If we were to create further Pacts in the future that contain some sort of relationship with either of our two APIs, we would use the same names that we've set out as parameters in `@Pact` so that when our Pacts were published later, they would be grouped under the same API name, making it easier to establish the relationships between each API in our platforms.

Next we create a `MessagePayload` like so:

```
MessagePayload message = new MessagePayload(
            "Mark Winteringham",
            "test@example.com",
            "012456789156",
            "You have a new booking!",
            "You have a new booking from Mark Winteringham. They have booked
            a room for the following dates: 2021-01-01 to 2021-01-03");
```

This POJO is helping us to define the structure of the request payload our `booking` API will send to the `message` API, which we then add to the `PactDslWithProvider`, along with other details that define how we expect the `message` API endpoint to be set up, like so:

```
return builder
            .uponReceiving("Message")
            .path("/message/")
            .method("POST")
            .body(message.toString())
            .willRespondWith()
            .status(201)
            .toPact();
```

As we can see, the `builder` allows us to set the following:

- *uponReceiving*—This allows us to give a natural language description of what is being sent from the consumer API to the provider API, which will be added to the Pact documentation that will go to our Pact Broker. In this instance, we're sending a simple message, so the name `Message` will do.
- *Path*—The URI for the `message` API we expect our request will go to.

- *Method*—The HTTP method we expect our request will use.
- *Body*—The request body we expect that the endpoint will use. Because we've created a basic payload structure, we're using an overridden `toString()` method that converts the `Message` POJO into the following JSON:

```
{
    "name" : "Mark Winteringham",
    "email" : "test@example.com",
    "phone" : "012456789156",
    "subject" : "You have a new booking!",
    "description" : "You have a new booking from Mark Winteringham.
    They have booked a room for the following dates: 2021-01-01 to
    2021-01-03"
}
```

Finally, we complete the definition by adding `willRespondWith()` and declaring that the provider should return with the status code `201` using `status()`. We then call `toPact()` to complete the definition that creates the Pact between the two APIs and configures the mock we will use in our contract test, which looks like this:

```
@Test
public void postBookingReturns201(){
    BookingDates dates = new BookingDates(
            LocalDate.of( 2021 , 1 , 1 ),
            LocalDate.of( 2021 , 1 , 3 )
    );

    Booking payload = new Booking(
            1,
            "Mark",
            "Winteringham",
            true,
            dates,
            "Breakfast",
            "test@example.com",
            "012456789156"
    );

    Response response = BookingApi.postBooking(payload);

    assertEquals(201, response.getStatusCode());
}
```

We're using a similar approach to what we discussed in chapter 6 to create a simple automated check that creates a booking and asserts that a positive response comes back from the booking API. But under the hood, as we saw earlier, as part of its flow, the booking API sends a message to the mocked version of the message API that we created with Pact. When we run this check, if the message being sent to the mock matches all the criteria we set in the `createPact()` method, a 201 message is sent back to the booking API to allow it to successfully complete its process and cause the check to pass. But more importantly, a JSON file is created in the target/pacts folder that documents the Pact or contract between the two APIs, as shown next:

```
{
  "consumer": {
    "name": "Booking API"
  },
  "interactions": [
    {
      "description": "Message",
      "request": {
        "body": {
          "description": "You have a new booking from Mark Winteringham. They
    have booked a room for the following dates: 2021-01-01 to 2021-01-03",
          "email": "test@example.com",
          "name": "Mark Winteringham",
          "phone": "012456789156",
          "subject": "You have a new booking!"
        },
        "method": "POST",
        "path": "/message/"
      },
      "response": {
        "status": 201
      }
    }
  ],
  "metadata": {
    "pact-jvm": {
      "version": "4.2.10"
    },
    "pactSpecification": {
      "version": "3.0.0"
    }
  },
  "provider": {
    "name": "Message API"
  }
}
```

9.3.3 *Setting up and publishing to a Pact Broker*

We've reached the point of creating a Pact that documents the contract between the `booking` and `message` APIs. Our next step might be to look to the provider API and establish the contract test for it. However, before we take that step, we need to consider how we store and share the Pact files created from our consumer contract test.

When creating a contract test for a provider API in Pact, we require the JSON files created from a consumer contract test to set the parameters against which the provider API is tested. (We'll explore this in more detail soon. For now, we simply need to understand that provider contract tests require Pact files.) This means we need to be able to store the JSON files in a location that the provider contract tests can access. This could be as simple as copying the files from target/pacts in the consumer API project to the provider API project. It becomes more complex if we're working in an organization in which teams don't necessarily have access to each other's projects, and we also have the overhead of configuring which project copies to what. Fortunately, the Pact Foundation team thought of this and created the Pact Broker.

The Pact Broker is essentially an API that stores JSON files (usually Pact files) created by our contract tests. It offers teams the ability to publish, review, and verify contracts, which is useful for the following reasons:

- *Centralized*—It offers a single point of truth as to what contracts exist between our APIs.
- *Versioning*—Pact Broker also offers the ability to version our contracts. This helps track the history of our contracts and gives consumers and providers the opportunity to select which version to use to prevent breaking changes. We also have the ability to "verify" changes, meaning we can track which proposed changes have been implemented and which have not.
- *Understanding*—By keeping all our contracts in one area, Pact Broker offers a relationship model of all our APIs to help us better understand the complexities and dependencies between each API.

Pact Brokers can be set up and run privately, which you can learn about from the Pact Broker GitHub repository (https://github.com/pact-foundation/pact_broker). However, for our project, we're going to use Pact's own implementation of their Pact Broker, Pactflow, which can be found at https://pactflow.io. Pactflow is a cloud implementation of Pact Broker that enables us to create a free project and push our Pact files to the cloud to see how a Pact Broker works.

With that in mind, the first step to getting set up with Pact Broker is to create a free "Starter Plan" at https://pactflow.io/, which will allow us to publish up to five free contracts. Once we set this up, we should have a project with its own subdomain; for example, https://restful-booker-platform.pactflow.io. The project URL is what we use to inform our projects where to send our Pacts, along with an API token to authorize our action. Before we update our project, make a note of the following:

- Your Pactflow project URL
- Your Pactflow API token (which can be found in Settings > API Tokens)

With those items noted, we next need to update our `booking` API project so that it can publish our Pacts to Pactflow, which we can do by adding this plugin to Maven:

```
<plugin>
    <groupId>au.com.dius.pact.provider</groupId>
    <artifactId>maven</artifactId>
    <version>4.1.11</version>
    <configuration>
      <pactBrokerUrl>https://restful-booker-platform.pactflow.io</pactBrokerUrl>
      <pactBrokerToken>TOKEN123</pactBrokerToken> <!-- Replace TOKEN with the
      actual token -->
      <pactBrokerAuthenticationScheme>Bearer</pactBrokerAuthenticationScheme>
    </configuration>
</plugin>
```

As we can see, we add our Pactflow project URL into the `<pactBrokerUrl>` element and our token into the `<pactBrokerToken>` element. With the plugin configured and our Pact JSON file in target/pacts, we can run the following command in our terminal to publish our Pact to Pactflow:

```
mvn pact:publish
```

Once run, we should see a positive message informing us that the publication was successful. We can also confirm that the publication has been successful by returning to Pactflow to see an unverified Integration in our Overview, similar to the one shown in figure 9.4.

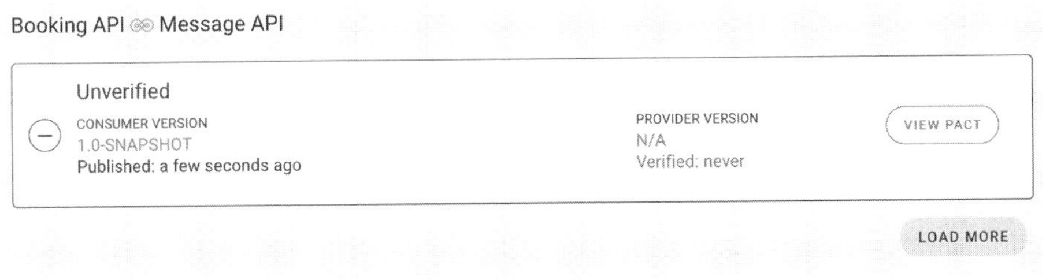

Booking API ∞ Message API

Unverified		
CONSUMER VERSION 1.0-SNAPSHOT Published: a few seconds ago	PROVIDER VERSION N/A Verified: never	VIEW PACT

LOAD MORE

Figure 9.4 Example of a published unverified contract in Pactflow

9.4 Building a provider contract test

With our consumer contract test now passing and published in Pactflow, we can now turn our attention to the provider to confirm it is following the expectations that the consumer has set out. To do this, we will

1. Configure our project to connect to our Pactflow project
2. Pull down related contracts to our provider API
3. Build and send HTTP requests based on each contract to verify that the request is accepted and the API responds in the correct manner

To help us better understand this, let's set up the `message` API with a provider contract test.

9.4.1 Building the provider contract test

As always, our first port of call is to add the necessary Pact dependency to our `mes-sage` API pom.xml, as shown here:

```
<dependency>
    <groupId>au.com.dius.pact.provider</groupId>
    <artifactId>junit5</artifactId>
    <version>4.2.10</version>
</dependency>
```

Notice that the `groupId` has changed from `au.com.dius.pact.consumer` to `au.com.dius.pact.provider`.

With the Pact library installed, we next create our test class `MessageBooking-VerifyIT` in our `com.example` package and add the following annotations to the class:

```
@Provider("Message API")
@PactBroker(url = "https://restful-booker-platform.pactflow.io",
    authentication = @PactBrokerAuth(token = "TOKEN"))

@ExtendWith(SpringExtension.class)
@SpringBootTest(webEnvironment = SpringBootTest.WebEnvironment.DEFINED_PORT,
    classes = MessageApplication.class)
@ActiveProfiles("dev")
public class MessageBookingVerifyIT {

}
```

Similar to the other test classes we've configured, we've added Spring annotations to the class to turn on the API before we begin verifying our contracts. But we've also added the following two new annotations:

- *@Provider*—This configures the name of the provider API we're running our contract tests against. Notice that we use the same name of `Message API` in this annotation as we did in our `@Pact` in the consumer contract test.
- *@PactBroker*—This configures which Pact Broker we want to connect to, including the URL of the Pact Broker (or Pactflow in our case) and our API token, which we provide using the `@PactBrokerAuth` annotation.

With our annotations added, we can set up our contract test by first adding in a `@BeforeEach` hook that will add some configuration details to our contract test, like so:

```
@BeforeEach
void before(PactVerificationContext context) {
    System.setProperty("pact.verifier.publishResults", "true");

    context.setTarget(new HttpTestTarget("localhost", 3006, "/"));
}
```

To break down this hook, we're doing two things:

- First, we're setting a system property that enables Pact to publish the results of our contract test back to Pactflow. Normally, `pact.verifier.publish-Results` is set as false, so failing to add this setting will result in any contracts in Pactflow not being verified.
- Second, we're passing a `PactVerificationContext` parameter to the hook so that we can update it with details of where the provider API is set up to run our contract tests against.

Finally, we complete the contract test by adding in the following:

```
@TestTemplate
@ExtendWith(PactVerificationInvocationContextProvider.class)
void pactVerificationTestTemplate(PactVerificationContext context) {
    context.verifyInteraction();
}
```

Unlike the consumer contract test, where we built an HTTP request and asserted the HTTP response, this time we're using JUnit5's built-in `@TestTemplate` feature and extending it with `PactVerificationInvocationContextProvider` to allow Pact to dynamically build a JUnit test for each contract in the Pact Broker that is labeled as `Message API`.

When we run the `pactVerficationTestTemplate()` method, it will download any contracts that are labeled as the Message API provider (as set by the `@Provider` annotation), create HTTP requests based on the rules that exist within the contract, and, if the expected response is returned, the contract is verified. Once the contract is verified, the details of the verification are pushed up to Pactflow, as demonstrated after a successful run in figure 9.5.

Booking API ⊘ Message API

	Successfully verified		
✓	CONSUMER VERSION 1.0-SNAPSHOT Published: 9 days ago	PROVIDER VERSION 0.0.0 Verified: 9 days ago	VIEW PACT

LOAD MORE

Figure 9.5 Example of a published verified contract in Pactflow

9.4.2 Testing out a change

We've now reached the point in which we've established a contract between the `booking` and `message` APIs. Now let's simulate a situation in which the consumer API, `booking`, changes the contract that the provider has to adhere to.

To do this, let's return to our consumer contract test in the `booking` API project and update the status code that is returned by the mock that we've established in the `createPact` method to something similar to this:

```
return builder
            .uponReceiving("Message")
            .path("/message/")
            .method("POST")
            .body(message.toString())
            .willRespondWith()
            .status(200)
            .toPact();
```

In our update, we've changed the status code from 201 to 200. A very simple change, but it will demonstrate what happens when slight changes to contracts occur, as well as their impact on API integrations. Now when we run our postBookingReturns201() contract test, we will see that our JSON file in target/pacts reflects our change with the following:

```
"response": {
  "status": 200
}
```

This is a change in our contract that needs to be pushed up to Pactflow, which we can do by running mvn pact:publish again. We can confirm the updated contract has been published because the integration is once again marked as Unverified.

Finally, now that we've made a change to the contract, we can return back to our message API project and run pactVerificationTestTemplate() again, only to find that the test logs a failure stating the following:

```
Pending Failures:

1) Verifying a pact between Booking API and Message API - Message: has status
   code 200

   1.1) status: expected status of 200 but was 201
```

As we discussed previously, this encourages us to speak with the consumer team to better understand their requirements and determine whether to update the status code to reflect what the consumer requires.

9.5   *Contract testing as part of a testing strategy*

What makes the contract testing approach novel when compared to other automated approaches is that it can be used both to confirm our assumptions about a system, similar to other automation approaches we've explored, and also to clarify misunderstandings and miscommunication between teams in a way that is similar to test API designs, albeit more limited. Our testing strategy model shows that contract testing can help us mitigate risks on the imagination side of our projects as well as confirm expectations, as shown in figure 9.6.

A failing contract test on either the consumer or provider side is an excellent opportunity to either establish a better understanding of how we expect our APIs to work together or to establish a conversation between owners of APIs. At times, the misunderstanding is a simple case of updating our code to conform to a contract, but at other times, it may lead to wider discussions, which may reveal new risks.

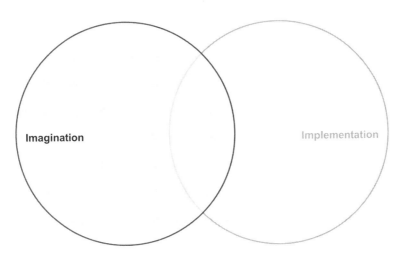

Figure 9.6 A model showing how contract testing helps supports our testing within the imagination area of a test strategy

Summary

- Contract testing is a programmatic way of ensuring the teams communicate API changes to each other.
- Contract testing works by creating a contract that is used to validate that both the consumer and the provider APIs adhere to the contract.
- A popular tool for creating contract tests is Pact, a collection of tools that allows us to run contract tests against consumer and provider APIs.
- We can also store the defined Pacts between APIs in a Pact Broker, which provides a way to store and version Pacts in a centralized location.
- When a consumer contract test passes, we publish the resulting JSON from Pact to our Pact Broker to be verified by the provider.
- We can configure a provider contract test to download contracts from a Pact Broker and use them to verify that a provider API matches those expectations.
- By changing the contract on either the consumer side or the provider side, a verified contract becomes broken and should either trigger a conversation between teams or inform the team to fix the contract.

Performance testing

10

This chapter covers

- How to manage expectations with performance testing
- How to plan and implement a performance test
- How to execute a performance test and analyze the results

Performance testing is an excellent example of why we should be motivated by quality characteristics in our testing strategy. Typically, performance is thought of as a "nonfunctional requirement," but as my colleague Richard Bradshaw once said, "If my application's features are all working, but it takes over a minute for it to respond to me when I'm using it, then it doesn't feel very functional to me."

The problem with the distinction between "functional" and "nonfunctional requirements" is that it can sometimes imply a hierarchy, or priority, over what testing to focus on first. This is why some projects end up in situations where performance testing is rushed at the end, with limited time and resources to plan, implement, execute, and analyze how our application performs in a specific context. However, if we consider performance as an equal quality characteristic to other, more "traditional" characteristics such as completeness, stability, and maintainability, we may begin to realize that performance for some contexts is a high-level quality characteristic, and it should take priority in a testing strategy.

Therefore, in this chapter, we'll not only learn what performance testing is and how to implement it as a testing activity but we'll also establish a process that enables us to iteratively manage our performance testing so that it is integral to a testing strategy.

10.1 Planning a performance test

The most common trap to fall into with performance testing is a lack of planning. Performance testing results in a lot of data to analyze and interpret. If we have no clear idea of what we want to know, how can we determine whether our product's performance is high or low quality? This, in my experience, results in situations where assumptions are made from performance testing results without any real evidence to back them up—resulting in ill-informed performance fixes and multiple test runs that show little improvement or contradictory results to previous runs.

Because performance testing requires at least a modest amount of investment in time and resources, it's important to put a plan together that considers questions such as

- What type of performance test do we want to do?
- What metrics do we want to measure during a performance test?
- What performance goals do we want our product to achieve?

10.1.1 Types of performance tests

Let's begin by digging deeper into what we mean by a *performance test* because the term is used interchangeably for a range of approaches. Depending on what we want to learn about, our product will determine what type of performance test we want to run. The most common types that are carried out include the following:

- Load tests
- Stress tests
- Soak tests
- Baseline tests

LOAD TESTS

A load test is used to help us understand how our application might behave when subjected to a reasonable or expected level of requests. During a load test, our application is subjected to a target number of requests that have either been estimated or are based on production statistics. A load test can help us assess whether our application meets performance targets for availability, concurrency or throughput, and response time (which we'll learn about soon).

Because the goal is to understand how the application works with the closest approximation to real application use, a load test will typically include delays and pauses that are experienced during interactions with our site, such as users filling in forms or other applications carrying out actions.

STRESS TESTS

Whereas a load test shows us how a product will handle an expected amount of load, a stress test seeks to push a product to its limit to understand what that limit is. Typically, a stress test will slowly ramp up the number of virtual users accessing our application until the volume of load begins to strain the application, perhaps causing it to exhibit errors or unacceptable response times for requests.

This information can help us establish the capacity of our application and determine whether that is acceptable. We might also learn what levels of capacity our application has, such as at what point the performance degrades versus the point at which an application is made unavailable. This technique can also be useful to better understand how our application might cope during attacks such as Distributed Denial of Services attacks (DDOS).

SOAK TESTS

Not all performance issues are related to the load volume an application is under. They may appear over time due to memory leaks or servers filling up with too much data. Therefore, with a soak test, the goal is to run a limited amount of load over a lengthy amount of time. Unlike load or stress tests that might run for an hour or two, a soak test might be run over many hours to attempt to trigger potential time-based performance issues that might manifest in a live situation. The goal is to see if spikes occur in later periods of a soak test in areas such as response times or hardware usage (CPU, RAM, disk I/O, etc.).

BASELINE TESTS

Baseline tests are usually run in conjunction with other types of tests, such as load and stress. Unlike other performance tests that generate a large number of virtual users, a baseline test is executed with a single virtual user for a set number of times. The information collated from this test can then be compared to load or stress test results to determine the amount of performance degradation that might occur as the load on our application increases. For example, a baseline test with a single virtual user might show that CPU usage is 30%, but when a load test is run with 100 virtual users, the CPU usage peaks at 35%. A 30% usage for a single run might not be ideal, but the comparison between results shows that the application is relatively capable of taking on load.

As we can see from these different approaches, we can acquire a range of information, from the limit of load our application can take before it fails to how it handles sustained load over a large period of time. It's not uncommon to run each type of test as part of a wider performance testing strategy, because what sets each approach apart is not *what* is being tested but the *amount of load* that is applied. As we'll learn, we can reuse performance testing scripts and simply modify the "ramp-up profile," which includes the number of virtual users we want to generate and the duration in which we want to apply them to achieve these different approaches.

10.1.2 *Types of measurements for performance tests*

Understanding the different approaches to performance testing helps us know how to apply a performance test, but we also need to be aware of the different ways in which we measure a performance test to determine success. Depending on what we want to learn about, our application will dictate what measurements we need to track. Some of the more common measurements include the following:

- *Availability*—When an application is under load, we want to ensure that it is up and its services are available. As we apply the load, we can measure whether the application is still running and available by tracking how the system responds. For example, we can measure 400 and 500 status codes to see if they start to appear when the system is under heavy load.
- *Response time*—Although availability is important, so is the speed at which an application can respond when under load. Therefore, to understand how an application responds, we can look at the time it takes for a request to be sent until the point at which a response arrives back. The longer the average response time or the longer the response times within a certain percentile are (e.g., the top 10% of response times), the slower the system is performing.
- *Throughput*—Throughput allows us to measure the rate at which application-orientated events occur or the amount of data successfully processed per time unit. For example, we could measure the number of requests that were processed within a second to see if the number increased as the load increased or whether it leveled off at a specific point.
- *Utilization*—As an application takes on load, it will use more resources, such as CPU, memory, and network bandwidth. Therefore, we might want to assess the percentage of capacity a specific resource type might use. For example, we might want to observe how much network bandwidth is being consumed by an application's traffic or the amount of memory used on a server when a thousand visitors are active. This information can also be useful to use in conjunction with the other metrics of availability, response time, and throughput to identify issues.

These are just a few of the more common measurements we might be concerned with, and many performance testing tools offer the ability to track these metrics and much more. It's tempting to track everything at once and then observe what happens at the end of a performance test. The challenge, though, is that the volume of information we get from each of these areas can be overwhelming. Therefore, establishing clear performance testing goals can help us to identify what we want to track and what we want to ignore (for now).

10.1.3 *Establishing performance testing goals and key performance indicators (KPIs)*

To create our performance testing goals, we need to be mindful of both the type of testing we want to do and what we want to measure. To help us understand this better, here are some examples of some performance testing goals we might set:

- The availability should be above 99% when 5,000 or more concurrent virtual users are connected.
- The response time average should stay under 1,000 ms when 200 concurrent virtual users are connected over a period of 24 hours.
- The network utilization should be less than 50% when 2,000 concurrent virtual users are connected.

As we can see, each goal hints toward the type of testing we want to do. Example one suggests a stress test, whereas example two might be a soak test. Each goal also clearly states quantitative goals to help us evaluate our results once a performance test has been done and determine what needs to be done next.

What will our performance goal be for restful-booker-platform? How do we determine a priority? Once again, the quality characteristics we identified as part of our strategy can play a role in determining what goals we want to set. Let's remind ourselves once again of the quality characteristics we identified. Our characteristics were

- Intuitiveness
- Completeness
- Stability
- Privacy
- Availability

To set our goal, we can think about how performance risks might impact the *stability* and *availability* of our product. If restful-booker-platform starts to send out errors when under load, these two characteristics would be negatively impacted. Therefore, our measurement might be around availability (the hint being the same word used for both the quality characteristic and measurement). With our measurement set, we would then need to determine what quantitative metrics we require to measure success. In restful-booker-platform's example, after some analysis, we might learn that

- We expect the regular number of users to be around the 40 mark because restful-booker-platform is aimed at small B&B businesses with small user bases.
- Our clients want restful-booker-platform to be available at least 95% of the time.

These details might come from conversations with users or analyzing metrics from tools that measure user behavior. From this information, we can put together a performance testing goal of

The availability should be above 95% when 40 virtual users are connected to the system.

This goal gives us an idea of the steps we now need to take when building our performance test. Perhaps we could create a load test for just the 40 virtual users, or perhaps we could stress-test the application beyond 40 users to see the true capability of our system. But before we create our test, we also need to consider what application data we want to capture to help us answer whether we've met our goal. This is why, in addition to capturing our performance goal, we also need to identify our key performance indicators.

Although measuring data that comes from a performance testing tool can help us understand the symptoms of a system under load, it doesn't necessarily share the underlying causes. To better understand why a system is behaving in a given way when under the load, it's important that we collect KPI metrics, so if we identify issues, we can do a root cause analysis of what is happening. We can also use these KPI metrics in conjunction with our performance testing tool metrics to determine whether our application is meeting our expected performance testing goals.

Examples of KPI metrics we might want to track include

- *Low-level KPIs*—Low-level KPIs focus on common resources that all software uses. This includes CPU or RAM usage, physical disk space, or I/O or network interface metrics such as bandwidth and throughput.
- *Server KPIs*—Server KPIs include any metrics that can be collected from the servers that make up our web APIs, which might include server tools such as IIS, Spring Boot, Tomcat, or Ruby on Rails.
- *Database KPIs*—If our application has some sort of persistence layer to store data, then we might want to track metrics from databases such as MySQL, Oracle, SQL Server, or NoSQL/XML. This can help us learn how much data is stored at a given time, the resources a database is using, or details on locks that are in place on specific records at certain points.

Which KPIs we track will depend on what tools and libraries we use within our applications. Therefore, some investigation is required to determine what we want to track and can track. For example, restful-booker-platform can be deployed using Docker; therefore, we have the ability to poll Docker to give us details on CPU usage, memory usage/limit, and net I/O. Knowing that these KPIs are available, we can factor those into our performance testing plan.

Tying together our performance testing goal and what KPIs we want to track will give us the detail we need to work toward. We now know what we want to measure in our performance tool as well as the other tools we require to poll and store KPI data. Our next step is to start developing the performance testing script itself that we intend to run.

Activity

Consider a performance test that you might want to run against your API platform. What would your performance test goal be? Take the time to work out the following:

- What type of test type would you run: stress, load, or soak?
- What do you want to measure: response times, availability, throughput, and so on?
- What KPIs do you want to track?

Then put together a performance testing goal you want to achieve.

10.1.4 Creating user flows

With our plan in place, our attention can turn to what exactly our performance test script will do when it's run, which requires us to plan out how our performance test script will run. Simply creating a script that lists each of our API's endpoints and then firing a large volume of load at them will not suffice (although it might help if we're considering understanding how our system would cope under a DDOS attack). The results returned would not be representative of any real-life scenario in which our product is used, which can contribute to wasteful decisions on what to fix and when to run performance tests again.

Instead, to build a performance test script that gives us relevant and valuable information, we need to be mindful of a core principle of performance testing:

> Our performance test should reflect real user behavior in our production environment as closely as is reasonably possible.

This means building a performance test script that emulates user behavior as close as possible. Although we won't always be able to exactly duplicate our user's steps and interactions, attempting to get as close as possible will result in metrics that are more accurate. We need to analyze and capture how users interact with our systems (or in the absence of user data, our expectations of how they will use it) and then use that information to capture user flows. To help us better understand what is meant by a user flow, let's look at an example that captures an admin creating a booking in our sandbox API, shown in figure 10.1.

```
User flow:        Admin makes a booking
Description:      An admin loads up the report view and makes a booking
Virtual users:    2
Injection profile: Ramp up 1 minute (1 admin per minute)
Duration:         31000 (Deviance 9500)

Step    Action                        Test Data              System time (ms)    User think time (ms)
1       Admin loads login page        None                   2000
2       Admin logs into site          None                                       5000 (Deviance 2500)
3       System logs admin into site   None                   2000
4       Admin clicks on report        None                                       2000 (Deviance 1000)
5       System returns report         <Rooms>, <Bookings>    2000
6       Admin loads up booking form   None                                       2000 (Deviance 1000)
7       System returns room details   <Rooms>                2000
8       Admin completes booking       None                                       10000 (Deviance 5000)
9       System confirms booking       None                   2000

<Rooms>
| roomNumber | roomPrice | roomId | type | image | features | description | accessible |

<Bookings>
| bookingid | checkin | checkout | depositpaid | email | firstname | lastname | phone | roomid |
```

Figure 10.1   An example user flow document that captures the flow of an admin creating a booking

The user flow can be broken into three sections:

- User flow description and load details
- User flow steps
- User flow data requirements

> **Example performance testing material**
>
> To help us learn about performance testing, a collection of example user flows, a performance testing script, and an example of performance testing results have been added to this book's supporting GitHub repository. You can view examples of a range of user flow diagrams in the Chapter 10 folder (http://mng.bz/lREj).

USER FLOW DESCRIPTION AND LOAD DETAILS

The user flow description and load details capture the name and description of the user flow as well as how much load or how many virtual users we want to apply in our performance test script. In our example user flow, the virtual user count is set very low: two virtual users. But this demonstrates that although the virtual user count is very low for this specific flow, we would expect our performance testing script to be made up of many user flows. Users interact with our system in many different ways, which means we should emulate real user interaction by capturing many different user flows. So although the virtual user count might be low right now, our performance test load will grow as we add new user flows.

The injection profile helps us capture how we want to specifically apply the load in our test. How users log on to our sites will differ depending on our context, and it isn't always the case that all our users log on at the same time. This means we can apply load with a big bang injection profile where all our load is added at the same time. Or we can have a profile in which load is applied steadily over a period of time, maybe quickly or slowly. For our example's injection profile, because the virtual user count is low, we have a short ramp-up period of one virtual user being added per minute.

Finally, the duration calculates the estimated time it takes for one cycle of a user flow to run with randomized deviance applied (more on that shortly). We can use this estimate to help us calculate how long we might think the performance test will take to run. When running our performance test, we have the option to set our user flows to loop indefinitely until we manually shut down our test. Or we might want it to stop after a user flow cycle is complete. If we choose the latter, we can use the duration along with the injection profile to learn how long we expect the user flow to take. For our example user flow, we would expect it to run for between 1 minute 31 seconds and 1 minute 45 seconds. Given that this is quite a short time for our performance test to run, we'll opt to run the user flows indefinitely for 10 minutes and then exit the script manually.

USER FLOW STEPS

The steps within a user flow allow us to capture each behavior we expect the user to do as well as how the system will behave. Look at one of the user steps, for example:

Admin completes booking

We can see that the step is designed to give us an indication of what we expect the user to do, but it doesn't go into granular detail. This allows us to capture expectations in our user flows from both technical and business team members. The step gives us enough information on what we need to capture in our performance test script. In the case of the example step, we'll need to send an HTTP request to `POST /booking/`. But it doesn't become so detailed that it becomes hard to read or maintain.

Each step also has details about what test data is required. Supporting data is an important factor in a performance test, so being able to identify what we need up front can save us time as we build our performance testing script. To ensure the steps table is easy to read, the test data columns contain references to data requirements which are then detailed below the steps. So, for example, with the step

System returns room details

we can see it requires test data of `<Rooms>` to send back. The column can be used to capture test data that is required to be in the system when the script starts or test data that the performance test script will use during the test that might be stored in .csv files or similar.

Finally, we have the system think time and user think time. Each column captures our estimates for how long we want the application to take to respond or how long the user will take to send a request. For the system think time column, each step has a generic 2000 ms because, at this time, we don't know how long the system will actually respond, so we add in a conservative estimate that is acceptable. The user think time is slightly different. Because we want our scripts to be representative of our users, we need to add in wait times that are similar to user behavior. No user is going to make all the requests required for a cycle one after another in less than 10 ms. Attempting that in a script will give us inaccurate results. Instead, we want to add wait times to steps that represent the time it takes a user (or other applications, depending on our context) to form a request and send it. Therefore, we add in an estimated time, plus a deviance time, which means with an example of user time such as

5000 (Deviance 2500)

we expect a user to take between 2.5–7.5 seconds to send their request. This variability is because not all users will interact in the same amount of time, and although this means no performance test run will truly be the same, it does add more realism.

USER FLOW DATA REQUIREMENTS

At the bottom of the user flow, we can then map out our data requirements in more detail. The titles of each data set are used as references in the user flow steps to make it clearer what we require. This is useful for clearly planning out what test data we require and can give us an indication of how to generate it. For example, when creating `<Bookings>`, I used a tool called Mockaroo (https://www.mockaroo.com/), which offers different random data sets to use. For example, if I can see that I require a phone number for my booking, I can use the phone number randomizer in Mockaroo to create my required data.

Once we have a finished user flow, we should have a clearer idea of what we require in our performance test script, such as

- The steps that will be taken during the user flow cycle
- The approximate timing of a user flow cycle to help time your performance test
- What data we require when the application is set up to have a performance test run against it
- What input data requirements we need when we run the performance test script; for example, booking details

These are all essential to planning our performance test script, but the true benefits of capturing user flows are that it allows us to begin to establish what our performance tests will do while production code is being developed, and it also allows us to iterate on our planning.

Ideally, we want our performance test scripts to evolve as our product evolves. Capturing user flows gives us a source of information on what our performance tests do that we can iterate over as new changes come in. Rather than wait for everything to be built up front and then run our first performance test, we have the opportunity to build up our user flows as our system does. For example, imagine that our sandbox API was still being built and we could only create a booking. We would capture the user flow for booking and execute a performance test based on that. Then, when the branding feature is created, we can create a new user flow for branding and add that to our performance testing script. This enables us to take an iterative approach to our performance tests in which we react to changes as we build our system and learn more.

> **Activity**
>
> A performance testing script is made up of multiple user flows, meaning we require more of them. Try creating a new user flow script for the guest booking flow in which a guest logs on to the site, finds a room, and makes a booking. You can compare your user flow with the additional example flows in the chapter 10 folder of the supporting repository (http://mng.bz/WM1x).

10.2 Implementing a performance test

With our user flows in place, we're now ready to translate the flow into a performance testing script. To do this, we'll go through each step required to implement our example user flow that emulates an admin creating a booking.

10.2.1 Setting our performance testing tool

Our performance testing tool of choice will be Apache JMeter, which is an open source performance testing tool that comes with a range of plugins and tools that we can take advantage of. Although a number of performance testing tools are available to use, both paid for and free, JMeter has been supported for more than 20 years (the first release was in 1998) and contains all the tools we need to create our performance test, such as

- HTTP samplers to make requests
- Variable management
- Cookie and HTTP header managers
- Logic controllers
- CSV data loaders

We'll take advantage of all of these as we build our script.

DISTRIBUTED SETUP

One of the challenges when working with performance testing is the resource requirements for creating load. A performance test will use a considerable amount of CPU, RAM, and network I/O, which can pose a problem if we attempt to run our script with limited resources. If a performance test doesn't have the necessary resources to run, it can impact our results. For example, if a performance test maxes out the network I/O, we may start recording high response rates, which is not the fault of the system under test but of our performance test harness.

We want to ensure that the results that come from our performance test are accurate. To counter the resource problem, we can leverage another feature of JMeter, which is running our performance test scripts in a distributed architecture, as summarized in figure 10.2.

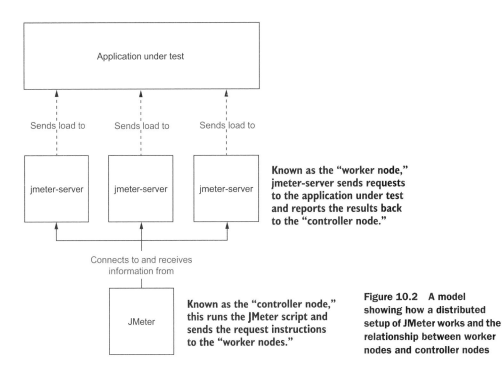

Figure 10.2   A model showing how a distributed setup of JMeter works and the relationship between worker nodes and controller nodes

A distributed model allows us to connect multiple jmeter-servers that are connected to an instance of JMeter. Typically, each jmeter-server is deployed on its own server, separate from others, and then connected to our main JMeter application via a network. This allows us to run our performance testing script from our main JMeter instance, which will then send instructions to each jmeter-server instance to generate load and send requests to the system under test. Each jmeter-server, once it has received a response, will send the information back to the main JMeter instance to be stored as results. This means we can create a test harness that generates load in a way that prevents resource overload and further ensures the accuracy of our results.

Working with distributed setups

When using jmeter-server, we have to be mindful of a few things. The distributed pattern works by having our main JMeter instance send a copy of our performance testing script to each instance of jmeter-server connected. This means when we set the number of virtual users for a specific flow in our performance test script, we have to divide it by the number of jmeter-servers we have. We also need to ensure that any supporting data files such as CSV files are copied across because jmeter-server will look locally for them and not via the network connection to the main JMeter application.

You can learn more about how a distributed setup works and how to create one from the Apache JMeter documentation (http://mng.bz/BZ5v). But for now, let's get JMeter installed and running.

INSTALLATION

As mentioned earlier, JMeter is an open source application and can be downloaded for free at http://jmeter.apache.org/download_jmeter.cgi. We will require the binary version, so download either the .zip or .tgz version of the application, and extract the contents, once downloaded, into a folder. Then move the folder to wherever you like to keep your applications.

With JMeter extracted, we simply need to run the application by opening the JMeter folder, followed by the `bin` folder. (You can either do this in a command prompt/terminal or via Explorer/Finder/etc.) Depending on your operating system, you then have the option to start up JMeter. For Windows systems, we can run `jmeter.bat`, and for Mac or Linux based systems, `jmeter.sh`. Once the `jmeter` script runs, we'll eventually be presented with a blank JMeter Test Plan, which we can begin to fill in to create our performance test script.

10.2.2 Building our performance test script

We're now ready to build our performance test script, starting with configuring our Test Plan and Thread Groups.

TEST PLAN AND THREAD GROUPS

The root of our JMeter is a Test Plan, in which everything that our script will execute lives under. Our first step is to click the Test Plan in the left-hand panel to call up its details in the larger, right-hand panel. Here we will update the Test Plan name to *Example performance test script*, and we'll add the following two User-Defined Variables, as shown in figure 10.3:

- Name: server, Value: localhost
- Name: port, Value: 80

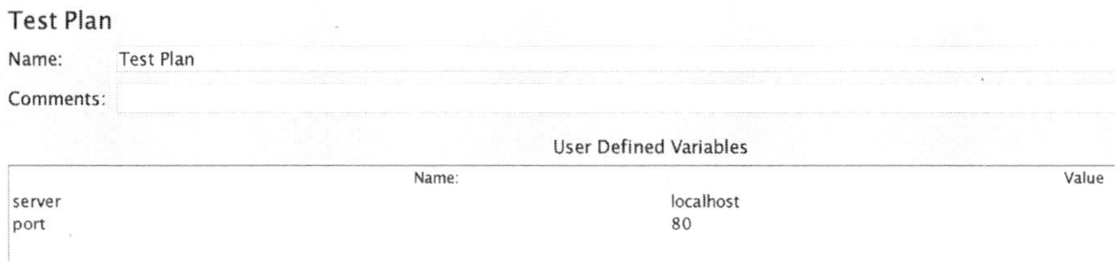

Test Plan

Name:	Test Plan
Comments:	

User Defined Variables	

Name:		Value
server	localhost	
port	80	

Figure 10.3   A screenshot of the JMeter Test Plan element

We'll come back to the variables soon, but that gives us everything we need to start adding Thread Groups to our Test Plan.

Thread Groups sit under our Test Plan and are responsible for organizing our user flows and configuring the amount of load a user flow might have. As we discussed earlier, a performance testing script will have multiple user flows being executed at once to emulate the many ways in which users will interact with our application. Therefore, it's not uncommon for a JMeter Test Plan to have many Thread Groups, each of which will contain a specific user flow.

We will explore more about how we configure Thread Groups later when the time comes to prepare our performance test run. For now, all we need to do is create a Thread Group by right-clicking the Test Plan in the left-hand panel to call up the menu and then selecting Add > Threads > Thread Group. We'll then name it by clicking the Thread Group and updating the name to *Admin makes a booking*, as shown in figure 10.4.

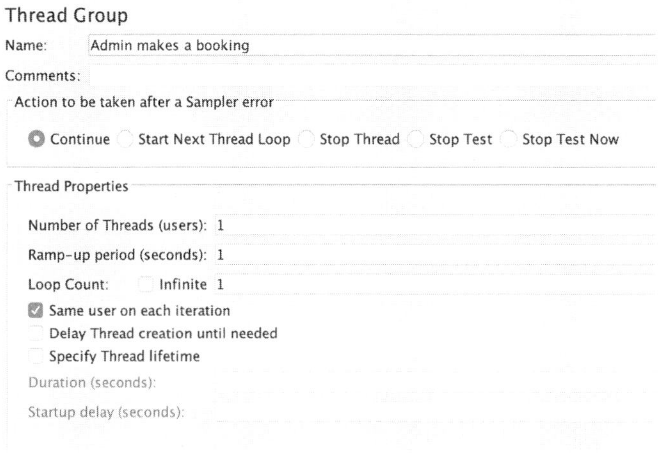

Thread Group

Name:	Admin makes a booking
Comments:	

Action to be taken after a Sampler error

○ Continue   ○ Start Next Thread Loop   ○ Stop Thread   ○ Stop Test   ○ Stop Test Now

Thread Properties

Number of Threads (users):	1
Ramp-up period (seconds):	1
Loop Count:	☐ Infinite 1

☑ Same user on each iteration
☐ Delay Thread creation until needed
☐ Specify Thread lifetime

Duration (seconds):

Startup delay (seconds):

Figure 10.4   A screenshot of the JMeter Thread Group element

Adding elements in JMeter

Throughout this example, we'll add many elements to our Test Plan. To make it explicit, elements such as HTTP samplers, logic controllers, and Config elements can be added to a JMeter Test Plan by either selecting an element in the left-hand panel and selecting Edit > Add in the main menu, or by right-clicking an element in the left-hand panel and clicking Add. Either approach will add your element as a child element.

Next, we need to add in requests that emulate an admin logging in to the application and then making a booking. To help us structure these two actions, we'll create two simple logic controllers to store our HTTP requests. The simple logic controller can be found in Add > Logic Controller > Simple Controller. With our controllers created, we rename them to the following, as shown in figure 10.5:

Figure 10.5   A screenshot of the JMeter Test Plan and how simple controllers are added under the Thread Group named "Admin makes a booking"

- Log into admin
- Admin makes booking

This gives us the structure we need to start adding in our HTTP requests.

HTTP HEADER MANAGER

Before we start adding in our HTTP requests, we'll streamline our plan by creating an HTTP Header Manager directly under the Thread Group (not inside one of the simple controllers) by navigating to Add > Config Element > HTTP Header Manager. The HTTP Header Manager allows us to configure what HTTP headers are added to any HTTP requests that we'll add to our Thread Group. We will add the following HTTP headers into the HTTP Header Manager, as shown in figure 10.6:

- Host: `${server}:${port}`
- Accept: `application/json`
- Accept-Language: `en-GB,en;q=0.5`
- Accept-Encoding: `gzip, deflate, br`
- Content-Type: `application/json`

HTTP Header Manager

Name: HTTP Header Manager

Comments:

Headers Stored in the Header Manager

Name:	Value
Host	${server}:${port}
Accept	application/json
Accept–Language	en–GB,en;q=0.5
Accept-Encoding	gzip, deflate, br
Content-Type	application/json

Figure 10.6   A screenshot of the JMeter HTTP Header Manager element

Every request we will send will have these headers automatically added. This means we don't have to add HTTP headers to each request unless we want to.

Additionally, notice how the Host header we've added has a value of `${server}:${port}`. These are JMeter variables, and they match up to the server and port variables we set in the Test Plan. Because we set the server variable to `local-host` and the port variable to `80`, when our script is run, `${server}:${port}` will translate into `localhost:80`. Using variables in this manner makes updating our script to use different environments easier.

LOGIN INTO ADMIN

With our HTTP Header Manager configured, let's add our first HTTP request into the `Login into admin` simple controller by selecting Add > Sampler > HTTP Request. The HTTP Request sampler is where we can configure an HTTP request and set details such as HTTP methods, URIs, request bodies, and so on.

Our first request is to emulate an admin attempting to validate whether they're logged in (which of course, they're not), so we add the following details:

- Name: `POST /auth/validate`
- Server name or IP: `${server}`
- Port number: `${port}`
- HTTP Request: `POST`
- Path: `/auth/validate`

We also need to select `Body Data` and add an empty object of `{}` because we don't have a token to send to validate, as shown in figure 10.7.

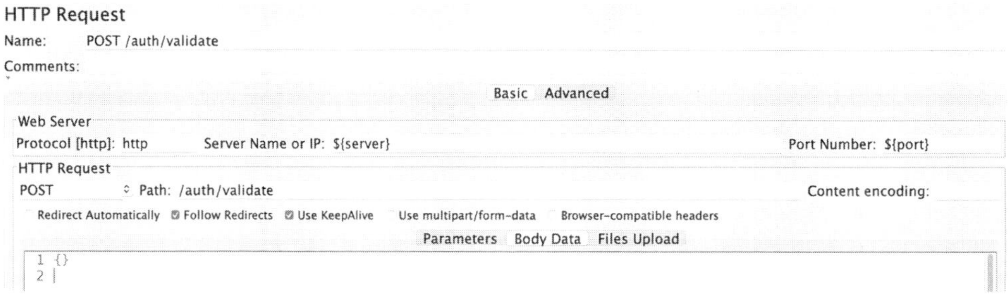

HTTP Request

Name: POST /auth/validate

Comments:

Basic   Advanced

Web Server
Protocol [http]: http   Server Name or IP: ${server}   Port Number: ${port}

HTTP Request
POST   ◇ Path: /auth/validate   Content encoding:

Redirect Automatically   ☑ Follow Redirects   ☑ Use KeepAlive   Use multipart/form-data   Browser-compatible headers

Parameters   Body Data   Files Upload

```
1 {}
2 |
```

Figure 10.7   A screenshot of the JMeter HTTP Request element

Next, we add in the remaining HTTP Request samplers we require for the login process:

- Name: `POST /auth/login`
- Server name or IP: `${server}`
- Port number: `${port}`
- HTTP Request: `POST`

- Path: /auth/login
- Body Data:

```
{
    "username":"admin",
    "password":"password"
}
```

Then add a request loading a message count:

- Name: GET /message/count
- Server name or IP: ${server}
- Port number: ${port}
- HTTP Request: GET
- Path: /message/count

And finally, we add a request for rooms:

- Name: GET /room/
- Server name or IP: ${server}
- Port number: ${port}
- HTTP Request: GET
- Path: /room/

Performance testing GraphQL APIs

Once again, because GraphQL works predominantly with HTTP, we can use HTTP samples to send GraphQL queries by updating the body data to contain a GraphQL query rather than a straight JSON object.

This all becomes a bit trickier when attempting to parse responses, but fortunately, JMeter is currently expanding its GraphQL features.

This gives us all the requests to emulate an admin logging in to our application. But we have one last element to add to the POST /auth/validate and the GET /room/ samplers, which are Constant Timers.

By adding a Constant Timer via Add > Timers > Constant Timer as a child element to a request, we're simulating the user wait time we captured in our user flow. For example, if we add a Constant Timer to POST /auth/validate and in the Thread Delay field we add ${__Random(2500,7500)}, we're adding in a randomized time delay in which the script will wait between 2.5–7.5 seconds before executing the request, as shown in figure 10.8.

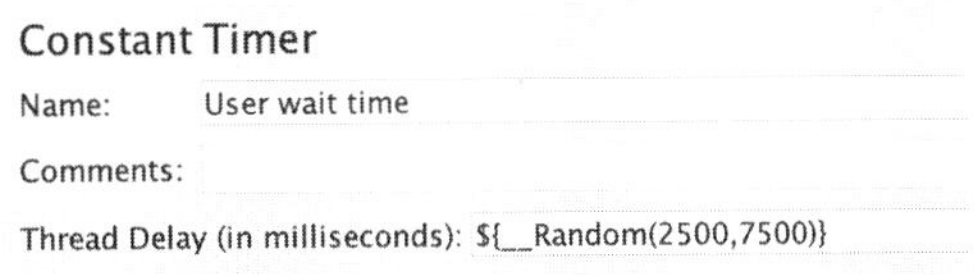

Constant Timer

Name: User wait time

Comments:

Thread Delay (in milliseconds): ${__Random(2500,7500)}

Figure 10.8 A screenshot of the JMeter Constant Timer element

To complete this section of the script, we add another Constant Timer to GET /room/ with a Thread Delay of ${__Random(1000,3000)}, which completes the first simple controller.

ADMIN MAKES A BOOKING

Next, we turn our attention to the "Admin makes a booking" controller. For this, we want to simulate getting a report to see currently available bookings, followed by room details, and then make a booking. We start by adding in the two following GET requests, the first being for /report/:

- Name: GET /report/
- Server name or IP: ${server}
- Port number: ${port}
- HTTP Request: GET
- Path: /report/

The second is for /room/:

- Name: GET /room/
- Server name or IP: ${server}
- Port number: ${port}
- HTTP Request: GET
- Path: /room/

This leaves us with our last request, which is to create a booking in the system. For this request, we require some additional elements to be added to our performance test script, starting with an HTTP request with the following details:

- Name: POST /booking/
- Server name or IP: ${server}
- Port number: ${port}
- HTTP Request: POST
- Path: /booking/

Next, we select the Body Data option and then add the following JSON object:

```
{
    "depositpaid": ${depositpaid},
    "firstname": "${firstname}",
    "lastname": "${lastname}",
    "roomid": 2,
    "bookingdates": {
        "checkin": "${checkin}",
        "checkout": "${checkout}"
    }
}
```

Notice how the majority of the values in this object are JMeter variables—for example, ${depositpaid}—and not hardcoded values. Once again, this is because we want to emulate real user behavior, and real admins or guests won't add in the same booking multiple times (plus, there are constraints in the application to allow duplicate bookings).

Therefore, we need to ensure that each time the `POST /booking` request is called in the thread, new booking details are sent. We can do this by data driving the request with a CSV file, configuring the request to pick a new row of data from a CSV each time it runs. This means we first need to create a CSV file with data that looks something like this sample data:

```
Silvie,Alyonov,salyonov0@wikispaces.com,92511364701,false,2020-01-01,2020-01-02
Ambros,Eary,aeary1@ox.ac.uk,41789748281,true,2020-01-03,2020-01-04
```

Each row contains a randomly generated first name, last name, email address, phone number, deposit paid, and check-in and checkout date. A normal CSV would have hundreds or thousands of these rows of data for JMeter to use, typically generated by tools—for example, a combination of Mockaroo and Excel.

Once we've created our CSV file and stored it in the same folder as our JMeter folder, we then add the CSV Data Set Config element into the "Admin makes booking" controller by selecting Add > Config Element > CSV Data Set Config. This config element allows us to import our CSV file and declare variables to use. In our CSV Data Set Config element, we'll set the following details, as shown in figure 10.9:

- Filename: `./bookings.csv` (or whatever you've named your .csv file)
- File encoding: `utf-8`
- Variable names: `firstname,lastname,email,phone,depositpaid, checkin,checkout`

CSV Data Set Config

Name:	CSV Data Set Config
Comments:	

Configure the CSV Data Source

Filename:	./bookings.csv
File encoding:	utf-8
Variable Names (comma-delimited):	firstname,lastname,email,phone,depositpaid,checkin,checkout
Ignore first line (only used if Variable Names is not empty):	False
Delimiter (use '\t' for tab):	,
Allow quoted data?:	False
Recycle on EOF ?:	True
Stop thread on EOF ?:	False
Sharing mode:	All threads

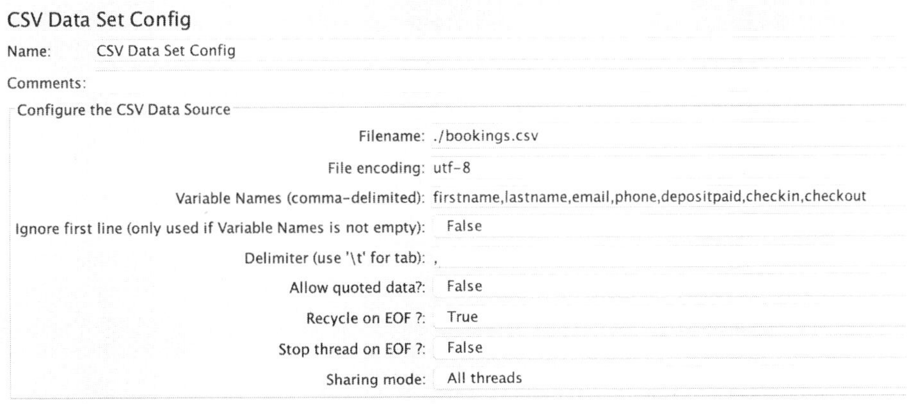

Figure 10.9   A screenshot of the JMeter CSV Data Set Config element

Notice how the comma-delimited fields in Variable Names match up with the columns in the CSV file and that the names of the variables match the variables used in the Body Data object. This means that, for example, if the first row of the CSV file has the first name `Silvie` when the performance test is run, the first booking that is sent in this Thread Group will add `Silvie` to the Body Data for `POST /booking/`, and when the second booking is sent, it will use the second row, which is `Ambros`, thus ensuring each booking that is sent will differ from one another.

Finally, to complete the script, we add Constant Timers to the following requests to emulate wait times:

- `GET /room/:` `${__Random(2500,7500)}`
- `POST /booking:` `${__Random(5000,5000)}`

This completes the user flow for our performance testing script, but we still need to configure JMeter so that it outputs the required metrics.

LISTENERS

At the moment, our performance test script has all the details we need to generate load against our web APIs. However, it's not storing those results anywhere at this time. To resolve this, we need to add Listener elements to the Test Plan. Specifically, we want to add two listeners directly under the Test Plan so that it captures all the metrics from each Thread Group. The listeners we want are as follows:

- *View Results Tree*—A listener that shows detailed results of every request and response that is sent. This is useful for debugging issues with a performance test script.
- *Summary Report*—A listener that groups information around response times, errors, and throughput based on each HTTP request sampler name. For instance, if there are many requests named `POST /booking` across multiple Thread Groups, their metrics are stored together. This is useful for grouping and exporting response times together based on endpoints for future analysis.

Each listener can be found by selecting Add > Listener, and as we'll see, there is a range of listeners that we could take advantage of. However, given that our goal is to measure status codes, the summary report will suffice. One final thing to configure is in the filename field in the Summary Report: we need to add in a filename such as jmeter-results.csv. This ensures that when the performance test script is run, the results are saved.

Turning off View Results Tree

View Results Tree listeners are excellent tools for debugging issues with performance test scripts. They provide a lot of detail on each request, as well as visualizations of successful and unsuccessful requests. However, because of this, the View Results Tree listener is a resource-intensive element, and it's advised by JMeter that when running a performance test, it is turned off. To do this, we simply need to right-click it and select Toggle, which will disable the listener and gray it out in the left-hand panel view.

> **Activity**
>
> As we've learned, performance test scripts contain multiple user flows. So far, we've added one for an admin making a booking, but there are more flows we can add to our script to run. For this activity, take the user flow you created in the previous activity of this chapter, add a new Thread Group to your JMeter Test Plan, and create the necessary elements to cover the user flow. Once again, you can get support by reviewing either the example flows or the JMeter script found in the chapter 10 folder of the supporting repository (http://mng.bz/WM1x).

RUNNING A DRESS REHEARSAL

Since our scripts are designed to replicate complex user behaviors, they understandably become complex themselves. Therefore, it's sensible to run a dress rehearsal before running the performance test properly. A dress rehearsal usually consists of running a performance test script with all the necessary data loaded into the script and the system, but with only one virtual user per Thread Group. By running it with a small amount of load, we can weed out any issues around Thread Groups interfering with one another or errors in our configurations. For example, when running a dress rehearsal for the example test script in the supporting repository, a series of 400 errors appeared. It turned out that one Thread Group was deleting rooms that another Thread Group was trying to send bookings to.

To save the headache of having a performance test script fail due to script errors, consider running a dress rehearsal each time considerable changes are made to a performance test script.

10.3 Executing and measuring a performance test

With our performance test script now in place, it's time to consider some additional factors we need to address before we run our performance test and analyze the results.

10.3.1 Preparing and executing our performance test

Before each performance test we want to run, we need to take a few steps to ensure our results are accurate. Let's look at what they are and why they matter.

PREPARING THE ENVIRONMENT UNDER TEST

Much like our goal with our performance test script was to emulate user behavior as closely as possible, it's important that our application is deployed in a manner that replicates a live environment as much as possible. Once again, this is to ensure that our results are as accurate as feasible. For example, if our application is deployed using tools such as Kubernetes, Docker, Ansible, or Puppet, which employ sophisticated infrastructures with scalable containers, load balancers, and database synchronization, running the performance test against a version of the application that is sitting on a lone server with limited resources is not going to be very accurate. We need to ensure that our performance test environment matches production as closely as possible within constraints such as project time and budgets.

In addition to ensuring that the infrastructure matches up, we also need to be aware of other items that make an application as close to live as possible, such as the following:

- *Loading up databases*—Databases aren't typically empty when users use our systems. Therefore, adding an expected average amount of data into the database will help increase accuracy.
- *Warming up caches*—A similar rule applies to caching. Users won't always hit an uncached system, so an initial run through the system with a tool or manually updating caches can also contribute to accuracy.
- *Cycling/loading up queues*—If there are scheduled events that take place in our system, having them up and running in a sensible fashion can help, for instance, by not turning on all queue processing at the same time.

These are just a few examples of ways we need to prepare our application for performance testing. By discussing our performance testing requirements with the team, we can learn more, which brings us to our next important step.

NOTIFYING STAKEHOLDERS

Imagine we're at the point of running our performance test. Our environment infrastructure is in place, and our application is deployed and configured. We start to run the performance test only to discover that someone has deployed an update to the environment or is running their testing and has changed the data we're reliant on. This is incredibly frustrating and a waste of time. This is why we take the time before we run a performance test to notify everyone who has some access or claim to the environment that we're performance testing against. Clearly communicating to each of these people when we intend to run a performance test, how long it will take, and that we will let them know when it's complete can save us from failed test runs that result in repeat testing or, worse, inaccurate data.

FINAL SETUP AND EXECUTION

Once everything is set up with the environment we intend to performance test and everyone is notified, we're ready to begin. All that is left for us to do is to set up our performance test harness and begin the performance test. This might include items such as the following:

- *Setting up a distributed framework*—As we discussed earlier, JMeter can run in a distributed setup, which allows us to create multiple jmeter-servers that we can use to generate load from a central instance of JMeter. Therefore, if we want to use this setup, we need to establish each instance of jmeter-server and configure JMeter to connect to them.
- *Review test data files*—We will need to make sure that all our necessary CSV files are in a location that our JMeter script can find. This might mean copying

necessary files to distributed jmeter-servers or making sure that the most up-to-date data files have been created.

- *Turn on monitoring tools*—Although our performance test tool will capture details based on each request sent, we'll likely need to collect other metrics as well. This means setting up tools to monitor KPIs such as system, server, and database metrics and ensuring they're collecting information for future analysis.
- *Configure Thread Groups*—Our Thread Groups will need configuring so that they generate our desired load. For example, for our "Admin creates a booking" Thread Group, we need to update the following fields based on the details we captured in our user flow:
  - Number of Threads: 2
  - Ramp-up period: 120 seconds
  - Loop Count: Infinite (so that we can manually exit our performance test script after a set amount of time)
- *Update the environment*—We parameterized the server and port options for our JMeter script so that we can quickly update them in the test plan to point to a specific environment. We should check to make sure they are pointing to the right environment, and if they're not, update them.

Once we're confident that everything is set up, we can begin our test run. A final thing to be aware of when using JMeter is to ensure it is run in headless mode and not via its UI mode. This is recommended by the JMeter team because running in UI mode is resource-intensive and may impact the accuracy of our results (again). So, we run it via a command-line interface, like so:

```
jmeter -n -t ./example-performance-test.jmx -l ./perfstats.csv
```

This will run our performance test script in CLI mode and output metrics into a file named perfstats.csv. Once it's time to finish the test, we manually exit the performance test, close down our monitoring tools, and collect the metrics for further analysis.

Activity

Running a performance test with our example performance test script against a fully deployed instance of restful-booker-platform with a distributed JMeter setup is a lot to take on as a first step. For an initial performance test to understand how they run and give us sample metrics to work with, run the sandbox API locally, and try to run JMeter in CLI mode for 5 minutes, along with a tool to measure your system's CPU.

10.3.2 *Analyzing results*

With our performance test now complete, next comes what is arguably the hardest part of a performance test: analyzing the test results to determine whether there are issues that require diagnosing. This is a difficult activity because typically the metrics we measure display symptoms of an issue rather than the issue itself. Add to this the numerous ways in which the performance of an application can be impacted, and it can be difficult to capture common issues. However, here are a few ways in which we can compare our performance test script data with KPI data to highlight areas for further investigation.

RESPONSE TIME MEASUREMENT

Response times can be measured against the number of users connected at a specific point in time during a performance test. If the application shows high response times, we may need to check the server and network KPIs to help determine whether an area of our application is using too many resources at that point.

THROUGHPUT AND CAPACITY

Reports showing how much data or transactions have been handled are measured against the number of users connected throughout the test. This can display how much data an application can process in a given time. It can display how fast an application can process an amount of data in a given time and highlight reductions in throughput, which might indicate that users are waiting to connect but are unable to do so.

MONITORING KPI: NETWORK

Network KPIs can be used to measure the amount of traffic coming in and out of an application. If we can see more traffic coming out of our application than is going into it, we might have issues around caching or larger-than-expected files being sent.

MONITORING KPI: SERVER

The KPIs we have set in our requirements can also be used to diagnose issues or measure whether our application is performant. For example, server KPIs, such as CPU and memory usage, may show a gradual increase or sudden jump in loss of performance, which may be due to different issues.

ERROR REPORTING

Measuring status codes such as 404, 503, and 500 can help show when a server may have become unresponsive. We can combine this information with other KPIs to understand the state of the system when error codes start to appear.

This brings us to our application and analysis of a performance test that I ran. First, let's recap the performance requirement we set out:

> The availability should be above 95% when 40 virtual users are connected to the application.

To help us determine whether our application meets this expectation, we can graph the percentage of error codes found in the last 30 requests throughout the test using the performance test results, as shown in figure 10.10.

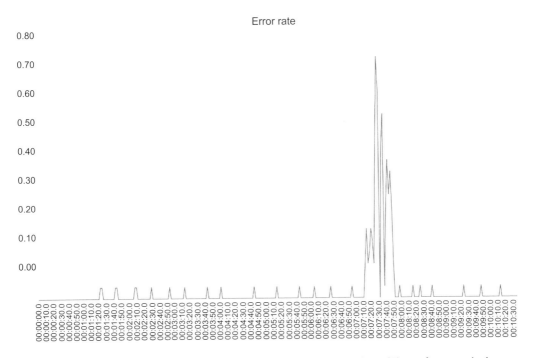

Figure 10.10   A graph showing the response time's track over the time of the performance test

We can also graph the CPU usage from our web APIs over time, as shown in figure 10.11.

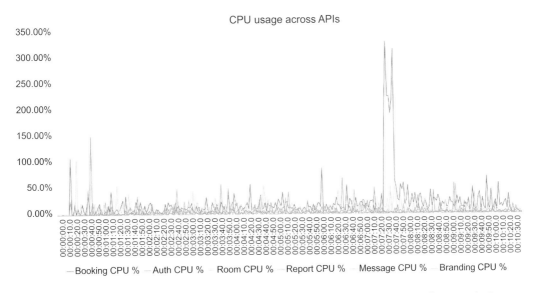

Figure 10.11   A graph showing CPU usage from each API over the time of the performance test

As we can see, there is a considerable spike around the 7.5-minute mark. It appears that the spike appears in both the response time and the `booking` API CPU usage (the CPU usage being the larger of the two spikes), which is more clearly shown in figure 10.12.

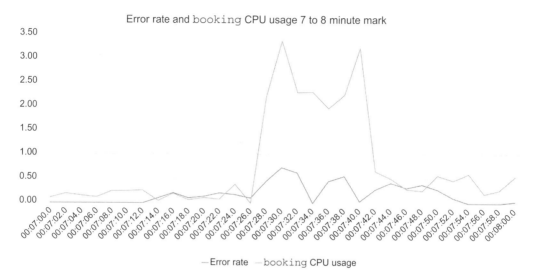

Figure 10.12   Graph showing more details of the response time and CPU usage

This gives us an indication that when the `booking` API spikes in CPU usage when under load, the API starts to error and means we don't meet our intended performance requirement. The team would need to take a look at the `booking` API in more detail to determine what is contributing to the heavy CPU use and resolve it.

STARTING AGAIN

As we've gone through this chapter, we've explored many aspects of performance testing that require planning. And although the initial setup requires a noticeable amount of investment, by iterating our user flows and performance test scripts, we have the ability to slowly grow our performance testing out alongside our application, which means a quicker turnaround for feedback from performance tests.

10.4   *Setting performance testing expectations*

Performance testing as a concept highlights how we can view our products from different perspectives. Regardless of whether we're testing to learn about the performance of a product or if the product has explicit requirements, we're still working with the same product. What changes is our mindset and motivations toward what we're hoping to learn. That's why if we apply performance testing to our test strategy model, as demonstrated in figure 10.13, it appears to cover areas of our model that are similar to those covered by activities such as exploratory testing or automation.

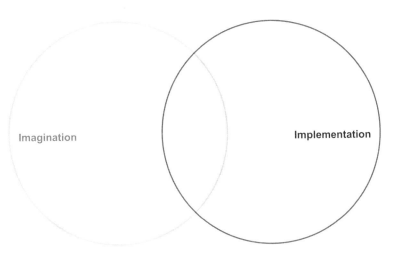

Figure 10.13   An example of the test strategy model, which demonstrates how performance testing focuses on the implementation side

However, by looking at our application from different perspectives, our considerations of what risks we need to mitigate can change. These perspectives, as mentioned earlier, can be driven by a user's idea of quality. A product that has working and correct features but poor performance can be a deal-breaker for some, which is why, if such a quality characteristic matters to our users, we need to be actively learning about the performance of our products as early as possible.

Summary

- Performance testing offers a way to discover information about a product that differs from other testing activities.
- The common types of performance testing include baseline, load, stress, and soak testing.
- We can measure statistics to determine the availability, response times, throughput, and utilization of an application.
- A clear performance testing goal is required to determine success when analyzing our performance testing results.
- Key performance indicators help us understand how our system behaves during a performance test and debug issues.
- We can track KPIs such as low-level KPIs, server KPIs, and database KPIs.
- When outlining a performance testing script, we want it to reproduce user steps as closely as is reasonably possible.
- We can plan out how to reproduce user behavior by creating user flow documents that capture the behavior of a user and our system.
- Apache JMeter is an open source performance testing tool that contains all the necessary features to create a performance testing script.

- We build a JMeter performance test script by adding Group Threads, HTTP Request samplers, Logic Controllers, Constant Timers, and Config elements.
- Our application should be as close to live as possible when performance-testing it.
- Analyzing results requires us to compare results from our performance test with KPI data to reveal issues that require resolution.

Security testing

This chapter covers

- The similarities in skill sets for those working in testing or security-focused fields
- Detecting security threats using modeling
- How to apply a security mindset to a range of testing activities

For some, the idea of security testing can conjure up images of individuals carrying out highly technical and complex attacks that discover unimaginable exploits in our systems. Although having knowledge of how systems work, how they can be exploited, and how to use tools to discover threats is a key ingredient to successful security testing, incorrect assumptions about security testing promote the idea that it is an exclusive club open only to those with superhuman technical skills. However, security testing isn't just about "hacking systems"; it requires intentional planning and analysis to detect threats and prioritize them. All of this involves a wide range of activities, skills, and techniques, some of which we've already learned in previous chapters.

If we take the time to explore the motivations and activities of those working in the security space, we find a great degree of overlap with what we've learned so far. Those who are involved in security testing are trying to discover and mitigate risks that might impact the quality of our products. The core difference is that security testing focuses on quality characteristics that revolve around security and privacy. By appreciating this similarity, we can begin our journey toward adopting a security mindset into our testing. As we'll discover, we can reuse the planning approaches and modeling techniques we've learned in previous chapters to help us carry out testing activities focusing on security.

Before we begin

Throughout this chapter, we will explore how security can be threaded into other testing activities. Therefore, it's assumed you have read chapters 2, 4, and 5 or are at least familiar with the concepts covered in those chapters. Additionally, it's important to note that this is not an exhaustive exploration of what can be done in the security testing space. It's an opportunity to start our security testing journey by familiarizing ourselves with common techniques used in security testing.

11.1 *Working with threat models*

There's no better example of the commonalities of security testing and the testing activities we've learned already than threat modeling. We learned back in chapter 2 how we can use models to help us better understand how our systems work and identify risks that could impact our systems, and threat modeling is no different. Threat models are used to make sense of how a system works and identify the key areas that we want to protect and then use that knowledge to determine what potential threats require mitigation. Similar to the modeling and risk analysis we've done in previous chapters, the value of threat modeling is that it helps us to both identify and prioritize the threats we need to address. Creating a threat model involves the following steps:

1 Create a model of the system that we can use to analyze.
2 Analyze the model for potential high-level threats.
3 Deep-dive into each threat using a technique called threat trees.

Similar to what we learned with modeling systems in chapter 2, we don't necessarily have to model a whole system in one go. Iterating on smaller slices of our systems will make it easier to digest and potentially identify issues that might be missed when analyzing the system as a whole. To demonstrate how this approach works, let's look at how we can carry out each of these steps against the `booking` API. Specifically, the `GET /booking/` endpoint should be available only to admin users.

11.1.1 *Creating a model*

Our first step in creating a threat model is to understand what exactly is at threat. Predominantly, when we're considering what we want to protect, we're usually concerned with sensitive data or the processes connected to that data. Therefore, unlike the models we created in previous chapters, we want to ideally create a model that attempts to illustrate the flow and storage of data. This is why a lot of threat models are presented as data flow diagrams (DFD) to help illustrate the flow of information, what processes use said data, and where it is stored. We can learn how a DFD is of use by looking at one that was created for the GET /booking endpoint, as shown in figure 11.1.

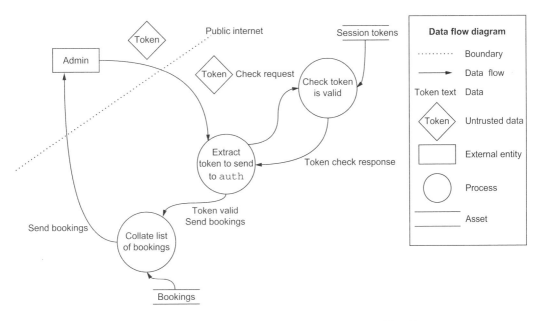

Figure 11.1   A data flow diagram showing how data is handled to get all bookings

The DFD model summarizes the process of an admin requesting the list of bookings, specifically showing the following:

1 An admin sends the request for bookings, providing a valid login token as part of the request.
2 The token is extracted from the request in the booking API and sent to the auth API for validation.
3 If the token confirms that the admin has access, the booking details are sent. (If not, then the forbidden status code is returned instead.)

The model also highlights different factors we can take into consideration when analyzing our system for potential threats. Through the use of standard DFD symbols, we can see the following:

- The external entity interacting with this process should be an administrator, as highlighted by the square box.

- There are multiple assets, session tokens, and bookings we want to keep protected, highlighted by the top-and-bottom-lined text in the model.
- We have multiple processes that handle incoming data and our assets, highlighted by the circles.
- We have untrusted data coming into the system in the form of a "token" that is highlighted in the diamond shapes in the model.

With these details in place, we can begin to understand how we expect our data to be handled in a given situation and who or what is interacting with it. This gives us the foundation we require to start analyzing our model to discover potential threats.

Mixing up models

Although using the DFD approach is common in threat modeling, don't be afraid to try different modeling approaches to help capture other information that might be important to us. DFDs allow us to focus on data, but they don't capture details such as what frameworks were used to build our system or the infrastructure it uses. The goal is to create a model that can be used to trigger ideas about what threats might occur. Take the time to experiment and learn how adding other elements to a model might help your analysis.

Activity

Pick a small slice of your application, and attempt to draw a DFD model of how it works. Models can be created as a collaborative effort, so take the time to speak to others to fill in gaps in your model or clarify assumptions you make. Also, don't be afraid to add any other additional information that you feel might be important.

11.1.2 Discovering threats with STRIDE

Perhaps one of the reasons why security testing is seen as having a high barrier of entry is the diverse ways in which the security of our work can be threatened. Threats can come from a wide range of actors, from organized criminals looking to steal data to sell, to activists defacing or taking down sites due to political motivations (a very unlikely scenario for a small B&B operation). Different actors will employ different attack vectors that we have to consider when analyzing our systems for threats, which is why tools like STRIDE have been created to make threat analysis easier.

Just like the heuristics we learned about in chapter 5, STRIDE is a mnemonic that helps us identify different types of threats to which we may be vulnerable. By iterating through each of the letters in STRIDE, which stand for different security considerations, we can review our DFD models and determine where they apply. For example, the D in STRIDE stands for denial of service (DoS), which helps us think about ways in which we might be vulnerable to an attack that seeks to bring down our services.

To apply STRIDE to a model, we first need to learn what each of the letters in the mnemonic stands for and what they mean, as described next:

- *Spoofing*—Spoofing refers to the act of impersonating someone else through the use of false information. For example, an attacker might seek to spoof a person's login details so that a system will give them access to data. Or it could be a scam caller pretending to be someone from a trusted organization, such as a bank, to extract account details from their victim. Spoofing can occur in many ways, so we want to be sure that we have the ability to authenticate a user correctly to ensure they are the right person being granted access to privileged information.

- *Tampering*—Tampering involves attackers gaining the ability to modify code or data that exists within a system or as it is transported from one location to another. One common example of this is a "man in the middle attack" in which HTTP requests that are sent across a network are intercepted and modified by an attacker before they arrive at the expected destination. Another example would be attackers injecting malicious programs, such as viruses, onto networks or PCs to interfere with our systems. To protect ourselves from these types of attacks, we need to consider ways in which we can secure communication between systems and validate the legitimacy of data arriving or being sent.

- *Repudiation*—Although spoofing and tampering are ways in which an attacker can exploit a system, repudiation relates to whether an attacker can claim they didn't carry out an attack. For example, if we lack the ability to log details of how entities are interacting with our systems, we cannot detect who is or isn't attacking our systems. This lack of information can be used by attackers to either go about their actions undetected or claim innocence if accused of malicious behavior at a later point. With repudiation, we want to ensure that not only do we have the ability to monitor suspicious behavior but also to ensure that monitoring cannot be bypassed or falsified during an attack.

- *Information disclosure*—Information disclosure relates to the leaking of information to individuals who are not authorized to view it. There are many examples of different types of privileged or confidential information being leaked, but what is less commonly discussed is how information can be leaked. This could be due to weak authorization controls, misconfigured access controls, or sensitive information not being secured in the event of different types of attacks such as spoofing or tampering.

- *Denial of service*—Unlike the other items in STRIDE, DoS involves attackers attempting to prevent someone from accessing their own information or services. Rather than attempting to infiltrate secure areas, DoS attacks seek to bring down systems or render them inaccessible in an effort to disrupt an organization or obtain a ransom. For example, attackers might carry out distributed denials of services, overwhelming services with high volumes of requests, or ransomware tools might deny services by locking individuals or organizations out of their services until a ransom has been paid.

- *Elevation of privilege*—Finally, elevation of privilege relates to attacks that allow an attacker to increase their level of privilege in an unexpected way. Elevation of privilege attacks involve attackers taking advantage of exploits and vulnerabilities to gain access rather than pretending to be someone they are not (like spoofing). Examples would include attackers finding ways to access other users' accounts (known as horizontal elevation) or bypassing access controls to elevate themselves to administrator privilege (known as vertical elevation).

After going through the different elements of STRIDE, we can begin to understand not only the different types of attacks we might be vulnerable to but also how they can be used in combination with one another. For example, spoofing might be used to grant an attacker access so that they can perform an information disclosure attack. This is what can make security testing challenging. A vulnerability in one part of the system might have a dramatic impact on another. This is why we should use STRIDE in conjunction with our DFD model to determine how different parts of our system can be vulnerable to different types of attacks. For example, we can start with spoofing and look at our model to see that the admin entity that interacts with our system could be spoofed. Instead of receiving a token from a legitimate user, it may be from an attacker. Therefore, we can label that part of our DFD model as potentially vulnerable to a spoofing attack, as shown in figure 11.2.

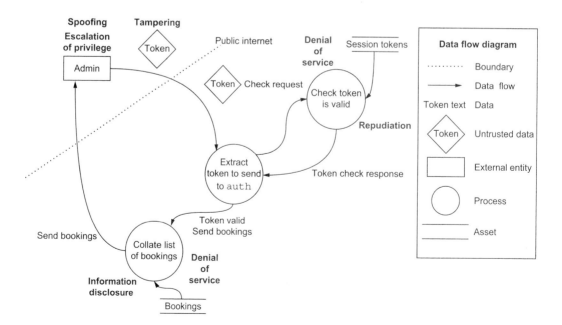

Figure 11.2   A data flow diagram updated to show potential threats using STRIDE

In this diagram, we've used our knowledge of the system and our understanding of STRIDE to identify where each type of attack could take place across the system. We've already discussed how spoofing might take the place of a legitimate admin user, but we can also see interesting threats, such as the following:

- Our `auth` and `booking` APIs might be susceptible to DoS attacks. `auth` is especially important because if it goes down, a large part of the system will be rendered inaccessible.
- If an attacker attempts to tamper or spoof tokens, the attack could be repudiated by the lack of logging and monitoring in the `auth` API.
- The list of bookings may be a target for information disclosure. A lack of encryption around bookings means that the data would be easy to parse if it was ever stolen or leaked.

The key point to this activity is that although we might not know the specific details of what an attack looks like or how it might occur, we have started to focus our attention on the types of vulnerabilities that might exist. Although this gives us an opportunity to begin prioritizing what we want to focus on—for example, we might care more about DoS attacks than information disclosure—the elements of STRIDE are quite broad. If we want to prioritize specific threats to our systems, we need to break down our STRIDE elements further using our knowledge from our models, which we can do using threat trees.

> **Activity**
>
> Using the DFD model of your system that you created, attempt to apply STRIDE to it. Label each of the areas of your model with the types of attacks that it might be vulnerable to. Discuss the ways that you currently mitigate them with others, or, alternatively, how they could be mitigated in the future.

11.1.3 *Creating threat trees*

Threat trees or attack trees enable us to decompose the threats identified using STRIDE into more tangible attacks that could be carried out against our system. As an example, let's return to the spoofing threat. We can begin to break down the many different ways an attacker can spoof the identity of a real admin user. We can start with high-level ways in which spoofing can occur before breaking them down into more specific attacks, as shown in figure 11.3.

As we can see, the threat tree is presented in levels that break down specific types of attacks by moving from an abstract idea into something more concrete. By creating a treelike structure, we have the ability to go broad—for example, listing potential high-level spoofing attacks such as guessing, credential stealing, or social engineering. Or we can pick one topic and dive deeper into it to begin identifying explicit attacks we could be vulnerable to; for example, the ways in which our access tokens might be publicly leaked via our own errors or third-party tools we depend upon that might leak details.

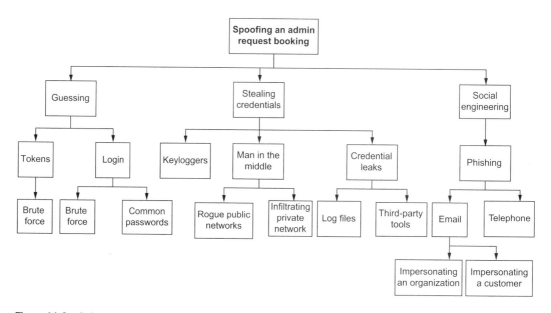

Figure 11.3   A threat tree that breaks down the different spoofing attacks that could be run against our application

What also makes a threat tree valuable is the diversity of threats we can capture. This is demonstrated in another threat tree that focuses on DoS in figure 11.4.

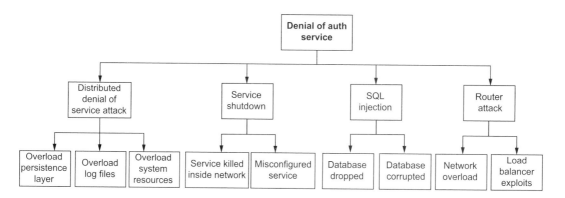

Figure 11.4   A threat tree that breaks down the different DoS attacks that could be run against our application

In this tree, as we begin to explore the ways our systems could be subject to a DoS attack, we can see a diverse range of attacks that we might be vulnerable to. The tree captures more well-known types of attacks, such as distributed DoS, in which a service is bombarded with requests across a wide range of locations. But it also demonstrates how DoS attacks might come from attacks that take advantage of our services being incorrectly configured. This could include accidentally making features that can switch off services publicly available (which can be done in the case of the API frame-work that the API sandbox uses, Spring-boot-actuator).

It's worth mentioning that these example trees are by no means a comprehensive list of every attack we might be vulnerable to. How we go about creating a threat tree depends on what we are most interested in exploring, our understanding of our systems, and our knowledge of the types of threats. When creating a threat tree, it's sensible to take the following steps:

- Create threat trees in a collaborative manner. Different perspectives and experiences bring a diverse range of ideas around what we might be vulnerable to.
- Research how others have been attacked in the past or any material security researchers have shared on specific topics or attack types.
- Investigate known vulnerabilities in the tools and technologies we are using, considering how those vulnerabilities might be used in an attack.

Threat trees allow us to let our imagination run wild. The more we can add to a threat tree, the more likely we are to discover and mitigate threats that matter to us. Taking the time to consider as many potential attacks as possible will make the next step of prioritizing and mitigating threats more effective.

> **Activity**
> Pick one of the STRIDE elements from your model and attempt to create a threat tree that captures the different ways in which your system specifically might be attacked. Take the time to research the different ways an attack might occur and add them to your tree.

11.1.4 Mitigating threats

Ultimately, when discussing threats in the context of security testing, we are simply working with a specific type of risk. Therefore, once our modeling is complete and we've discovered a series of threats/security risks, our next step is to prioritize which risks matter to us so that we can begin to mitigate them. To do this, on a basic level, we can reuse the approach we learned in chapter 3 to prioritize risk by considering the likelihood and severity of each threat and using that information to determine what to focus on. If a security risk has a high likelihood of being carried out and causing a high severity of damage to our systems and business, then we should seek to mitigate the risk as a priority.

Alternatively, the Open Web Application Security Project (OWASP; https://owasp.org), which offers a wide range of materials on security testing, promotes a prioritization technique called DREAD. Created by Microsoft (which also created the threat-modeling mindset and related tool sets that you can find at http://mng.bz/deND), DREAD stands for the following:

- *Damage*—How damaging to us and our users would an attack be?
- *Reproducibility*—How easy can a threat be reproduced by attackers?

- *Exploitability*—How easy is it to exploit a threat?
- *Affected users*—How many users would be affected?
- *Discoverability*—How easy is it for an attacker to discover the threat we've identified?

Unlike the more traditional likelihood and severity approach to prioritization, DREAD allows us to be more granular by giving each of the items in DREAD a score of 1–10 to determine priority. For example, say we're concerned that an attacker could use a SQL injection in which some SQL in our database is exploited to reveal privileged information, in turn allowing the attacker to trigger a denial of service by shutting down the application with the privileged information. We can apply DREAD to it to create this score:

- *Damage: 7*—Sensitive data that we want hidden could be revealed.
- *Reproducibility: 8*—Once identified, the attack could be repeated easily.
- *Exploitability: 3*—It requires strong knowledge of SQL injections and how our databases are structured.
- *Affected users: 10*—If our databases are lost, it could affect all our users.
- *Discoverability: 8*—Our APIs could be hit with different injection attacks to discover vulnerabilities.

We would then calculate this score using DREAD's scoring model, which involves adding all the scores together and dividing by five. So, in our example, it would be 7 + 8 + 3 + 10 + 8, which equals 36. Divided by 5, it gives us a priority score of 7.2. We would then apply this DREAD model to every threat that we're concerned about and rank the threats by the score, with the highest priorities being closer to 10.

The technique of threat modeling has demonstrated that the entry level into security testing is much lower than what people normally think. We've seen how threat modeling reuses a lot of the skills we've established from other testing activities by taking advantage of modeling skills and risk analysis. By honing these skills in relation to threat modeling, we can begin to identify a diverse range of risks that don't require us to know the exact technical details of how each attack could take place but can help encourage our teams to build more secure applications.

11.2   Applying a security mindset to our testing

Although threat modeling gives us a great start in becoming more security-minded, we can go further in security testing by threading our security mindset into other testing activities. We can do this by combining the results from our threat modeling sessions to identify other testing activities we can carry out that will help us learn more about how secure our applications really are.

11.2.1   Security testing in testing API design sessions

Typically, when creating a threat model, it is best to do so as a team in a collaborative environment. We've already discussed how a diversity of ideas and experience helps with threat modeling. But it also offers the opportunity for our teams to learn about the threats together and, crucially, agree on a plan to manage them.

As we learned in chapter 4, by taking the time to discuss the design of our APIs up front as a team, we can do the following:

- Learn more about why we're building the feature in question
- Ensure everyone has a clear understanding of what we're being asked to build
- Capture any potential risks that could threaten the quality of what we are about to build

Threat modeling in a collaborative manner during an API design session can help with the final point. Once threats are identified, we have the opportunity to discuss them and decide how we might mitigate them. This might result in us implementing a feature in a different way. For example, a discussion of password resets might uncover a need to handle an attacker that deliberately resets a user's password and locks them out of their accounts. Therefore, we expand the feature work to add a password reset confirmation email and time limits for resets. This helps teams because it is easier to "bake in" security design at the time the feature is being built rather than having to go back at a later date (potentially after an attack has taken place).

Naturally, we might not want to create a threat model for every change we make. It's up to us as a team to determine when a threat modeling activity will be of use. But if we encourage threat modeling on a regular basis, perhaps iterating on previous models with new knowledge to save time, we can develop a habit of building in security before a line of code is started, saving us a lot of time and headaches later on in our work.

11.2.2 *Exploratory security testing*

So far, our investigations into security risks have been somewhat abstract, focusing on what *could* happen. But what about exploring the product to discover actual real-life risks that currently live in our systems? This is where we can leverage the exploratory testing skills we learned in chapter 5 by using the same approach of time-boxed sessions of focused testing, but with a focus on security.

CHARTERING FOR SECURITY

We learned in chapter 5 that we could create charters that are used to guide our testing, and they are based on risks on which we feel it is important to discover more information. Chartering is no different when it comes to security threats.

Once again, threat modeling can be an asset to us in terms of identifying what charters we might want to create around security risks. Although some threats might be mitigated earlier by changing our API designs, we might still want to explore the product for threats to determine whether they exist (especially if we're implementing security testing at a later stage in our project). Therefore, we could simply select specific threats from our threat trees, turn them into charters, and get to work.

However, one other source that we can draw inspiration from that is worth mentioning is the OWASP Top 10 (https://owasp.org/Top10/). Designed to capture and communicate the top 10 most common threats to web applications, we can use this list to create security-focused charters. It's useful to do this in conjunction with threat modeling because the Top 10 offers us a different perspective on potential threats. Threat modeling is only as good as the individuals who contribute to it, and that will mean there are gaps in our analysis. By using the Top 10 as a guide, we can ensure that the gaps we will inevitably leave in our work are not the most common threats that exist in web applications.

The OWASP Top 10 applies to many different types of web-based applications, which means that not all of the entries would apply in an API security-focused context, such as cross-site scripting, because there is no front end to render it. But we can pick from the list and use it to create an exploratory testing charter. To demonstrate this, let's create a charter influenced by entry seven in the list, Identification and Authentication Failures, and write it out as a charter as follows:

Explore the `auth` API

With Burp Suite and a list of common passwords

To discover whether a password can be brute forced

We can then briefly explore how a charter like this might be executed using the tool Burp Suite to discover more about the potential threat in our `auth` API.

EXPLORING WITH THE USE OF TOOLS

The charter goal is to discover how the `auth` API responds when we brute-force the password. Will it just accept the requests? Will it start to error after a period of a time? Will we be able to get in? To do this, we'll use the security testing tool Burp Suite, which contains a collection of scanning and attack tools that we can use to run our attack. We'll use the Community Edition of Burp Suite, which can be found at https://portswigger.net/burp/communitydownload. With the Burp Suite Community Edition, we have everything we need to run a brute-force attack.

Options with security tools

It's worth mentioning that the professional, paid-for version of Burp Suite has a range of additional tools we can use in exploratory testing sessions to discover vulnerabilities, but it does come at a cost. If price is a concern, you can use other tools such as OWASP ZAP (https://www.zaproxy.org/), which is open source and free to use but has a higher learning curve.

To set up our session, we need to carry out the following two initial steps:

1 Run the sandbox API application. We can either run the complete application using the provided run scripts, or, because we're focused on just the `auth` API, we can load up the `auth` API by itself.

2 Install and open Burp Suite Community Edition. Because we are using the Community Edition, once it opens, we can only select a temporary project to run, which is perfectly fine. Use Burp Suite's default settings if asked.

Managing the Burp Suite proxy

One of the features Burp Suite comes with is a proxy that is used for capturing requests and responses for further analysis. Although we won't use it in this demo, we do need to be aware that it is running, especially because it runs on a default port of 8080, which is the same port that the sandbox API runs on. Therefore, if you come across an issue in which you go to load the sandbox API and get a response from Burp Suite instead, simply go to Proxy > Options in Burp Suite, and either turn off the proxy in the Proxy Listeners section or click the entry in the table, select Edit, and then change the Bind to port field to 8081 or any other port that works. Then you can restart the sandbox API.

With everything set up, we can begin creating our attack. For this, we'll use the Intruder feature of Burp Suite, which can be found in the tab list at the top of the application. Before we can fill in the details for the Intruder attack, we require an HTTP request to send with our fuzzed details. Because our focus is the POST /auth/login endpoint of the auth API, we need to extract the details of the HTTP request; however, that isn't our focus right now, so the HTTP request that follows can be used:

```
POST /auth/login HTTP/1.1
Host: localhost:8080
Content-Type: application/json

{
    "username": "admin",
    "password": "fuzzme"
}
```

With our HTTP request identified, we can begin to set up our Intruder attack, starting with the Target tab. In the Target tab, we want to enter the host and port of the application we're going to fuzz. Depending on whether the full application is loaded or just the auth API, we set the following:

- Host: localhost
- Port: 8080

If the full sandbox is live, and if just the API is up, then the details are

- Host: localhost
- Port: 3004

What is added here must match the Host header from our HTTP request. Otherwise, we'll get an error.

Next, we open the Positions tab to see an area where we can paste our HTTP request for POST /auth/login. Once the request is pasted into the text box, we need to configure it to indicate which fields we want to fuzz. Because our goal is to try out different passwords, we should select the value fuzzme within our JSON object (don't include the quotes) and then click Add, which can be found on the right-hand side of the application. This tells Burp Suite that we intend to replace the contents of fuzzme with different fuzzing options that we set up in the Payloads tab.

Once our request is configured, we need to add in a list of attacks we want to carry out. This is set up in the Payloads tab, where we will use some of the following default settings to establish our attack list:

- *Payload set*—This can stay "1" because we have set up only one parameter to change in our HTTP request: fuzzme.
- *Payload type*—Burp Suite offers a range of options for the types of payloads we want to add, depending on what type of attack we want to carry out. However, because we will brute-force with a list of common passwords, the Simple list type will work for us.
- *Payload options*—This is where we add our list of common passwords that we want to use. To gain a list of common passwords, we can search online with the keywords "Common Passwords txt list" to return results containing lists of passwords. (I found one at http://mng.bz/rnYg.) Once you have found a list, copy it, and click Paste in Payload Options to paste the list in.

We're now ready to run our attack. We have pointed Burp Suite to the correct host, updated the HTTP request with a parametrized password field, and added in a list of passwords to fuzz with. Click Start attack in the right-hand corner to begin the session. We'll begin to see output similar to figure 11.5.

Results	Target	Positions	Payloads	Resource Pool	Options

Filter: Showing all items

Request ∧	Payload	Status	Error	Timeout	Length
0		200			138
1	123456	403			101
2	12345	403			101
3	123456789	403			101
4	password	200			138
5	iloveyou	403			101
6	princess	403			101
7	1234567	403			101
8	rockyou	403			101
9	12345678	403			101
10	abc123	403			101
11	nicole	403			101
12	daniel	403			101
13	babygirl	403			101
14	monkey	403			101
15	lovely	403			101
16	jessica	403			101
17	654321	403			101
18	michael	403			101
19	ashley	403			101
20	qwerty	403			101
21	111111	403			101
22	iloveu	403			101
23	000000	403			101
24	michelle	403			101

Figure 11.5   The results of an example intruder report run within Burp Suite

We can see in the results the details of what password is being sent, followed by a status code response. We can click each request to get more details, but what is interesting about this session is the number of requests and their status codes—specifically, that we were able to get a 200 with one of the passwords and that all the others returned 403s and not some sort of error that relates to requests being denied from the system. This tells us we have the following security issues:

- The default password for an admin is incredibly weak, being the fourth most common password in the list we used.
- There are no controls to prevent the brute-forcing of a password.

The conclusion of this brief exploratory testing session with the assistance of security testing tools has uncovered two potential issues that need addressing. If we take a step back and observe what has occurred during the session, it is no different from other exploratory sessions we've analyzed in this book. We followed a charter to learn about a specific risk and used tooling to support our exploration. The focus is simply on a different type of risk. We are proving once again that applying a security mindset to existing testing activities can pay dividends quickly.

Activity

Try running an exploratory testing session using the Intruder feature of Burp Suite. Here are some suggested areas of the application you could consider fuzzing:

- `POST /message`—Fuzz the message payload for SQL injections.
- `GET /booking/`—Fuzz the query string `roomid` for potential exploits.
- `POST /auth/`—Fuzz the login payload with content that might cause the API to send server errors back.

11.2.3 Automation and security testing

Our example exploratory testing session has demonstrated to us that we can take advantage of security tools to help us learn more about threats. And although the ET example showed us how we could use them to support our testing, we can add other tools as part of an automated pipeline that requires minimal operation. We learned in chapter 6 how automated checks could be used as indicators to warn us if something has changed in the system, and we can analyze whether that change has impacted the quality of our application. We can do similar things in the context of security, using tools to tell us whether there have been changes in the awareness of vulnerabilities.

When we build systems, we rely on a wide range of third-party libraries and dependencies and use popular design patterns in our code. Although we always try to do our best to ensure that there aren't vulnerabilities in our work, it's impossible to prevent every possible threat. Design patterns can be discovered at a later date to be vulnerable to specific types of attacks, and dependencies can be found to have vulnerabilities as well (e.g., I'm writing this chapter just as the log4js vulnerability has been announced). The key is how we react when those vulnerabilities are discovered. If they're known by attackers, then it's only a matter of time until tools are created that weaponize said vulnerabilities to an attacker's advantage. In order to protect ourselves, we need to ensure we're made aware of these discovered vulnerabilities as they are identified, determine if they exist in our systems, and mitigate them before they become a bigger problem.

To do this, we can use automation to help highlight when existing or new vulnerabilities have been discovered in our codebase. Let's look at two ways in which we could use tools to highlight potential vulnerabilities that we can resolve.

STATIC ANALYSIS

Static analysis, the process of analyzing our codebase for issues, is an excellent way to detect potential threats in our work. Tools like SonarQube and open source linters all have a range of plugins or integrations that review code before it's deployed to warn us of threats. In fact, there are so many to pick from that it can be a bit overwhelming (http://mng.bz/Vy7X).

Let's look at one example of static analysis that can be used as part of a pipeline by analyzing the `auth` API code base with the tool SpotBugs (https://github.com/spotbugs/spotbugs) and a plugin called Find Security Bugs (https://find-sec-bugs.github.io/) to see what issues might exist in the codebase. First, we add the following plugin into the `auth` pom.xml:

```
<plugin>
    <groupId>com.github.spotbugs</groupId>
    <artifactId>spotbugs-maven-plugin</artifactId>
    <version>4.5.0.0</version>
    <configuration>
        <plugins>
            <plugin>
                <groupId>com.h3xstream.findsecbugs</groupId>
                <artifactId>findsecbugs-plugin</artifactId>
                <version>1.10.1</version>
            </plugin>
        </plugins>
    </configuration>
</plugin>
```

Once the plugin has been added, we can open a terminal and run `mvn spotbugs :check`. This will run an analysis of our codebase and then output a list of warnings that we need to fix. For example, the following was detected when it was run at one point:

```
[ERROR] Medium: Cookie without the HttpOnly flag could be read by a malicious
    script in the browser [com.automationintesting.api.AuthController] At
    AuthController.java:[line 30] HTTPONLY_COOKIE
[ERROR] Medium: Cookie without the secure flag could be sent in clear text if
    a HTTP URL is visited [com.automationintesting.api.AuthController] At
    AuthController.java:[line 30] INSECURE_COOKIE
```

With this feedback, we're now able to proactively update our code to make it more secure.

DEPENDENCY CHECKING

Static analysis is useful for analyzing our code for potential vulnerabilities, but what about the libraries we depend on to build our systems? Keeping dependencies up-to-date has become an important part of securing our systems, with sites like GitHub offering dependency checking as standard. GitHub scans codebases regularly to inform us of newly discovered vulnerabilities in our dependencies.

However, these issues are discovered after our code is committed and stored in a third-party site, which might not be ideal for some contexts. As an alternative approach, we can use tools such as OWASP Dependency-Check (https://jeremylong .github.io/DependencyCheck/), which allows us to run checks locally before we commit our code.

Let's look at how we can use Dependency-Check with the `auth` API to discover vulnerabilities. First, add the Dependency-Check plugin to the `auth` pom.xml by adding the following XML:

```
<plugin>
    <groupId>org.owasp</groupId>
    <artifactId>dependency-check-maven</artifactId>
    <version>6.5.0</version>
    <executions>
        <execution>
            <goals>
                <goal>check</goal>
            </goals>
        </execution>
    </executions>
</plugin>
```

After it's added, open a terminal and run `mvn verify`. Once all the automated checks are run, we'll see Dependency-Check run and create a report that can be found in target/dependency-check-report.html. This report gives us a breakdown of the dependencies we rely upon, as well as which have known vulnerabilities. For example, a quick run against `auth` showed me that the `jackson-databind` dependency had a critical vulnerability that I needed to take care of immediately by updating the dependency to a version that had patched the exploit.

RELYING ON AUTOMATION

These are just two examples of the types of tools that we can add into our pipelines to scan our codebase and inform us of any potential security risks. But there are many more tools to take advantage of. For example, Burp Suite, which we used in the exploratory testing session earlier, has command-line features (some of which are paid for) that can be used as part of a pipeline (OWASP ZAP proxy has similar features). What has been demonstrated, though, is that tools like these don't require much investment to add if, once again, we're looking at how automation can help us from a security perspective.

A word of warning, though: similar to how automated regression checks won't find every issue, security scanning tools won't find every vulnerability. They can help bolster our security testing response to threats, but we must ensure that our security automation doesn't lull us into a false sense of security (pun intended), resulting in us getting a nasty surprise from attackers.

11.3   Security testing as part of a strategy

Security is a vast topic, and unfortunately, there is a wide range of ways in which we can be vulnerable to attack. However, this chapter has demonstrated that many of the skill sets and approaches used in security testing are no different from what we've learned in previous chapters. When we think of security testing, we can think of it as a mindset that uses existing testing techniques such as modeling, analysis, collaboration, automation, and exploratory testing skills with a focus on the topic of security when considering security testing as part of a wider strategy. We can apply it across the entire strategy model, as demonstrated in figure 11.6.

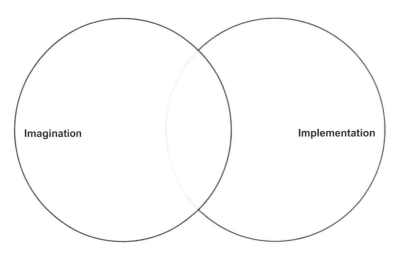

Figure 11.6   A model showing that a security mindset is needed across our entire testing strategy to keep our applications secure

We've seen how threat modeling can be carried out collaboratively when testing API designs so that we can encourage our team members to bake security into their work. We've learned that discovering potential threats in our systems is exploratory testing in nature, allowing us to charter testing sessions that focus on specific security threats. And finally, we've learned that we can use automated tools to warn us of security issues and encourage us to keep systems up to date and protected from known threats. All of these activities are no different from what many teams do already in the name of quality, but by simply infusing our testing with a security mindset, we can all contribute toward building more secure systems.

Summary

- Security testing follows similar motivations to other testing activities.
- It uses common techniques and skills, such as modeling and risk analysis, to discover risks related to security-based quality characteristics.
- We can use threat modeling to discover and prioritize which threats we want to mitigate in our systems.
- Threat modeling starts by creating a model of the system using tools like data flow diagrams or something similar.
- We can then apply STRIDE to a model to identify threats. STRIDE stands for spoofing, tampering, repudiation, information disclosure, denial of service, and elevation of privilege.
- We can identify specific attack types by creating threat trees based on each of the elements of STRIDE.
- Once our attacks have been identified, we can prioritize which attacks we focus on using the DREAD prioritization technique.
- We can use what we've identified in threat models to guide other testing activities.
- Threat modeling while testing API designs allows us to capture threats earlier and modify our plans to mitigate them.
- We can leverage exploratory testing by creating and executing charters that focus on security threats.
- Exploratory testing sessions can be aided through the use of security testing tools such as Burp Suite and ZAP.
- We can bake in security scanners and linters such as SpotBugs or Dependency-Check to discover vulnerabilities in our code or the libraries we use.
- We can apply a security testing mindset across the testing strategy model.

Testing in production

When Eric Ries wrote *The Lean Startup* in 2011, the strategy and mindset he proposed influenced various industries, including software development. The center of Eric's thesis is that we want to ensure that we're delivering something of quality with as minimal waste as possible. As he puts it in a blog post on linkedin.com (http://mng.bz/xMO8),

> *"The problem is that quality is really in the eye of the beholder. For a for-profit company, quality is defined by what the customer wants. So if we are misaligned with what the customer wants, then all the extra time we take to polish all the edges and get everything right is actually wasted time because we end up pushing the product away from what the customer wants."*

There are two lessons to be learned from Eric's attitude toward quality as being in the "eye of the beholder." The first is that quality is "defined by what the customer wants," a topic we've discussed in depth throughout this book. The second is that we need approaches that enable us to successfully measure both how our users and systems behave to help inform us of our product's quality. The opportunities for this second lesson are wide-ranging, but one way a testing strategy can help is by embracing a testing-in-production mindset.

The phrase "testing in production" can conjure a feeling of anxiety for some. Visions of stray test data appearing on live sites, production systems crashing, or insecure accounts that leave vulnerabilities for attackers to exploit spring to mind. But when thinking about testing in production, it's important to take a step back and remind ourselves of the overarching goal of testing.

As we've discussed before, testing is about learning as much about the imagination (what we want) and implementation (what we have) of our product to bring those two factors into alignment. Yes, to achieve that goal, we can exercise our products in different ways to observe what happens. But we can also learn a lot by observing the system and how others use it. So when we say testing in production, we're thinking less about exercising our live systems to discover issues and more about measuring and reacting to metrics that come from our system as users interact with it, all of which will become more apparent as we look at how we can get started with testing in production.

12.1 Planning out testing in production

Testing in production is motivated by learning how our users interact with our product and how our system behaves in a "live" context. We need a plan for collecting metrics and analyzing them. Therefore, before we can begin to implement any type of tooling that supports our testing in production, we need answers to these questions: What metrics should we be tracking, and how do we determine whether the metrics are pointing toward a potential decline in quality?

12.1.1 What to track

To determine what to track, we can use techniques developed by site reliability engineers (SRE) to determine the following:

- The necessary level of availability and reliability for each product feature
- What metrics to track to help us determine those levels

By answering these two questions, SREs are able to develop a plan to track whether the product they are responsible for is meeting business and end user expectations. We can similarly use this approach to learn how our users are interacting with our system and how the system itself is behaving, both of which will help us understand whether we're delivering a quality product. To demonstrate this, let's look at how we can answer those questions within the context of our sandbox API to determine what we might want to track.

To understand how we go about addressing the two questions of what levels to track and what metrics to use to determine those levels, we need to learn about three things:

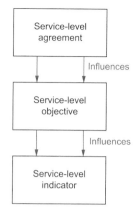

- Service-level agreements
- Service-level objectives
- Service-level indicators

These each have a relationship with one another that is summarized in figure 12.1.

We'll discuss each of these levels in more detail shortly, but the key thing to remember is that the objective captured as part of a higher service level will influence what is tracked at a lower service level. To better understand each of these levels, let's discuss an example for restful-booker-platform.

Figure 12.1   A model showing the relationship between service-level agreements, service-level objectives, and service-level indicators and how they influence each other

12.1.2 *Service-level objectives*

It may seem odd to start with the middle level within this model, but because a service-level objective (SLO) is what is directly managed and tracked by a team, it's a sensible place to start. This becomes more necessary if we find ourselves in situations where no clear service-level agreement (SLA) exists and we're required to determine our own SLOs.

An SLO is a measure or threshold that a team sets to determine whether a product meets certain expectations, such as availability, reliability, and responsiveness. For example, one SLO might be that our product should be available at a minimum of 95% of a given time frame (24 hours, a week, a month, etc.). Setting this SLO means that we can use it to measure whether our product is meeting that expectation as it's being used. If we're not meeting our SLO, we can respond accordingly and identify and address issues that might cause us to miss our SLO targets.

What is interesting about SLOs is their similarity to the quality characteristics we discussed back in chapter 3. Traditionally, SLOs have a more explicit technical focus because they are determined through the measurement of system metrics. But that doesn't mean they aren't focused on the same things as quality characteristics, that is, the user and their experience. When determining our SLOs, we're actually identifying quality characteristic measurements, similar to how we have identified our characteristics for our strategy, which help us understand the level of our product's quality.

With that in mind, let's return back to the work we did in chapter 3 and remind ourselves of the quality characteristics we identified for restful-booker-platform to see if we can capture a relevant SLO for tracking. Our test strategy aims to support our team in improving the following quality characteristics of restful-booker-platform:

- Intuitiveness
- Completeness

- Stability
- Privacy
- Availability
- Tailorability

For this chapter, we're going to pick one of these characteristics to turn into an SLO. Which should it be? As we look through the list of characteristics, there are some that could be quite complex to measure. For example, there is no obvious metric for intuitiveness. We could use metrics such as time between requests to infer a user's ease of navigating through a system, but that doesn't eliminate other factors. However, other characteristics such as availability can be more quickly measured. So with availability in mind, we'll set the following SLO:

> The availability of restful-booker-platform will be 99% over a 24-hour period.

With this SLO in place, we'll then need to consider what metrics we're going to measure. But before we do that, let's take a look at another input when determining SLOs.

12.1.3 Service-level agreements

Simply put, a service-level agreement is the same as a service-level objective with the following caveats:

- It's been explicitly stated in a binding contract with a user.
- Some sort of penalty is attached to failing to meet the agreed level.

For example, let's say that for each B&B owner we take on as a client, we agree to and sign an SLA with them. That SLA may have a stated section about availability, similar to the one we picked ourselves, with the extra details about penalties. For example:

> The availability of RBP will be 95% over a month's period, with a penalty of $1,000 paid to the client if availability is under 95%.

Obviously, this is not a perfect example of legal text, but it does highlight a few interesting differences between an SLA and SLO. First, the figure of 95% differs from the 99% stated in the SLO. In this example, the 95% SLA might have been thrashed out with the client by a different team (perhaps legal or client services), whereas as mentioned earlier, the team has more control over what SLOs they want to meet. By setting a higher target threshold of 99% as a team, it gives us time to react if we drop below our SLO before penalties might be triggered.

Balancing cost and levels

Although it might make sense to set a higher threshold for an SLO to allow time to react to situations in which our levels are dropping, we do need to consider the cost of a high threshold. Keeping a system at 99% availability is more costly in terms of time and resources and potentially provides more interruptions to day-to-day work than at 95%. It's sensible when working out our SLOs to pick a target that isn't prohibitively costly but potentially offers space to breathe.

As we've discussed briefly, the second key difference between an SLA and SLO is the introduction of a penalty if targets are not met. Penalties are likely put in place as a way to compensate clients for loss of revenue or as a means to motivate a business to meet certain standards. But the penalties also give us an insight into the mindset of the client/user, which is useful when thinking about what quality means to them. Levels that appear in an SLA as a priority or that come with a higher financial penalty can tell us a lot about which quality characteristics matter most so that we can factor them into our testing in production and other testing activities. This helps us to identify higher-priority risks and select which testing activities to use at given times.

In conclusion, if an SLA exists, the levels of service that have been contractually set will determine, at a minimum, the SLOs we use. Beyond any SLAs, engineering teams should identify SLOs based on research on a user's ideas of what quality means to them. Once our SLOs are in place, we can then begin to determine what metrics we'll track to measure whether we are meeting acceptable levels.

12.1.4 *Service-level indicators*

If service-level agreements and service-level objectives describe what levels of specific metrics a product should meet, then a service-level indicator is what we use to track the success or failure of meeting a given expectation. For example, let's return to our SLO:

The availability of restful-booker-platform will be 99% over a 24-hour period.

We need to work out a way to measure the availability of restful-booker-platform. To do this, we could

- Capture the status code of each request made by a user
- Record the results of each ping we do to each API
- Query hardware metrics and determine their levels

Although the easiest approach might be to ping each API at a regular interval and measure the return status code, we want data that reflects the user's experience. That's why we will track the status code of each request made by a user for our SLI.

As each response is returned, we would add that status code to all the status codes we've captured within a 24-hour period (set by our SLO) to determine whether we're at a 99% availability limit. This would mean that if we start to collect error status codes or network timeouts within our 24-hour time that cause us to drop below the 99% level, we would know we're no longer delivering our SLO and are at risk of breaching our SLA.

This example gives us a basic idea of what an SLI is, but we need to consider a range of things beyond what we're going to measure. Tracking a status code is a start for our SLI, but we might need to do the following as well:

- *Track based on different locations*—Our RBP instances may be deployed across different server regions. Being able to determine which locations are unavailable might help us diagnose issues earlier.

- *Review historical data*—Although our indicator would trigger actions to fix contributing factors to our reduction in availability, we may want to review historical data to analyze trends, such as slow deployments that cause spikes in unavailability.
- *Track response times*—An API that takes 20 seconds to respond isn't a great deal better than an API that is down. In fact, our SLA might define availability as either down or taking more than five seconds to respond. Tracking response times can help us measure our availability and diagnose issues around a lack of availability (such as performance bottlenecks or third-party applications adversely affecting our product).

These are just a few examples of additional considerations we might need to decide upon when defining our SLIs. Not only is this important to define how we're measuring whether we're meeting our SLOs/SLA, but it will also determine how we pick and set up our tooling.

12.1.5 What to save

Although our SLIs help us determine what metrics we want to measure, we still need to consider the execution of our SLIs and how we will set up our measuring instruments. It may be tempting to pick a tool that allows us to capture a broad range of metrics, point it at our application, and see what happens. But as our systems grow, so does our metrics gathering, so we need to ensure that we don't end up with issues such as incurring high costs for managing data and losing or missing out on the use of historical data. To help ensure we pick the right tool for the job, we should consider a range of topics that we'll briefly explore now.

METRIC STRUCTURE

Although many libraries and frameworks offer logging as standard, their structure and scope might not necessarily be the best structure of output for us to use. Traditionally, logs are used as a means to inform us about actions or issues that occur within the system. But our goal is to track information that tells us about the interaction between our users and our system. This becomes all the more complex when working with systems that employ a distributed range of web APIs with each responsible for specific services. Imagine trying to diagnose an issue across over 100 web APIs by trawling through a series of log files.

Therefore, we should consider structuring our metrics through the use of *events*. A collection of relevant information is captured after each request is made. We can capture common attributes, such as HTTP request headers, payloads, and HTTP response status codes as standard. But we can also add in other interesting information, such as unique identifiers and user details. Additionally, events can be tied together easily to help us trace the journey of a user's request across our API platform, making it easier for us to analyze at a later date.

By employing a tool that encourages the use of events over log files, we can shift our focus onto tracking users' behavior across our platform.

STORAGE LOCATION AND LENGTH

Another factor to consider is where we want to store our metrics and for how long. When tracking metrics for service levels, we have a choice of either keeping data for the lifetime of a service level before deleting it (e.g., 24 hours) or keeping it longer to help us analyze issues or identify trends over a larger period of time. We could also consider compromising between the two options and rolling up our data into smaller, less detailed data sets that allow us to search historically but with less information.

Each of these approaches has benefits and costs. The volume of data our API platforms can generate could be enormous, and we will have to pay to store and analyze it. Additionally, as we are tracking data from real users, privacy and security concerns need to be considered, and how strict we will be depends on our domain. One option is to anonymize and even downsample the data once your SLO window has been completed, that is, remove nonessential data. This provides a low-fidelity and more costly view for an extended period of time.

ADDITIONAL INFORMATION

We might have a clear idea of some metrics we want to collect—like status codes or response times in our restful-booker-platform example—but we may want to spend some time considering what other metrics we might need. If we want the ability to analyze historical metrics, it is important to capture useful information that we can't get back by other means. If data such as user locations, user agents, or system-specific state is lost, it will make analyzing problems harder. However, the trade-off is similar to storage length: the more we track, the more we have to save and process.

COST OF TIME AND BUDGET

We must establish an understanding of what metrics we want to collect and how they will help to identify the tooling that works better for us. For example, the factors of storage length and historical analysis will guide us toward tools that support an observability mindset, whereas other tools might lead us down the monitoring path. Regardless of the choices we make around our metrics, there are other considerations that we need to make when selecting our tools that tap into the wider strategic themes.

For example, the range of tools for gathering metrics and setup alerting is vast. Quickly search for monitoring or observability tools, and you'll discover many open source tools available, including a range of paid options with different price points. As with most tooling, there are choices and compromises to be made. Some tools offer cloud setup with easy integration into existing systems but come with a price tag. Others offer the ability to set up your own instances but require a great deal of configuration and maintenance of setups, data management, and backup. A discussion should be had to determine how much we are willing to spend both financially and timewise on the tooling we want to use for testing in production. Also, as these data-metric-gathering tools become more sophisticated, the learning curve increases. An investment is required in up-skilling a team to become comfortable with using these tools and ensuring that knowledge stays with the team as it grows and changes.

In the end, to succeed with testing in production, a clear plan is required. We've learned that defining what our service levels are and how we intend to meet them will give us a clear direction to follow. From there, it's a case of identifying what we need to execute our testing in production and taking the time to research our options. Once we've established our approach, the implementation of testing in production should go much more smoothly.

12.2   Setting up testing in production

As the mindset and techniques behind monitoring, observability, and testing in production have grown, the options for tooling have exploded. There is a range of different paid-for or open source tools available for us to take advantage of. To help us get set up with testing in production for restful-booker-platform, we'll use the observability platform Honeycomb. Honeycomb is a popular tool that allows us to quickly drop in tooling to track events within our application and review them. The core of Honeycomb is an SaaS application that we can access via the web to analyze events sent by specific Honeycomb libraries that are embedded in our software. Honeycomb will give us all we need for this chapter, but when selecting your own tooling, take the time to look at the options available to determine which tools will help you the most in implementing your SLIs.

12.2.1   Setting up a Honeycomb account

For our purposes, we require a tool that is able to capture event data from our APIs and send it to a central location for processing and analysis, which Honeycomb offers. As we'll see during setup, Honeycomb offers a range of features, such as easy API integration, rich querying and easy-to-set-up alerts, all for free. Of course, there is a wide range of other features available in their paid-for tier, but the free version will give us everything we need to establish our testing in production for now.

To begin our setup process, we first need to create an account with Honeycomb. Our Honeycomb account will be the central location to which our event data will be sent when the application is up and running. To do this, simply head over to https:// honeycomb.io and click Get Started to create your account.

Once your account has been created, you will next need to create a new team. Enter in the name of your demo team; for example, I named my team rbp and pressed Enter. Your account will be set up and will wait for event data to be sent. You should also see your API key, which will be used to authenticate event data from our APIs. Make a copy of the API key for future use. Now let's turn our attention to setting up our APIs with Honeycomb.

12.2.2   Adding Honeycomb to APIs

As you may have already noticed, Honeycomb has been set up in the `branding`, `booking`, and `auth` APIs in the codebase for restful-booker-platform to help demonstrate how it works. But if we want to track events from our other APIs, we need to integrate Honeycomb into the other APIs. In this section, we'll set up the `room` API with Honeycomb.

One of the advantages of Honeycomb is its ease of integration with a range of open source API frameworks. Whether it's Java, JavaScript, or C#, the Honeycomb team has worked hard to integrate web APIs with their services as easily as possible.

During our exploration of restful-booker-platform, we've learned that the APIs are built using SpringBoot. This is great news for us because Honeycomb has an easy-to-use library to connect Honeycomb and SpringBoot APIs. All we need to do to add Honeycomb is to add the following dependency to our `room` API's pom.xml:

```
<dependency>
    <groupId>io.honeycomb.beeline</groupId>
    <artifactId>beeline-spring-boot-starter</artifactId>
    <version>1.5.1</version>
</dependency>
```

NOTE Update the version to the latest version, if appropriate.

The `beeline` library is used to collect event data and send it to our Honeycomb account. This means that to complete the setup, we'll need to configure it by adding the following into the application.properties file:

```
honeycomb.beeline.enabled=true
honeycomb.beeline.service-name=rbp-room
honeycomb.beeline.dataset=rbp-room-dataset
honeycomb.beeline.write-key=<APIKEY>
```

The `enabled` and `write-key` options are straightforward, allowing us to enable Honeycomb and then store the API key that will be used by `beeline` to connect and send events. The `service-name` option allows us to add a service name to the event being sent to help us identify the event's origin with Honeycomb. The final option, `dataset`, allows us to determine what data store all our events are going to be sent to in our Honeycomb team. We may choose to have one data store in which all events from all APIs are sent, or we may opt to have one data store for each API. How we want to search for data and what SLIs have been identified will determine which approach we might want to choose.

Don't save your key in your code

It should go without saying that you should never save your API keys in your repositories. It's better to send your Honeycomb write key to your API when deploying the application through the use of environmental variables and to call the following when running a SpringBoot API: `Dhoneycomb.beeline.write-key=$HONEYCOMB_API_KEY`.

With our API configured to connect to Honeycomb, you can either start the API by running the `room` API in your IDE or by building it with `mvn clean install` before running it with `java -jar java -jar restful-booker-platform-room-{version-number}.SNAPSHOT.jar`. The API will load up and automatically make the connection to Honeycomb, ready for events to be sent.

To test the integration, open up a new terminal window and run the following request multiple times to generate some events:

```
curl http://localhost:3001/room/
```

After generating some events, head back to the control panel on https://ui.honey comb.io/ and either log back in or refresh the page. You'll find that the home page has updated and is showing not your API key but event metrics for the API. This means we're ready to add triggers based on our SLIs.

GraphQL or REST? They're all events!

Another string to Honeycomb's bow is that regardless of the structure of your HTTP request, whether it uses REST or GraphQL, Honeycomb will capture them as events. Regardless of your API architecture, tools like Honeycomb allow you to execute your testing in production approach in a similar fashion.

Activity

With the `room` API configured with Honeycomb, complete the set by adding Honeycomb to the `report` and `message` APIs. You can also update the settings in the other APIs to enable them to all point to your Honeycomb team.

12.2.3 Advanced querying

Now that we have data appearing in our Honeycomb data set, we can begin to query the data to learn more about the events stored and create alerts, known as triggers in Honeycomb, to inform us when we're not meeting our SLOs. Let's first familiarize ourselves with how to build useful query events before turning them into triggers.

As we learned earlier, all our events sent from our APIs are stored within data sets. To query events within a data set, we first need to select the data set we want to interrogate. If we opted to add all our events to one data set, then select New Query to begin. But if we had multiple data sets, we can view them all by selecting the Datasets menu item and then selecting the data set we want to query. Either approach to navigating to the query page will result in the query form shown in figure 12.2.

Figure 12.2   A screenshot of the Honeycomb query tool that we can use to query events

We can use this query tool to build our event queries. For example, if we want a count for each status code within a specific time frame, we can run the following query:

- Visualize: COUNT
- Group by: response.status_code

Clicking Run Query will present counts for each response status code that has been sent back within a two-hour period, as shown in figure 12.3.

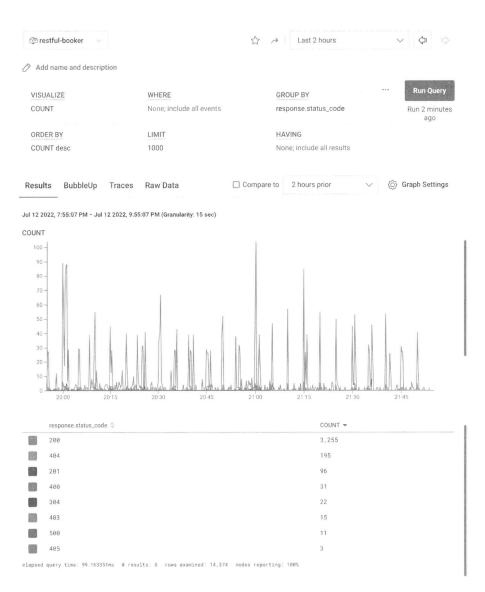

Figure 12.3   A screenshot of query results after counting all the HTTP response status codes within the last two hours

It's a simple demonstration of how to build queries within Honeycomb, but if we take a step back to an empty query form and click the Visualize field, we'll see a range of different methods to make sense of our events, including averages, percentiles, and heatmaps.

The range of query features can be as much a curse as it is a blessing. The options available to us mean that there are many ways in which we could approach building queries for our SLOs, so we need to think carefully about how we design our queries. For example, if we remind ourselves of our SLO for restful-booker-platform, we want to ensure

The availability of restful-booker-platform will be 99% over a 24-hour period.

Using our current query of counting status codes isn't going to work because we would be ignoring the relationship between error codes and success codes that make up the percentage of availability. We could build a trigger that goes off every time the error code count goes over a certain number, such as 100. But for those 100 error codes, there may be 10,000 success codes, meaning our actual availability is still above 99%, and our time is wasted trying to resolve an issue that isn't there. If we don't design our queries in a correct manner, we can suffer from false negatives as much as we can suffer from false positives.

With that in mind, let's look at how we can create a more robust query for our trigger. Honeycomb doesn't offer an out-of-the-box way to query the percentage of error codes in a given time (at least not for free), so we will need to create our own query function, known as a derived column.

Before we get into what derived columns are, let's first locate them in Honeycomb. Click the Datasets menu item on the left and then the Settings button for the data set we created. Once in the data set settings, click the Schema tab to load the Derived Columns section. Finally, click Add new Derived Column to open the editor.

Derived columns grant us the ability to create expressions that will process our event data in any way we want and then allow us to query data based on the output of the expression. For example, we need to know what percentage of all status codes are error codes within a time frame, so in the Function field we add the following

```
IF( GTE( $response.statuscode, 500), 1, 0)
```

and name the function `http_error_rate` within the Column alias field. We've created a derived column that, when used in a query, will do the following:

1 Inspect each event's response status code
2 Determine whether the status code is greater than or equal to 500 and return either a score of 1 if true or 0 if not

This function alone gives us only a binary score based on the error, but we can use it to achieve our goal when we combine this into a query. To do this, we save the derived column and create a new query, this time with the following query settings:

- VISUALIZE: `AVG(http_error_rate)`

Note that the `http_error_rate` in the query matches the name of our derived column. What we're doing is working out the average of all the 1s and 0s that have come from each event's status code to give us an average somewhere between 1 and 0. If it's 0, then there are no errors; if it's 1, then all the responses are errors. The average could be anywhere between 1 and 0, which gives us a metric upon which to build our trigger.

12.2.4 *Building SLO triggers*

Now that we have our query and derived column in place, building the trigger itself is relatively straightforward. To start, we click the Triggers menu item and then select New Trigger. Depending on the data sets that you have, you'll be asked to select the data set you want to create the trigger for. Once we've selected a data set, the following details are required to create our trigger:

- *Name*—If we intend to have multiple queries, a simple, concise name will do; for example: `Error Rate >= 1%`.
- *Description*—Honeycomb supports teams with multiple accounts, so it's worth getting into a good habit of describing alerts in more detail for others to read.
- *State*—We want this to be set as Enabled, but it can be used to turn off a trigger if it's temporarily not required.
- *Query*—Here we add our query of `AVG(http_error_rate)`.
- *Threshold*—Our threshold determines whether an alert needs to be sent to the team to let us know that we are no longer meeting our SLO. As our SLO states, we want availability to be 99%, so we should set a threshold of `>= 0.01`. The higher the threshold, the more our availability statistic is being reduced.
- *Recipients*—This is who we want to notify. Notification can be via email or via integrated tools like Slack. For now, let's add our email address to help us test out the trigger.

With those details added, we can save our trigger, which will begin a scheduled query and analysis of event data that will trigger an email alert (which we can test by clicking Test) if the error rate creeps over 0.01% of all responses. We now have the required feedback loop in place to react to any events, code changes, deployments, and so on that might impact our ability to meet both our service-level objectives and service-level agreement.

12.3 *Taking testing in production further*

The tooling we've put in place helps us gain real insights into what a user is experiencing at a given time with our production systems. That insight can help us measure whether we are meeting our objectives and, as an extension, measure the quality of our product. This will provide a lot of value to our testing strategies, but there is still much more we can take advantage of when using this approach to testing. With tools like Honeycomb, we open up a wealth of feedback from our live systems to combine with other testing activities to learn more about our product and our end users. Let's take a brief look at a few of these options.

12.3.1 *Testing with synthetic users*

One of the benefits of implementing a tool like Honeycomb is that the events it collects can come from either a real flesh-and-blood end user or from a synthetic user. A synthetic user is a term used for actions carried out in a production environment that simulate how a real user might interact with our product. This would be carried out either by a member of the team or, as is more commonly done, using automated tools interacting with the system.

For example, with our `room` Honeycomb/API setup, we could use automation to make a series of API calls that replicate the user flow of creating a room and then updating its details. If we run this automation against our production environment while Honeycomb is receiving events, we can observe whether any alerts are triggered, which might indicate issues with our production systems that could contribute to us missing our service-level objectives. Our synthetic users can be used to help us flush out unexpected issues and increase our confidence that our production systems are working at expected levels.

> **Synthetic users compared to smoke tests**
>
> Another testing technique used in production environments is the idea of a smoke test, in which the most common flows through the system are tested to ensure our product is functioning on a high level. Although the actions are very similar for smoke tests and testing with synthetic users, using tools to simulate "happy path" behavior, the intent of each approach is different.
>
> For me, smoke testing is about focusing on integration risks. The imagery behind a smoke test is to blow smoke down a pipe to see where the smoke comes out in order to locate gaps or holes. The same principle applies when smoke-testing a production system. The goal is to exercise every part of the system once to ensure that all parts are running correctly and integrated with one another. This differs from testing with synthetic users, which is focused on generating events in a synthetic manner to check that we're meeting SLOs.

As we've discussed before, our context is key to whether this is an activity we can take advantage of. To help better understand whether this is a viable technique, here are some considerations:

- *Can you keep your testing hidden from real users?* Although testing on a production system isn't a complete deal-breaker, we do want to ensure the actions of our testing don't impact others. For example, we don't want the embarrassment of test pages with stock text appearing or the frustration of real users finding that their activities are blocked by our testing (think booking the last room for a specific date). To avoid this, we need control over what we're testing, and that crucially means control over the data we're interacting with. If we cannot set up and tear down data easily or manipulate access to information in a clean way, then using synthetic users becomes very difficult.

- *Can you ensure that your test data doesn't impact security?* Working with live environments may mean we have to adhere to tighter security controls. We also don't want to carry out testing that might compromise or leak real user data, for example, if we were replicating an admin user who could reveal sensitive profile information. Additionally, there may be infrastructure security concerns that prevent us from accessing a production environment in the same way as a test environment. All of these considerations may impact whether we can use synthetic users.

- *Can you discern between test events and real user events?* A final thing to consider is whether we have the ability to separate test events from real user events. With tools like Honeycomb, we can filter on a wide range of attributes in an event. For example, if we can filter user agents, we could use a fake user agent for our synthetic users to help us filter them out of real user events. This can help us diagnose issues and analyze results because we don't want our test events to skew activities such as A/B testing, which we'll learn about next.

These considerations demonstrate that a certain level of planning is required to create and use synthetic users. It's not as straightforward as pointing existing automation at a production system or carrying out other testing activities while we have tools like Honeycomb switched on.

One of the compromises of this approach is that our synthetic users will be based on an assumption of how users will behave. They won't give us a 100% accurate indication of how real end users will interact with our product. We must always consider using this in conjunction with tracking real events from users to expand the feedback we get.

12.3.2 *Testing hypotheses*

When examining event data against SLOs, we're determining whether the metrics from the product are meeting our expectations and those of our customers. However, there is a lot more to be learned from the historical data we collect. When done correctly, the event data can also be analyzed to learn more about users' behavior and attitudes toward our product and its value. But what do we analyze, and what are we hoping to learn? To answer these questions and more, we need to plan out clear hypotheses that we want answers to before setting out an experiment to test our hypothesis through the use of techniques such as A/B testing, which will help us compare and contrast the behavior of different users based on what features we present them.

To help illustrate this approach, let's say that as a team, we want to discover how users react to a new feature in which the GET /room/ endpoint starts to paginate lists of rooms instead of showing them all in one list. We can toggle the pagination feature for a subset of users using A/B testing; for instance, 50% see the pagination feature (group A), and 50% don't (group B). We then time-box the duration in which users might be added to each of these groups. Once the time-box is complete, we analyze the event information we have on each group to determine whether there is an increase or decrease in traffic depending on features, whether users send unexpected requests that might result in errors, and so on. The goal is to learn more about how users really interact with and feel about the assumptions we've made around improving the quality of a product. If the new feature is received negatively, we know that our thinking needs to change.

Using A/B testing techniques with tools like Honeycomb can help us learn more about our users. But similar to the other activities we've explored, they require upfront planning to succeed. Here are some considerations for implementing A/B testing and measuring results:

- *Planning*—Although we'll never be able to successfully predict the outcomes of A/B testing, it's important to have a clear idea of what constitutes success and what doesn't. Taking the time to determine what we want to learn first is essential before diving in with different iterations. Failing to do so opens us up to ambiguity and disagreement.
- *Setup*—Techniques like A/B testing will require development work to enable a product to be configured into different states based on the user visiting. A wealth of A/B testing tools exist to help aid the adoption of this activity, but they will require experience and time to get set up.

Simply put, to run a successful A/B testing session, we need to clearly define what our hypothesis is and how we plan to test the hypothesis and then execute the testing. If each step is considered carefully, then the information received will give us a wealth of information that other testing activities might not offer so easily.

At the start of this chapter, we mentioned the book *Lean Startup* by Eric Ries, which explained that for a business to succeed, it needs to understand what quality means to a customer, and failing to do so results in waste and potential failure, an idea that follows along closely with our testing goals. Our testing is focused on helping teams deliver high-quality products. That is why testing in production, when done well, can reward us with clearer insights into what customers or users want than any other activity we've explored in this book. To be clear, this doesn't mean that everything else we've learned is made redundant by testing in production. But as part of a holistic strategy, it offers a testing perspective that focuses more on real-life interactions between our systems and our users.

12.4 Expanding your strategy by testing in production

Throughout this book, we've explored a wide range of testing activities, and one thing that ties them all together is that they focus on discovering information before new features or products go live. We do this to help establish a solid understanding of what we've built, which in turn helps increase our confidence in what we're delivering. But what if that confidence is misplaced? On the imagination side of our strategic focus, what if we've misunderstood a user's needs? For the implementation side, what if a blind spot has resulted in us missing a critical risk in our product? We may be in for a rude awakening when we finally present our work to our users.

The key to this dilemma is not to double down on more testing but to accept that sometimes we carry out wasteful testing—at best, delivering little value and, at worst, giving us a false sense of confidence. We've discussed before that what we can test will always be eclipsed by what can be tested, and the consequences of this are potentially wasteful testing and gaps in our efforts. It's unavoidable, so by accepting that this will happen, we can begin to put a strategy in place to handle the times when we "go off course" with our testing.

That's why adopting the testing-in-production approach can enable us to learn about both imagination and implementation at the same time, as shown in figure 12.4.

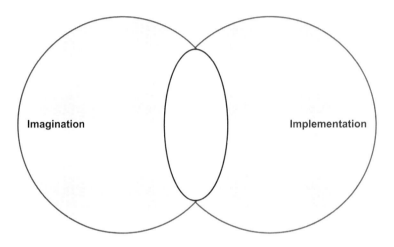

Figure 12.4   A testing strategy model that shows how testing production informs both how our application works in real-life scenarios (implementation) and how our users interact with our application (imagination)

By utilizing testing in production, we can do the following:

- *Improve our understanding of the imagination space by observing how our users interact with our product*—For example, if a new feature is hard to use or unwanted, we can observe metrics that share usage.
- *Improve our understanding of the implementation space by observing any issues that might occur as our product is used*—For example, if an increase in latency appears after a release, we might need to take time to discover what is causing the slow-down.

Essentially, with testing in production, there is nowhere to hide, and that's what can scare teams away from implementing it as a testing approach. But by learning more about how the product is truly used, we can increase our understanding of both the user's attitudes toward our work and how our product really behaves in a real-life context, all of which can help us improve quality.

Summary

- Testing in production is about observing how users interact with our system and how our system behaves to help us better understand our users.
- Testing in production can help us identify issues that are missed during other testing activities, which we can resolve and reflect on to improve other testing approaches.
- We can use techniques created by site reliability engineers to help us track whether we're delivering a quality product by measuring the behavior of our system and comparing its levels of expectation.
- We determine what we want to measure through the use of service-level agreements, service-level objectives, and service-level indicators.
- Service-level objectives are used to set clear levels of specific behaviors that a system should meet that are set by the team.
- Service-level agreements are similar to service-level objectives in that they set levels of expectations but are also associated with financial penalties and are typically decided by the business.
- Service-level indicators are what are used to measure whether we are meeting a service-level objective within a specific time frame. They also help us to determine what tooling we require for measuring our systems.
- We can easily integrate tools like Honeycomb into our APIs to start tracking event data.
- We build queries within Honeycomb to analyze data as well as to create triggers that inform of us when we're no longer meeting our SLOs.
- Testing in production tooling allows us to try out other testing activities such as synthetic users and A/B testing.

appendix
Installing the sandbox
API platform

Setting up restful-booker-platform

To help aid our learning, we'll attempt different testing activities against a sandbox API platform called restful-booker-platform. Restful-booker-platform is a web API platform that has been designed as a teaching aid to help us explore and learn about testing using Java and JavaScript. The source code can be found at http://mng.bz/AVWp. To install restful-booker-platform, you will need a version of the following:

- Java SDK
- Maven
- NodeJS LTS

The specific versions for each dependency can be found in the README document. They are regularly updated.

> ### Why do I need NodeJS?
> The JavaScript component of the platform is used for creating the user interface for restful-booker-platform. This part of the application won't be discussed as much throughout the book (because we're focusing on the web API side of the product), but it is required to get the application up and running.

To build the application locally, all you need to do is run either bash `build_locally.sh` for Linux or Mac or `build_locally.cmd` on Windows to build restful-booker-platform and get it running. It may take a while to build on the first run because it downloads dependencies, but it will speed up afterward. Once the application has been built, you will be able to access it at http://localhost:8080. You can use either `bash run_locally.sh` for Linux or Mac or `run_locally.cmd` on Windows to start restful-booker-platform up again.

Alternatively, a publicly available version of restful-booker-platform can also be found at https://automationintesting.online.

index